WITNESS
THROUGH
TROUBLED TIMES

WITNESS THROUGH TROUBLED TIMES

A History of the Orthodox Church of Georgia, 1811 to the Present

With contributions by
Zaza Abashidze
Nino Abashidze
Eldar Bubulashvili
Gocha Saitidze
Sergo Vardosanidze

Edited by
Tamara Grdzelidze
Martin George
Lukas Vischer

*Published with the support of
the Swiss National Science Foundation*

BENNETT & BLOOM

First published
in 2006 by

BENNETT & BLOOM
www.bennettandbloom.com
PO Box 2131
London W1A 5SU
England

Typeset and designed by Desert♥Hearts

Printed and bound by
Newton Printing, London, England

British Library Cataloguing in Publication Data
A catalogue record for this book is available from the British Library

ISBN 1 898948 68 2 • 978-1-898948-68-1 (hardback)
ISBN 1 898948 69 0 • 978-1-898948-69-8 (paperback)

Contents

A note on dates

The Orthodox Churches uniformly followed the Julian ('Old Style') calendar, which at present runs 13 days later than the Gregorian ('New Style') calendar used in secular society. In 1923 an Inter-Orthodox Congress in Constantinople moved to revise the system and so the Gregorian calendar was introduced in March 1924. This change was not accepted by Georgia, Jerusalem, Russia, Serbia, Poland and Mount Athos, who all continue to follow the Old Style calendar. In this book, therefore, alternative dates are sometimes provided to reflect the two systems, e.g. the feast day of St Nino, January 14/27, where the first date is Gregorian and the second Julian.

Acknowledgements

The editors wish first of all to thank those who collaborated in working on this book: the Georgian, Swiss and German scholars participating in the preparatory symposium at Spiez, Switzerland, and Professor Dimitri Oikonomou of Oxford, England for proofreading and refining the English version.

We also would like to express gratitude to the institutions whose contributions made possible the aforementioned symposium and the further preparatory work on the publication: the Swiss National Foundation, the Beer-Brawand-Foundation (Berne), the Department of International Relations of the University of Berne, the Hochschulstiftung der Burgergemeinde (Berne), the Faith and Order Secretariat at the World Council of Churches, and the Association of the Friends of Georgia in Switzerland.

Finally our appreciation and thanks are due to the Swiss National Science Foundation, and the Foundation for Ecumenical and Historical Theology, both in Berne. The printing of this book would have been impossible without their publication grants.

The Editors

Georgia at the beginning of the 21st century

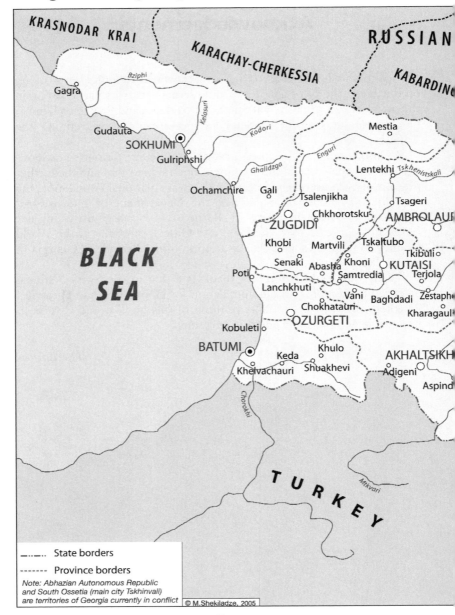

KRASNODAR KRAI

KARACHAY-CHERKESSIA

RUSSIAN

KABARDINO

Bziphi

Gagra

Kelasuri

Gudauta

Kodori

Mestia

SOKHUMI

Gulriphshi

Ghalidzga

Enguri

Lentekhi *Tskhenistskali*

Ochamchire   Gali   Tsalenjikha   Tsageri

Chkhorotsku   AMBROLAURI

ZUGDIDI

Khobi   Martvili   Tskaltubo   Tkibuli

Senaki   Abasha   Khoni   KUTAISI

Poti   Samtredia   Terjola

Lanchkhuti   Vani   Baghdadi   Zestaphoni

Chokhatauri   Kharagauli

Kobuleti   OZURGETI

BATUMI   Khulo

Keda   AKHALTSIKH

Khelvachauri   Shuakhevi   Adigeni

Aspind

Chorokhi

BLACK
SEA

T U R K E Y

Mtkvari

_.._.._ State borders

------- Province borders

*Note: Abhazian Autonomous Republic
and South Ossetia (main city Tskhinvali)
are territories of Georgia currently in conflict* © M.Shekiladze, 2005

8

**REGIONAL SYSTEM
AT THE BEGINNING OF THE 21ST CENTURY**

1. Abkhazian Autonomous Republic .... Sokhumi
2. Ajarian Autonomous Republic .... Batumi
3. Tbilisi .... Tbilisi
4. Samegrelo (Mingrelia) - Zemo (Upper) Svaneti .... Zugdidi
5. Racha-Lechkhumi-Kvemo (Lower) Svaneti ... Ambrolauri
6. Guria .... Ozurgeti
7. Imereti .... Kutaisi
8. Samtskhe-Javakheti .... Akhaltsikhe
9. Shida (Inner) Kartli .... Gori
10. Kvemo (Lower) Kartli .... Rustavi
11. Mtskheta-Mtianeti .... Mtskheta
12. Kakheti .... Telavi

Mtskheta

Preface

For reasons that will become obvious, until recently, little has been known about the Orthodox Church of Georgia. Persecuted and oppressed, only scant information about church life and witness could be transmitted to the outside world. According to the theories of Marxist-Leninism, the Church was destined to disappear as a historical reality. Official scholarship, therefore, held no interest in the details of its history and the Church was presented as an irrelevant relic of the past. But, in spite of enormous difficulties, the Orthodox Church of Georgia survived and has re-emerged as the "soul" of the Georgian nation.

This volume tells the story of the Church's witness through extremely troubled times. It sheds light particularly on ecclesiastical life over the past two centuries, since the annexation of Georgia by Russia. In order to place the events of this period into its correct context, this account is preceded by a general survey of Georgia's long and turbulent history.

This publication is the result of a joint venture. Initiated some years ago by the Swiss Association of Friends of Georgia, it took shape in collaboration with the Theological Faculty of the University of Berne, Switzerland. We were fortunate in finding a group of specialists in Georgia who were ready to contribute the various chapters that were eventually translated into English. In 2002, the Georgian authors spent some days in Spiez, Switzerland at a colloquium with a group of Western scholars. As a result of these discussions, they were able to revise their papers; the English texts were subsequently worked through by the three editors and again checked by the Georgian authors. It is our hope that this working method has brought into being a monograph that represents the view of the Georgian people and at the same time speaks to readers from other countries.

Clearly, this oeuvre is no more than a first attempt. Both authors and editors are aware of its limitations. Fortunately, much information could be used that was hitherto inaccessible. Other details only partially known have, thanks to the industry of the authors, acquired consistency and colour. It is clear, however, that additional research must be undertaken in the future. There is a wealth of information in other archives, particularly in Russia, which will undoubtedly shed new light on periods, events and persons little known today. It is our hope that this study will serve to stimulate further efforts and we very much look forward to the new insights they might reveal.

This volume is dedicated to the Orthodox Church of Georgia and, in particular, to His Holiness Ilia II, Catholicos-Patriarch of All Georgia, who has welcomed, encouraged, and blessed our initiative.

Tamara Grdzelidze
*Faith and Order
Secretariat,
World Council of
Churches, Geneva,
Switzerland*

Martin George
*Institute of Historical
Theology,
University of Berne,
Switzerland*

Lukas Vischer
*Association of the
Friends of Georgia,
Switzerland*

Geneva & Berne,
Epiphany 2006

Part I

A general survey of the history of Georgia

The Caucasus and Middle East in ancient times

Map of the Ancient Near East

KARTS

KULHA

DIAUHI

River Mtkvari

Lake Sevan

ETIUNI

URARTU

River Araks

Caspian Sea

Lake Van

Tushpa

MANNA

River Tigris

Lake Urmia

MEDES

MITANNI

Nineveh

River Euphrates

Assur

ASSYRIA

KASSITES

ELAMS

BABYLONIA

Babylon

SUMERIA

Map by Desert♥Hearts

From Antiquity to the 18th century

The king of all mountains is the Caucasus.
—Aeschylus

Georgia in the ancient world

Just to the south of the main ridge of the Caucasus mountains lies the country of Sakartvelo, known as "Iberia" to the ancient Greeks but today known as Georgia in almost all European languages.

In the 13th century BC, ancient historical sources, mainly Assyrian, refer to the earliest Georgian states as Diaokhi or Diauehi (later also as Taokhi and Tao) and Kolkha (Colchis/Kolkheti). Diaokhi was defeated in a lengthy war with the Assyrians; Kolkha could not withstand the invasion of the Cimmerians, who came from the north, and in due course also fell. On the cusp of the 7th and 6th centuries BC, a new and powerful Georgian state, Egrisi, was created in Western Georgia. During the last quarter of the 4th century BC another new state, that of Iberia (Kartli), appeared in the territory of Eastern Georgia. A little earlier, the Greeks had founded trading stations along the east and north shores of the Black Sea: Dioskurias (Sokhumi), Pitius (Bichvinta), Phasis (Poti) and Gienosi (Ochamchire). Thereafter, Georgia remained an ally and inherited the benefits of Greek civilisation.

Colchis and the Caucasian mountains were known to the Greeks from times of Homer. Of the Greek myths associated with Georgia and the Caucasus, the best known is that of Jason and the Argonauts and their voyage in search of the Golden Fleece and the tragedy of the Colkhian Princess Medea (*The Argonautica*). The legend describes the "golden country of Colchis with its capital Cutaia (Kutaisi), and the king of Colchis, Aeetes, son of Helios".

According to the ancient Georgian chronicles, the first king of Kartli, and of a united Georgian state, was Parnavaz. His reign, at the beginning of the 3rd century BC, was notable for uniting the western and Eastern Georgian states. The Georgian historian, Leonti Mroveli[1] records that "King Parnavaz became head of all Kartli and Eguri". Georgian sources ascribe to him the foundation of the first Georgian alphabet. Georgia did not remain united for long since King Parnavaz's heirs were unable to preserve the integrity of the state.

Roman rule

At the end of the 2nd century BC, Egrisi (Colchis/Kolkheti) was conquered by the king of Pontus, Mithridates VI Eupator (132-63 BC; r. 121-65 BC). In 65 BC, following the defeat of Pontus and Armenia, Georgia was invaded by Roman forces led by the great general Gnaeus Pompey. Whereas Rome was content with Iberia's half-vassal status, Egrisi was made a Roman province.

The Greek geographer and historian Strabo (64 BC-20 AD) provides informative details about Georgia. He describes the social, economic, and cultural life of its dwellers and refers to the existence of four main castes or classes in Iberian society during the Classical period. These were the royal family, the priesthood, free warriors, and free farmers. To these are added the common people, who were slaves of the king and performed all the services that pertain to human livelihood. Strabo describes Iberia as a rich country with a rather dense population and with "many towns and meadows". Ships sailed from the Black Sea to Shorapani along the Phasis-Kvirila waterway. Through Iberia and Egrisi ran the road by which goods arrived from India to Europe via Middle Asia, the Caspian Sea, along the Mtkvari (Kura), Dzirula, Kvirila, and Phasis (Rioni) rivers up to the Black Sea, and on to Europe. Since such a significant trade route ran through Georgia and also because of its very advantageous economic and strategic position, Georgia had always been a most significant target for foreign conquerors. Throughout the centuries Romans, Persians, Arabs, Byzantines, Mongols, Turks and, finally, the Russian Empire had occupied this small country. The history of the Georgian people therefore became a history of Georgia's constant struggle for independence and freedom.

Archeological materials, found near Mtskheta, Georgia's ancient capital, clearly testify that this was a country that possessed high cultural and economic standards of living. Archeologists have discovered the Mtskheta acropolis, Armazi, with its solid walls, living rooms, and a

---

1. Leonti Mroveli was the bishop of Ruisi (Eastern Georgia) in the 11th century. To him are attributed some of the books of *The Life of Kartli* (*Kartlis Tskhovreba*).

water-pipe. Impressive baths and a necropolis with rich royal tombs have also been unearthed. Extraordinary precious articles have been found in abundance: gold and silver, jewels decorated with precious stones, weapons, plates, and dishes.

According to ancient Greek sources, the people of Colchis worshipped Aeetes (in mythology, the son of Helios) as their principle god. They also worshipped Uranos (the sky) and Gaia (the earth). Other references are made to the goddess Phasis, who was related to the cult of the "Great Mother" Rhea. In pagan Kartli, before the time of King Parnavaz, anthropomorphic statues of Gatsi and Gaim were worshipped. As in the whole Hellenistic area, so in Egrisi and Kartli, both the Persian cult of Mithras and Zoroastrianism were widespread. Parnavaz instituted a cult named after himself, Armazi (Persian for Parnavaz), and erected an idol and an acropolis under this name. Armazi remained the principal god before the Christianisation of Kartli.

The 1st to 2nd centuries AD was a period when Iberia possessed considerable might — one that was facilitated by the weakening of neighbouring Armenia, an internecine war between Rome and Parthia, and friendly relations with her northern neighbours, the Alans. In the thirties of the 1st century, Parthia and Rome waged a war over the possession of Armenia. Iberia's king at that time, Mithridates V, entered the hostilities and finally annexed Armenia to his kingdom where he appointed his son, Mithridates VI, as ruler.

After him the new Georgian king, Parsman I (mid 1st century), made his son, Radamist, king of Armenia instead of his own brother. It was not long, however, before the Armenians revolted against Radamist, driving him back to Iberia. In Armenia, the youngest branch of the Arsacid dynasty of Parthia ascended to the throne, and acknowledged its vassal dependency on Rome. These events temporarily weakened the position of Iberia in Transcaucasia.

Independence from Rome and Persian subjugation

In the early part of the 2nd century AD, the kingdom of Iberia achieved its strongest position in antiquity. Its frontiers moved further to the southwest as far as the Black Sea. King Parsman II (who ruled Georgia from the thirties to the fifties of the 2nd century) refused even nominally to be subject to the Roman emperor. Invading Armenia, he drove out the Romans and then attacked Parthia with the help of the Alans.

Although the Roman emperor Hadrian (115-138) tried to improve relations with Iberia, when he summoned Parsman II to his headquarters in Cappadocia, the king refused. The emperor then attempted to gain concessions by sending Parsman precious gifts — as many as "no one before had given him" remarked the Roman writer and historian, Flavius Arianes. In return, Parsman only conveyed a few presents to the Roman court, firmly keeping Iberia independent of Rome.

Relationships between Iberia and Rome improved during the reign of Emperor Antoninus Pius (138-161) when Parsman II visited the emperor with his wife, son and a large entourage, the visit was considered worthy enough to number among the most important events of that year in Rome. At the emperor's order, a statue of the Georgian king on horseback was erected in Rome in the Forum of Mars. The most important consequence of this encounter was the fact that Rome confirmed the borders of the kingdom of Iberia: from the south-eastern coast of the Black Sea to the lower reaches of the Mtkvari (Kura) river and from the Caucasian ridge to the Arax river.

During the 3rd century, Georgia and all of the Caucasus faced a new, stronger and more dangerous enemy: the Persian dynasty of the Sassanids which had replaced the Arsacid dynasty in Parthia. In several military engagements the Persians defeated the Romans; they overpowered Armenia and Albania,[2] and constituted a serious threat to Iberia.

The christianization of Georgia

In 320s the most remarkable and important event in the history of Kartli took place. During the reign of King Mirian (first half of the 4th century) Christianity was proclaimed as the state religion, a circumstance that for many centuries shaped Georgia's political, social and cultural development.

As revealed by recent archeological excavations of a number of early Christian tombs, the populations of Kartli had been aware of Christianity from the first century. According to the oldest Georgian and Byzantine chronicles, Christ's message had been proclaimed in Georgia in the first century by the Apostles Andrew the First-Called, Simon the Canaanite and Bartholomew. In addition, Mtskheta claims to have preserved the most sacred of all relics for Christians — the seamless robe of Jesus Christ, which had been retrieved from Calvary after the

---

2.   Albania (no connection with modern Albania in the Balkans) was an independent Caucasian state on the territories of what is now Azerbaijan, Southern Daghestan and part of the South-East of Georgia, stretching from the Caspian Sea to the Iberian border. Christianized in the 4th century, it was occupied by Persia in the 6th, Arabs in the 7th, and Turks in the 11th centuries, its people finally being assimilated into their neighbouring Azeri, Georgian, Armenian and Daghestani populations.

St Nino

The Illuminator of Georgia named as 'Equal to the Apostles'. The relics of St Nino are in the monastery in Bodbe (Kakheti, Eastern Georgia). The Orthodox Church of Georgia commemorates her feast day on January 14/27.

She was born in Asia Minor, and as a young girl, around 330, she was sent to Kartli to preach Christianity. Nino was so successful that she converted first Queen Nana and later her husband King Mirian.

Sources relate that Mirian was unwilling to give up his belief in his pagan gods. But one day, when he was out hunting, a total eclipse of the sun took place. Out of fear, the king started praying to the gods to dispel the darkness but received no response. Then he remembered Nino, and he prayed to her God in his desperation. At once the sun reappeared in the heavens. Mirian thereupon announced he would be baptised and decreed that Christianity should become the official religion of the kingdom of Kartli.

Crucifixion and brought from Jerusalem to the capital by a local Jew named Elioz. The significance of Georgia's conversion to Christianity can hardly be exaggerated. It had an extraordinary effect on art, literature, culture and every other aspect of life. The event is particularly connected with the name of a young woman from Cappadocia, Nino, who was later canonised as the Illuminator of the Georgians. All through their subsequent history the Georgian people have venerated her and continue to do so today.

When King Mirian, converted to Christianity by St Nino, sent ambassadors to the Roman emperor Constantine the Great between 323 and 326 requesting that clergy be sent to Kartli, the emperor despatched a bishop, priests and deacons. The bishop had been consecrated by Eustathios, himself bishop of Antioch between 325 and 330. Priests arrived in Kartli approximately from 325 to 326.

The Church historians Gelasius of Caesarea, Rufinus, Gelasius of Cyzicus, Sozomen, Socrates and Theodoret mention in their works that the Armenians and Iberians adopted Christianity during the reign of Constantine, that is, before 337 (the year of the emperor's death).[3] From the very beginning, the Patriarchate of Antioch was regarded as the Mother Church by the Church of Kartli, and it was from Antioch that the Georgians received partial autocephaly around 480. At that time the head of the Church of Georgia was given the title of catholicos.[4]

During the same period, or perhaps a little earlier, Christianity had been adopted by the Western Georgian state of Kolkheti — called Lazika by the Byzantines — which was geographically and politically closer to the Christian centres of the Roman empire. According to Gelasius of Caesarea and Gelasius of Cuzicus, the conversion of Lazika took place together with that of Kartli, but other sources do not concur. According to the acts of the Council of Nicaea (325), Stratophiles, bishop of Pitius (today Pitsunda) in Abkhazia, was in attendance. Moreover, there is archeological evidence of a Christian cathedral in Pitius dating from the first half of the 4th century. This would indicate that the conversion at least of parts of the population of Lazika took place earlier than the conversion of Kartli.

3.   According to *The Ecclesiastical History*, the adoption of Christianity in Georgia took place around 330, in the year when the philosopher Metrodoros made his journey to India. Historians today agree on a date around the 320s. For sources, see: *Georgica, Scriptorum Byzantinorum Excerpta ad Georgiam Pertinentia*, vol. 1, edited by A. Gamkrelidze & S. Kaukhchishvili (Tbilisi, 1961).
4.   See Part II, chapter 1, 'Abolition of Autocephaly and Formation of the Exarchate'.

Between Byzantium and Persia

In the meantime, invasions by the Persian empire into Kartli became more and more frequent. Yezdigerd II, shah of Persia (438-457), carried out an aggressive religious policy in his attempt to spread Zoroastrianism throughout Armenia, Albania and Kartli. In the Transcaucasus certain *aznaurs* (noblemen) were forced to adopt Zoroastrianism (at least nominally). In 451, as a result of the decisions of the Fourth Ecumenical Council of Chalcedon which anathemised monophysitism, Byzantium and Kartli formally adopted dyophysitism. Meanwhile, monophysitism held sway in Armenia and Albania. Under persecution by the Byzantines, Persia had, in the past, tolerated monophysitism but now it supported the heresy wholeheartedly and bolstered its efforts to quell dyophysite Kartli.

Kartli's outstanding king Vakhtang Gorgasali (440s-502/3), himself a remarkable military commander, led a successful uprising against the Persian invaders in Transcaucasia (482-484). Vakhtang also is remembered for consolidating royal power and for joining Western Georgia to Kartli. He was also responsible for a praiseworthy building programme: a number of new churches were constructed, especially Mtskheta's new stone-built Svetitskhoveli cathedral that was founded at the place where the seamless robe of Jesus Christ had been buried. New fortresses and towns were also raised, and under Vakhtang the plan was mooted to move the capital of Kartli from Mtskheta to nearby Tbilisi. This finally came about during the reign of his son, Dachi, who became ruler at the beginning of the 6th century.

Vakhtang's church policy is also worthy of note. On his initiative, and in full agreement with the local ecclesial authorities, the Church of Kartli achieved partial autocephaly. The head of the Church in Kartli was now an archbishop with the title of catholicos, and many new eparchies were founded.

Vakhtang was wounded in the Samgori valley near Tbilisi during the war with Persia. Shortly thereafter he died in Ujarma — a fortress that he had built himself — and was buried in Svetitskhoveli cathedral. The Georgian church canonised him as a king who sacrificed his life for Christianity and for the freedom of his country. He is commemorated on December 13/November 30. After the king's death, Georgia continued its unending struggle against the Persian invaders. In 523, under the leadership of King Gurgen of Kartli, the people rose in rebellion against the Persian occupiers, but the Persians won and Gurgen was obliged to leave for Byzantium. The Persians abolished the king's power and sub-

Georgia in the 4th-7th centuries

Invasion route of the Khazars, 627-8

Campaign route of Heraklius-Caesar of Byzantium, 627

© M.Shekiladze, 2005

From Antiquity to the 18th century

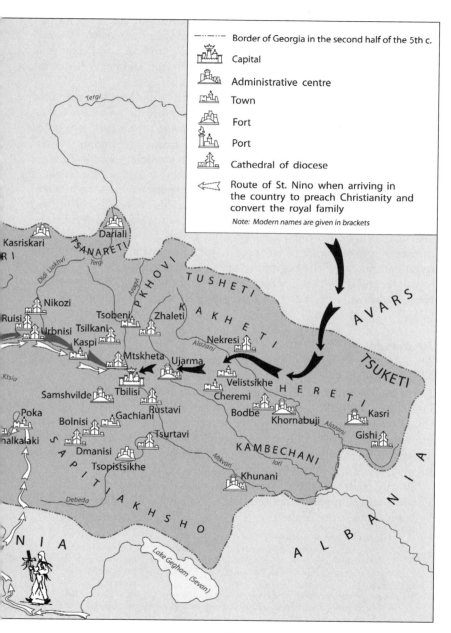

Border of Georgia in the second half of the 5th c.

Capital

Administrative centre

Town

Fort

Port

Cathedral of diocese

Route of St. Nino when arriving in the country to preach Christianity and convert the royal family

Note: Modern names are given in brackets

jugated all of Eastern Georgia. In Western Georgia the kingdom of Egrisi struggled against the expansion of Byzantium and later against Persia, having conquered Kartli, the latter also laid claim to Western Georgia. The clash between the interests of Byzantium and Persia gave rise to a succession of battles, which resulted in ruin and heavy losses for Egrisi, which remained a vassal of Byzantium.

In the second half of the 6th century, Kartli's chief *aznaurs*[5] managed to restore state power in the country. A number of *eristavis*,[6] taking advantage of the king's loss of power had enlarged their property holdings and enjoyed complete independence from any higher central authority. They were naturally loath to lose this privilege and so decided to elect a titular head of state to replace the king as a "first among equals" — he was accordingly given the title *erismtavari*. A member of the Bagrationi family, Guaram (according to the dynastic chronicles) became the first erismtavari. The Bagrationi family had come from the province of Speri (in today's Turkey) but as early as the 6th century, its members rose to power in Georgia. Later it became a royal dynasty and ruled Georgia until the beginning of the 19th century.

By the end of the 6th century, Persia's changing politics meant Kartli became almost entirely free of the empire. But the respite was not destined to last for long.

Arab rule

After 620, the armies of the Khazars (originally Turkic nomads who later adopted Judaism as their national religion) and Byzantium invaded Kartli and by the mid 7th century the former had founded a state in the lower area of the Russian Volga river east of the Northern Caucasus, called Khaganate. They had joined forces with the Byzantine emperor Heraclius (610-641) in his forays against Kartli; the Byzantines reached as far as Tbilisi, which they occupied. When, in 628, Heraclius was on his way back from Persia he once again attacked Tbilisi.[7]

Shortly thereafter the Byzantines themselves, together with the Persians and some other nations, were confronted by a new, strong and dynamic enemy: the Arabs.

5. *Aznauri* — Georgian nobility.
6. *Eristavi*, from *eri* meaning "people, nation" and *tavi* "head", signifying the head of a Georgian province whose office gradually became hereditary. The institution of *eristavi* was established as far back as the reign of King Parnavaz, the first Georgian king.
7. Heraclius was attempting to subdue the non-Chalcedonians to his south-east, and he had to pass through Kartli (627-627) which was under Persian occupation. In Tbilisi a regiment of 1,000 Persian troops had occupied the central fortress.

Since the 630s, Arab forces had steadily been conducting rather aggressive strategies against territories both near and far. As early as the 640s Arabs appeared in the Southern Caucasus and managed to occupy Dvin, the capital of Armenia. Georgia at that time was spared from an invasion. Following the defeat of Persia and the victory over Byzantium in Armenia, Arab forces approached the borders of Georgia and, the erismtavari of Kartli finding himself faced with so strong an enemy, felt obliged to submit to Arab supremacy.

At first the command appeared to be nominal, acceptance of the Arab supremacy in Kartli in the middle of the 7th century was all that was required; but, by the 8th century, death and destruction were the order of the day. In the 730s, the Arab commander, Marwan ibn Muhammad (later the last of the Umayyad caliphs), using both fire and sword, devastated all of eastern and Western Georgia. In spite of promises of honour, fame and riches, the Arabs brutally tortured and then executed the erismtavari Archil and the princes David and Constantine Mkheidze, who refused to betray Christianity by adopting Islam. Archil, David and Constantine were later canonised as martyrs. In 853 the Arab general Buga invaded Georgia, captured Tbilisi, and burnt it to the ground: more than 50,000 people perished in the conflagration.

As a result of long and uncompromising warfare, however, the territory under Arab rule began to diminish and in the end, it covered only Tbilisi and a small area to the south of the city. By the end of the 8th and beginning of the 9th centuries independent principalities and kingdoms began to rise in western and Eastern Georgia: to the west, the kingdom of Abkhazia; to the south-west the principality (*samtavro*) of Tao-Klarjeti; to the east the kingdoms of Kakheti and Hereti. The Arab emirate of Tbilisi constituted a separate political unit.

Attempts at unifying Georgia

Georgian kingdoms and principalities fought each other for supremacy. Ultimately, this became a struggle for the unification of all the Georgian lands centred around Georgia's central province, Kartli. Possession of this territory would provide enormous political, economic, and moral advantages. Of no small significance was the fact that Georgia's religious centre, the catholicosate of Mtskheta, was situated in Kartli.

In the 9th century, the kings of Western Georgia (Abkhazia) implemented several religious, cultural and political measures to establish a closer union with Kartli. In due course, the Byzantine eparchies in Western Georgia, which celebrated Church services only in Greek, were

Grigol Khandzteli (Gregory of Khandzta, 8th-9th centuries)

Grigol played an important role in the life of the church. Born into a noble family and having received the best education, he dedicated his whole life to the church.

He became one of the founders of a large monastic movement in south-east Georgia in a period when Kartli (Eastern Georgia) was under Arab rule. A cultural revival in the south-east of Georgia, helped by the newly built monasteries, contributed to the political stability of the region.

At the end of the 10th century, Giorgi Merchule ('the Legislator'), the author of the Life of Grigol, linked territorial integrity and development of national identity with the church's integrity and identity. He declared that "the lands where church services are proclaimed in the Kartuli (Georgian) language constitute the state of Kartli (Georgia)".

The authority of the Church in Georgia gained considerably through the efforts of Grigol, in particular the preparation of the Holy Chrism locally, one of the marks of autocephaly.

The increase of the authority of the Church and revival of monastic life also had major political implications which bore fruit later when the independent Georgian lands became united under the One Church in the 11th century.

He is commemorated by the Church on October 5/18.

closed down and in their place eparchies with services in Georgian, part of the newly established Abkhazia catholicosate, were created. Later, these fell under the jurisdiction of the catholicos of Mtskheta, who, from beginning of the 11th century (around 1020), came to be known as the Catholicos and Patriarch of All Georgia.

The ecclesiastical unification of Western and Eastern Georgia effectively promoted the process of political unification for the country. Its integration, together with the establishment of a single monarchy were responses to the social, economic, political, and cultural developments throughout the country. Cultural achievements increasingly excelled hand in hand with Georgia's political unification to the point that they competed strongly with comparable Byzantine accomplishments.

Unifying impact on language and culture

With the official recognition of Christianity as the country's official religion, Georgian culture became thoroughly Christianized. At the same time, it is true to say that Christianity destroyed significant monuments of Georgia's ancient pagan culture and supposedly its pagan literature (if the narrative about the first Georgian alphabet created by King Parnavaz is true).

Nevertheless, a Georgian monastery in Palestine (dating from 433) and the Bolnisi Sioni (end of the 5th century) preserve monuments with Georgian inscriptions and provide evidence that a literary tradition in Christian Georgia existed from early on. Churches and monasteries within Georgia (Mtskheta, Gareji, Khandzta, Shatberdi, Opiza, Ishkhani, Anchie, and others) and Georgian religious foundations abroad (in Syria, Palestine, Sinai, Cyprus, Mount Athos) served as cultural and educational centres at the time.

A united kingdom of Georgia

Bagrat III (975-1014), a descendant of the ancient Georgian Bagrationi dynasty, became the first king of a united Georgia. On his father's side he was a progeny of the "king of the Kartvelians", and on his mother's an heir of the "king of the Abkhazians". King David III (974-1001, king of the Kartvelians in Tao, a historical province in south-western Georgia), whose Byzantine title was kyropalates,[8] played a major role in

8.   "Kyropalates" was the traditional title given to the head of palace security from the 4th-6th centuries in Byzantium. He was second only after the emperor. At first, this was solely a position held by members of the royal family. From the 8th century, however, it became an honorary title for foreign sovereigns (among them, the Georgian kings after the 9th century). The first Georgian monarch who rejected this title was David IV.

uniting the Georgian lands and in promoting Bagrat III. David III adopted Bagrat as his son and declared him to be his heir.

At the outset (975), David established authority over the *aznaurs* of Kartli and actively supported Bagrat in his claims on the throne of Abkhazia. Thus, Kartli, Abkhazia and most of south-eastern Georgia were subject to Bagrat by the end of the 10th century. Later, from 1008-1010, Bagrat placed two other Eastern Georgian kingdoms, Kakheti and Hereti, under his authority and by the end of his reign (1014), only the Tbilisi emirate, which remained under Arab rule, and the estates of David III in Tao (seized by the Byzantines)[9] remained outside the united Georgian kingdom.

During the whole of the 11th century, the Georgian kings Giorgi I (1014-1027) and Bagrat IV (1027-1072) fought to take these territories, but without success. The final unification of all Georgian lands is linked with the name of King David IV the Builder ("Aghmashenebeli"; 1089-1125), who left a strong monarchy to his successors.

The Golden Age

David IV ascended the throne amidst times of difficulty for Georgia. The country had already undergone considerable turmoil during the reign of his father Giorgi II (1072-1089), and the monarch's rule had been weakened as a result of the zealous feudal lords who had been raging and defying the central authorities. Kakheti and Hereti also broke away from the united state and the entire situation was further aggravated by Seljuk Turks — they had invaded Georgia as early as 1064 and now occupied almost entirely its eastern areas.

David took decisive measures to bridle the feudal nobles. In an attempt to reform his army, he created small military units to produce a well-disciplined mobile force — one of the strongest in the east, and initiated the gradual expulsion of the Seljuks from Georgian lands. The result was that people once driven from their homes now returned; there also ensued a gradual revival of the economy.

David implemented important financial, administrative, and judicial reforms and paid due attention to the Church. On his initiative an ecclesiastical council was convened at which many disreputable figures who, because of their noble origin occupied high clerical posts, were forced to retire. Measures such as these strengthened the king's authority and led to stability in the country.

9.   David III supported a rebellion against Emperor Basil II (976-1025) and as a result Tao was seized by the Byzantine army.

Svetitskhoveli: symbol of a united Georgia

Dating from the 11th century, the cathedral building bears witness to the strength of a united Georgia under kings Bagrat III and Giorgi I. It replaced a basilica which in turn was erected on the site of one of the first churches in Georgia.

The story of Mtskheta's first church is found in all Georgian sources dealing with the events of the conversion of the kingdom of Kartli to Christianity. It was built of wood and its roofing was supported by pillars.

According to tradition, one of these pillars was made from the same cedar which had grown on the burial place of the robe of Christ in Mtskheta. Considered to be miraculous, the column was named "Svetitskhoveli", the "Life-Giving Pillar".

The present church is dedicated to the Twelve Apostles.

At the battle of Didgori in 1121, David the Builder inflicted a shattering defeat on a vast army of Seljuk and Arab forces. Shortly thereafter, in 1122, he emancipated the town of Tbilisi, which became the capital of the newly united Georgia (Kutaisi had been the capital prior to this). Following his victory at Didgori, David then expelled the Seljuks from Shirvan and incorporated the territory into Georgia in 1124. In the same year, envoys from the Armenian capital of Ani came to David requesting his assistance to free their town from the Seljuks and unite it with Georgia; this eventually transpired.

David implemented an important governmental reform by creating at his royal court the *darbazi*, a council of representatives from high aristocracy and from the church hierarchy. The king ruled the country by means of a complex staff of officials: each domain had its own minister (*ukhutsesi*) while the government was led by the "secretary of letters" (*mtsignobartukhutsesi*). By the king's decree the latter was to be the archbishop of Chkondidi (the most important eparchy in Western Georgia) and who was also head of the highest legal body, the *saajokari* (supreme court). The provinces were administered by local governors (*eristavi*). David's successors, Dimitri I (1125-1156) and Giorgi III (1156-1184), inherited a vast territory stretching from Nikopsia (near Tuapse) to Derbent and from Alania (now northern Ossetia) to Mount Aragats (in Armenia).

During the reign of Queen Tamar (1184-1210/1213), Georgia continued to prosper culturally and economically and also increased in political power. Georgians referred to her as Tamar "Mepe", i.e. "King" Tamar. Under her rule, the country gained a number of important victories over neighbouring Turkic rulers, further expanding its borders. By the beginning of the 13th century, Georgian power extended across almost the entire Caucasus: all of the northern and south-eastern Caucasus, southern and Iranian Azerbaijan, and Armenia now were dependent upon Georgia. The creation of a buffer state, the kingdom of Trebizond on the southern coast of the Black Sea, constituted a crucial victory for Georgia, for its throne had been given to the Byzantine prince Alexios Komnenos only by consent of the Georgian royal family. Trebizond remained under the strong political influence of Georgia for as long as it existed (1204-1462).

The Georgian state was acclaimed for its hegemony all over the Islamic and Christian world. Even the Crusaders, facing disastrous circumstances in Palestine, anticipated support from Georgia. Indeed, the idea of a Georgian campaign in remote Palestine to liberate Jerusalem from the Muslims had been cultivated during the reign of Queen Tamar's son Giorgi IV (1210/1213-1223). Having received Pope Honorius' proposal to participate in a crusade, Giorgi actually began preparations for the campaign, but the plan never materialised, having been thwarted by the arrival of the Mongols in Georgia.

The era of invasions

At the precise moment that Georgia perceived itself to be virtually invincible (even to the point of organising, as mentioned above, a campaign to save Jerusalem), a destructive avalanche of Mongols began to move westwards from Central Asia. Up until 1206, the Mongols had led a nomadic life on the plain of Central Asia, usually in constant conflict amongst themselves. In time the Mongolian nobility called a *kurultai*, or political council, on the banks of the Ononi river in Mongolia and appointed Genghis Khan as their supreme commander. He proved able to unite the Mongols, who subsequently began to occupy neighbouring territories, forcing them to pay large tributes.

Between 1211 and 1215 the Mongols had occupied a large part of China and by 1220 they had taken all of Central Asia, including Khorezm, east of the Caspian Sea. That same year they appeared in Azerbaijan and then in Georgia, after which they entered large parts of Russia. The Mongol invasions hindered the development of many kingdoms and khanates, most of which lost their statehood forever and their economies crumbled irreparably. The same was true of Georgia, where a century-long Mongolian rule resulted in disastrous consequences.

When the Mongols first entered Georgia in 1220, during the reign of Giorgi IV, they achieved two important victories. By the end of the 1230s, they had already occupied all of Eastern Georgia. Queen Rusudan (1223-1245), forced to acquiesce, recognised their rule and for a century, while the western part of the country remained free, Eastern Georgia fell under the Mongolian yoke. All spheres of life: political structures, the economy, and culture, fell into decay. And whenever rebellions were staged against the occupants, the Mongols responded by new raids, further destruction and crippling devastation.

Only in the 1320s, did King Giorgi V Brtskinvale ("the Glorious": 1318-1346) first manage to weaken the Mongolian presence in Georgia. Through astute diplomacy he was eventually able to liberate Georgia from bondage and, in the 1330s, to reunite both parts of the country by reviving statehood and the economy. During Giorgi's rule, Georgia regained power to the extent that neighbouring and distant countries

Georgia at the beginning of the 13th century

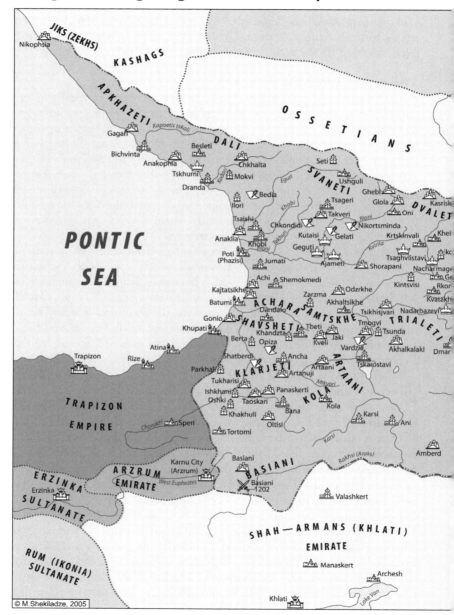

JIKS (ZEKHS)
Nikophsia
KASHAGS
APKHAZETI
OSSETIANS
Gagari
Kapoetis tskali
DALI
Besleti
Bichvinta
Anakophia
Chkhalta
Seti
Tskhumi
Mokvi
SVANETI
Ushguli
Dranda
Eguri
Ghebi
Bedia
Tsageri
Glola
Kasrisk
Ilori
Khobi
Takveri
Oni
DVALET
Tsaishi
Chkondidi
Rioni
Nikortsminda
Khei
Anaklia
Khobi
Kutaisi
Gelati
Krtskinvali
Takhi
Rioni
Poti
Geguti
Kvirila
Tsaghvlistavi
Ikc
(Phazisi)
Jumati
Ajameti
Shorapani
Nacharmage
Achi
Shemokmedi
Kintsvisi
Ge
Kajtatsikhe
Zarzma
Odzrkhe
Rkor
Batumi
Akhaltsikhe
Kvatakh
ACHARA
SAMTSKHE
Dandalo
Tsikhisjvari
Nadarbazevi
Gonio
SHAVSHETI
Tbeti
Tmogvi
TRIALETI
Khupati
Khandzta
Jaki
Tsunda
Berta
Opiza
Kveli
Vardzia
Atina
Shatberdi
Ancha
Artaani
Akhalkalaki
Dmar
Trapizon
Rize
Parkhali
Artanuji
ARTAANI
Tskarostavi
KLARJETI
Tukharisi
Panaskerti
KOLA
Ishkhani
Oshki
Taoskari
Bana
Kola
Khakhuli
Karsi
TRAPIZON
Oltisi
Ani
EMPIRE
Chorokhi
Speri
Tortomi
Karsi
PONTIC SEA
Amberd
Karnu City
Basiani
ERZINKA
ARZRUM
(Arzrum)
BASIANI
Rakhsi (Araks)
Erzinka
EMIRATE
West Euphrates
Basiani
1202
Valashkert
SULTANATE
SHAH—ARMANS (KHLATI)
EMIRATE
RUM (IKONIA)
SULTANATE
Manaskert
Archesh
© M.Shekiladze, 2005
Khlati
Lake Van

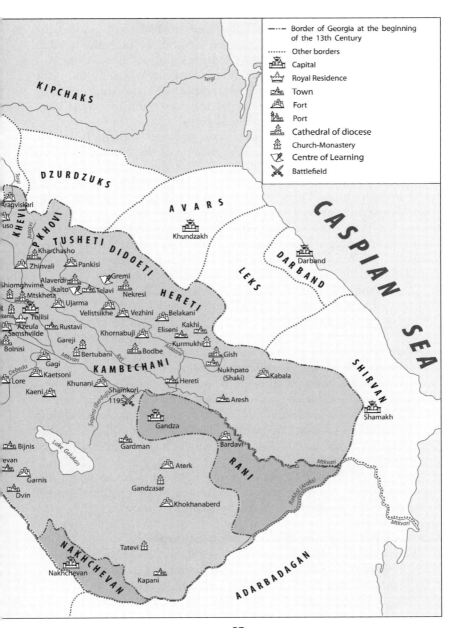

recognised that it was a force to be reckoned with. Georgia's authority became so highly regarded in the international arena that the Egyptian sultans, who ruled over all the holy places in Palestine, granted the Georgians special privileges. They were allowed, for example, to enter Jerusalem on horseback, with unfolded flags and without paying customs. Of singular significance was the fact that many sacred sites in the Holy Land (earlier the property of Georgia and of Georgians) including Calvary and the keys to the Holy Sepulchre, were returned to the kingdom and to the Orthodox Church in Georgia.

Notwithstanding these events, the vigour and supremacy of the Georgian monarchy again declined at the end of the 14th century as a result of the repeated incursions of the hordes of Timur Leng (or Tamerlane; 1336-1405). At the head of a turkified Mongolian group based in Samarkand, Timur Leng invaded Georgia no less than eight times during the period 1386 to 1403. His army's assaults were widely known for their extraordinary cruelty to people and property. They destroyed and ravaged everything they could find: cutting down gardens, vineyards, and forests, burning cornfields, destroying crops and virtually all buildings, including residences, churches and fortresses.

Timur Leng's offensive resulted in so great a catastrophe for Georgia that the country was never fully able to restore its shattered economy. Though King Alexander I ("the Great") (1412-1442) did much to revive Georgia from its ruins, he failed to achieve his goal. Indeed, during the reign of Alexander's sons, Vahktang IV (1442-1446) and Giorgi VIII (1446-1466), the united Georgian state began to disintegrate further. Internal problems, the weakening of the monarchy, civil dissension, feudal faction, economic decay, and an aggravated international situation — namely the fall of Constantinople in 1453 and with it the Byzantine empire, a catastrophe for the eastern Christian world, followed by the disintegration of the kingdom of Trebizond — had an extremely negative impact on Georgia.

Now cut off from Europe, its new neighbour was the aggressive Ottoman Empire, not the Christian Byzantine Commonwealth. Georgia found itself surrounded in the south by Islamic countries.

Consequences of the fall of Constantinople

By the end of the 1480s, the Georgian monarchy had finally split into three kingdoms — Kakheti, Kartli and Imereti — in addition to the principality of Samtskhe-Saatabago. Later, provinces in Western Georgia: Guria, Samegrelo, Abkhazia, and Svaneti, became semi-independent, no longer recognising the central authority of the king of Imereti.

The political situation in Georgia became even more complicated in the 16th century. Thereafter, the Georgian kingdoms and principalities became involved in a relentless 300-year struggle against Persia and Ottoman Turkey, both of whom were anxious to establish their own rule in Georgia and to divide it between them. The heroic efforts of the Georgian people, led by kings Luarsab I (1527-1556) and Simon I (1556-1569, 1578-1600) of Kartli, against its 16th-century assailants were of paramount importance for the country's future. Enemy powers were hindered from strengthening their presence in Georgia and from establishing their own law and order. However, the southern and south-western regions of the country suffered enormously in this struggle. The Ottoman Empire eventually annexed the historic Georgian provinces of Samtskhe, Javakheti, Tao, Klarjeti, Shavsheti and Ajara in which most of the resident populations were forcibly converted to Islam.

The 17th century was characterised by even greater difficulties. Reprisals against the Persian invaders were led by the outstanding military leader, Giorgi Saakadze. In March 1625, resurgent Georgians led by Saakadze almost completely annihilated the immense Persian army, frustrating the plans of its eminent military leader, Shah Abbas I (1589-1629). Saakadze was also involved in constant conflicts against Ottoman Turkey, attempting to expel the Ottomans from the Transcaucasus and, more especially, from Georgia. It was the shah's intention to exterminate the populations of Eastern Georgia (Kartli and Kakheti) and to establish Muslim rule on the territory in order to set up bases for further military campaigns. He did not, however, succeed in conquering Georgia.

In addition to Ottoman and Persian aggression, incursions by Daghestani feudal lords became frequent during the 18th century. Increasingly menacing, they caused further devastation in the already weakened country.

Suffering martyrdom

Many of Georgia's best sons fell in the unevenly-matched campaigns. The priest Tevdore from the village of Kvelta sacrificed his life by leading Ottoman invaders along a false trail, thereby enabling the Georgians to avert an unexpected attack and to re-assemble their forces. The Ottomans tortured and assassinated Tevdore for misleading them. The Orthodox Church of Georgia has recently canonised the martyred Father Tevdore.

By her life and death too, Queen Ketevan of Kakheti set an admirable example of courage and faith. The mother of King Teimuraz I and the widow of King David, her entire reign was simultaneous with the Persian occupation. Together with her grandchildren, Alexander and Levan, Ketevan was exiled to Persia — then ruled by Shah Abbas I. In an attempt to occupy Kakheti and prevent Teimuraz from attacking Persia, Abbas kept them as hostages but was unable to realise his objectives. Teimuraz negotiated an alliance with the Russians and also sought help from the Ottomans against Persia, thereby kindling the ire of the shah. As a consequence, Abbas cruelly punished the royal family by castrating the two princes, which caused Alexander's death and made Levan turn insane. The shah then demanded that the Queen convert to Islam but Ketevan adamantly refused. She expressed, instead, her readiness to undergo any torture in order to preserve her faith in Christ: "The shah may injure my body and thus save my soul."

Ketevan's rejection of Islam led to a brutal martyrdom: on 26/13 September 1624 in Shiraz she suffered burning by hot tongs, after which the executioners cut off her breasts and hands before pouring boiling water over her. But the queen withstood the torments and died heroically. Numerous examples of bravery and valour such as hers gave the people courage and hope.

Ottoman and Persian domination

Hoping to draw Georgia out of this impasse, King Vakhtang VI (ruler of Kartli, 1703-1714; king of Kartli, 1716-1724) attempted to establish favourable relations with a number of European states. His intention was to heighten their concern for Georgia and to gain support for the country's struggle against the Islamic states. To this end he sent his adviser Saba Orbeliani on a mission to Rome and to Paris. But the effort was unsuccessful; Western Europe had no resources to help Georgia at that time.

Vakhtang also tried to befriend the Russian tsar Peter I for the same purpose. However, this failed as well; it produced no positive results. On 12 July 1724, Russia and the Ottoman Empire concluded an armistice according to which the former recognised the claims of the Ottoman Empire in the south-eastern Caucasus. Vakhtang was forced to leave Georgia for St Petersburg where he continued efforts to encourage Russia in solving the Georgian problem and to secure support. Another failure.

Prior to Vakhtang's departure from Georgia, while he was preparing for his journey in Tskhinvali, his son Bakar ruled Kartli for a period.

However, when the Ottomans invaded Georgia, it was difficult for Bakar to resist and so he was replaced by Vakhtang's brother Iese, a convert to Islam who became faithful to the invaders. Supported by King Konstantine of Kakheti, local feudal lords organised a large-scale insurgence. Its defeat left Iese in power until his death in 1727 when the Ottomans abolished the local authorities in Kartli and appointed the Pasha of Akhaltsikhe head of the region.

The Ottoman domination of Kartli (a period known as the *Osmaloba*) lasted until 1735 when Persia exploited Georgia's struggle against the overlords, which ended in the expulsion of the Ottomans from the south-eastern Caucasus. This, however, did not create a free and independent Eastern Georgia since Kartli and Kakheti found themselves under Persian rule (known as the *Kizilbashoba* period). Meanwhile, the raids by Daghestani feudal lords continued to cause great devastation throughout Kartli and Kakheti.

Restoration of a kingdom in Eastern Georgia

In the face of insurmountable difficulties, the Georgian people continued to labour for their independence. Several theatres of war were successfully staged against the Persians, to the point where Shah Nadir, unable to break down the resistance of Kartli and Kakheti, was forced to make concessions. In June 1744, he was obliged to confirm the accession of Teimuraz II (Vakhtang VI's son-in-law) to the throne of Kartli, and that of Teimuraz II's son, Erekle II, to the throne of Kakheti. On October 1, 1745, Teimuraz's enthronement in Mtskheta at Svetitskhoveli cathedral was acclaimed as a great victory for the Georgian people. For the first time in a hundred years, Christian kings once more occupied the thrones of Kartli and Kakheti.

Teimuraz II (1744-1762) and Erekle II (Kakheti, 1744-1762; Kartli-Kakheti, 1762-1798) pursued policies that helped strengthen the Eastern Georgian kingdoms. Indeed, they not only managed to divest themselves of Persian influence, but also forced the khans of Yerevan, Ganja, and Nakhchevan to recognise their subordination to the kings of Kartli and Kakheti. The Lori and Borchalo regions, previously sequestered by Persia, were also returned to Kartli. Gradually, the economic and cultural situation in Eastern Georgia became relatively normalised.

Georgia, however, continued to be threatened by Persian and Ottoman hostilities and by the Daghestani feudals. Teimuraz and Erekle had far-reaching plans to liberate and revive the country — and in those plans the Russian empire had a special part to play.

Georgia and Russia

Relations between Georgia and Russia can be traced back to the 11th and 12th centuries; they were then disrupted in the 13th century as a result of the invasion of the Mongol hordes in both countries. The Kakheti kingdom was the first among the Georgian kingdoms and principalities to establish relations with Russia after the disintegration of the united Georgian state.

Once Russia had finally rid itself of the Mongol occupiers in 1480, it gained in strength and self-reliance. Moreover, with the collapse of the mighty Byzantine empire, Russian political circles launched their proposition that Moscow was now the "Third Rome". This was intended to send out the message that Russia was prepared to undertake the task of protecting all Orthodox peoples. Kakheti turned out to be the first region that recognised the validity of this mission. In 1483, a diplomatic envoy of the Kakheti King Alexander I (1476-1511) arrived at the court of Grand Duke Ivan III the Terrible (1533-1584) in Moscow. In his letter, the Georgian King referred to Ivan III as "protector of all Christians and pillar of Orthodoxy". Later, at the end of the 16th century when King Alexander II (1574-1605) ruled in Kakheti, even though the kingdom officially came under the protection of Russia, no tangible results ensued. On the contrary, this step only succeeded in aggravating relations between Kakheti and Persia.

The kingdom of Kartli also established relations with Russia in the early 17th century. In 1604, the Russian tsar Boris Godunov instructed his envoy Prince Tatishchev to offer King Giorgi X of Kartli (1600-1606) a Russian protectorate similar to that extended to Kakheti. At the same time, the Russian envoy was instructed to inform the Georgian royal court that Boris Godunov was willing to unite himself to the Bagrationi royal family by finding in Georgia a wife for his son, the crown prince, and a husband for his daughter. All matters were soon settled, but in 1605, Godunov died unexpectedly. The Pretender Dmitri I ascended the throne in Russia after exterminating the Godunov family.

Prelude to the Treaty of 1783[10]

In order to understand the events that befell the Orthodox Church of Georgia after 1801, and to appreciate their implications for the political and spiritual life of the Georgian nation itself, it is necessary to turn to a

10. This section on the pre-conditions of the treaty is based on the study by the late Georgian historian, Iase Tsintsadze, *The Protecting Treaty of 1783: Material on the History of Russian-Georgian Relations* (Tbilisi, 1960).

key period in the relationship between Russia and Georgia — the Treaty of Georgievsk, signed between the two countries on July 24, 1783. How did this treaty come into existence and why did the interests of both sides coincide?

Key factors that played their part in preparing the ground for the signing of the treaty between Eastern Georgia and the Russian Empire were Georgia's political and economic instability, the weakening of Persia, Russia's interests in Persia, and Russian-Ottoman relations, particularly with respect to hegemony in the Caucasus. During the 18th century, especially after the death of Peter I (1689-1725), the kings Teimuraz and Erekle took advantage of instability within Persia and forced the khans of Ganja, Erevan and Nakhchevan to pay taxes to them instead of to Persia.[11] This aroused grave concern in Russia because, having already made this first move, there was every possibility that Georgia would now interfere even deeper in the affairs of Persia and upset the status quo. This was already worrying Ottoman Turkey and, should the situation escalate, there was a very real prospect of conflict between the Ottomans and Georgia. Since Georgia was clearly unable to resist the might of the Ottoman Empire, the inevitable outcome would pave the way for Ottoman supremacy in the Caucasus, a situation the Russians clearly did not desire. The Ottomans, however, saw the threat of a prospective alliance between Russia and Georgia, and they therefore marshalled Muslim peoples in the Caucasus to stage a series of destablising raids into Georgia.

But a new balance of power in the Caucasus arrived with the First Russian-Ottoman war of 1768-1774 — by its end the weaknesses of the Ottoman Empire were clearly exposed. Prior to this, during the 18th century, Russia's politico-religious consciousness had developed a self-image that it was the rightful heir to Christian Constantinople and the long-gone Byzantine Empire. At the same time, Russia was beginning its expansion towards the Black Sea, and Empress Catherine the Great was proving a formidable opponent for the Ottomans. The "Greek Project" was hatched by the empress's advisor Count Grigori Potemkin and her chancellor Alexander Bezborodko as part of a wider blueprint for expansion of the empire. The project aimed at breaking up the Ottoman Empire by removing the Ottomans from Istanbul (Constantinople), to distribute their territories between the Russian and Austrian empires. The Christian Greek (Byzantine) empire would be re-established with a Russian monarch at its head, although it was

11. See p39.

41

intended that there would be no union of the two thrones of Russia and Byzantium. Catherine joined forces with the Austrian emperor Joseph II (1765-1790) in jointly attacking the Ottoman Empire, and Russian sources also refer to this as the "Great" or "Famous Plan".

Serious steps were taken by the Russians towards achieving these goals: first, the Crimea, the Taman area and then the Kuban peninsula along the northeastern Black Sea coast were annexed by Russia. The Ottoman Empire's surrender of its North and South Caucasian territories was inevitable. And once the Crimea had fallen into Russian hands, it could now face the Caucasian issue with confidence as the crumbling Persian empire provided further inspiration to enlarge its imperial dominion over the Caucasus and beyond.

From 1751, Persia had been divided into small principalities. The internal weakness of the empire was well known to the tsar's court but Russia could not go ahead with its plans to move southwards because of Ottoman support for Persia, which lasted until the 1780s. Through a defeat of Persia, however, Russia planned to create buffer states in the Caucasus and therefore supported the existing state of Kartli-Kakheti — the Christian Caucasian states would help Russia's plans to expand its trade in the east

It is therefore clear that the Caucasian issue formed part of a far wider foreign policy. As part of their imperialist blueprint, Potemkin and Bezborodko envisaged that the Georgians would support the creation of buffer states. The Armenian hierarch, Joseph Agrutinian, wrote to the imperial court, informing the count that King Erekle II had ample power and possessions in the Caucasus, including Ganja, Erevan and Nakhchevan, and could assemble an army of 40,000 men in time of emergency. Hardly intending acts of charity in the Caucasus, these implementers of Russian diplomacy continued to cultivate friendly relationships with the Caucasian rulers while at the same time working to increase their control and influence over them.

Such were the conditions in 1782 under which King Erekle commenced his negotiations with the Russians. Although the Russian state, for its part, planned to support Georgia, the Georgian king himself had been intending to seek Russian protection. And yet there had already existed a separate history of Russian-Georgian relations prior to this period and the treaty. As already mentioned,[12] during the 16th century the king of Kakheti, Alexander, had asked for help from Ivan the Terrible of Russia. And though no contemporary evidence exists to confirm it, 17th-century documents claim that in the preceding century Kakheti was under the juridical

12. See p40.

protectorate of Russia. An "Award of Mercy", granted in 1587 by Ivan's son Theodor (r. 1584-1598) to Alexander, declared that the Georgian monarch was obliged to remain faithful to the Russian tsar until his death.

It was a common in its foreign policy for Russia to negotiate with weaker political units and offer help; the practice amounted to a gesture that suggested subordination. In this instance, however, the interests of the two countries coincided: Russia obliged Georgia to support the empire in fighting the Ottomans and in return promised to provide protection. Russia also demanded tribute such as kilims, fabrics with gold and silver embroidery, silk and well-bred horses. In 1752, the kings Teimuraz and Erekle sent their ambassadors to Russia, to Empress Elisabeth I (1741-1761), in order to renew the benefits for the country provided by the Award of Mercy. But their mission ended in failure.

By the 1770s it became clear to Erekle that the situation in the Ottoman Empire might be generating sufficient concern among the Russians to take Georgia under its protectorate once more. He accordingly sent his ambassadors Prince Levan and Catholicos-Patriarch Anthony II (1762-1827), together with an entourage of about sixty fellow Georgians, on a journey to St Petersburg at the beginning of 1772. The Georgian legates were, however, kept in honorary exile by the Russians in Astrakhan for almost twelve months. In April of the following year they eventually reached St Petersburg and handed over Erekle's letter to the tsar's minister of external affairs.

Among the Georgian king's requests were the following:

—to rid Georgia of non-Christian invaders;
—to provide a regular army of 4,000 to defend Georgia against attacks from Persia and Ottoman Turkey;
—to help in liberating the Georgian territories from Persia and Ottoman Turkey on condition that they remain loyal to the Georgian king;
—on the basis of help provided, Georgia to send one royal prince, several princes, and nobility to the Russian royal court as a sign of loyalty;
—to make offerings of silk and wine.

Although Russia found these proposals themselves of little interest, Catherine nevertheless promised to help Georgia in its struggle against the Ottomans. This was helped by the Treaty of Kuchuk-Kainarji.[13]

Several years later, in 1781, Georgia fell actively into the agenda of

13. Signed on July 21, 1774, between Russia and the Ottoman Empire after the Ottomans were defeated in the Russo-Turkish War of 1768-1774.

Russia's large-scale plans against the Ottoman Empire. In that year Russia made an effort to influence Erekle through the mediation of his German personal doctor, Reinegs. The intention was for Reinegs to draw up a new set of requirements for the acceptance of Georgia under Russian protection. In this new plea, Erekle essentially reiterated his former demands but with a few additions. But he also now reflected on the possibility of seeking protection from the Ottomans and Persia.

There is a letter from Catherine and her chancellor Bezborodko to Count Potemkin that instructs the latter on the Georgian question. With diplomatic subtlety the document reflects Russia's true agenda, suggesting that a treaty be made with the Georgians who are named as "allies", to be protected by the Russian Empire. It demands the abolition of tax payments (a reasonable decision at that time), the taking of only a 50 per cent share of Georgia's natural resources and minerals, as well as a demand for good wine, silk and horses. It goes on to demand the prohibition of direct diplomatic relations with the other European empires, that two regiments of the Russian army be sent to Georgia and the appointment of Russian as local rulers to combat the instability in the Caucasus. Crucially, it recommends links between the Georgian hierarchs and the Synod of the Russian Church, and the installation of the Georgian Primate as one of the senior hierarchs of the Russian Synod (in this way, for example, Roman Catholic clergy would be deprived of direct contact with the Georgian hierarchs — their contact would be indirect, through the Russian Synod).

This letter to Count Potemkin is most instructive. It is clear that Russia was trying to protect Georgia from non-Christian invaders but was also seeking complete control over the protectorate, especially in its relations with other powers. And by submitting the more ancient Orthodox Church of Georgia to its own synod, Russia was stealthily moving into the spiritual heart of Georgia. The Russians were well aware that the Orthodox Church for centuries had been the rock upon which the national identity and integrity of the Georgian nation had been founded.

When Erekle II sent his first petition to the Russian court in 1773, he demanded that the Georgian primate be retained along with himself as king. But were Erekle and his court actually aware of the church structure in Russia?[14] In view of the fact that Anthony, the Catholicos of Georgia, had spent several years in Russia and had most probably par-

---

14. Under Peter the Great, patriarchal rule in the Russian church had been replaced by a governing synod.

ticipated in the discussions surrounding the first petition, it would seem reasonable to assume that the situation of the Russian Church would have been known to Erekle.

The Treaty of Georgievsk itself is revealing about the new Church regulations in Georgia. Article 8 of the first part of the treaty refers specifically to church affairs. Until its final draft, arrangements had been made whereby the Georgian primate was ranked as the fifth hierarch of the Russian Synod, after the metropolitans of Kiev, Novgorod, Moscow

and St Petersburg. Furthermore, he was first among the "second class" hierarchs of the same Synod. The situation, however, changed radically in the final version: now, the Georgian primate was to be given a lower place in the Russian Synod after the metropolitan of Tobolsk. Article 8 ends with a note stating that a new article on church matters would be prepared. However, no new bylaws were ever discussed.

The feelings of the Georgian court with regard to the structure of the Russian Church remain unknown to us. We do not know whether or not Georgians sympathised with the close links that existed between church and state. What is known, however, is that after the official signing and adoption of the Treaty, Erekle despatched a special petition to the Russian court, asking it to retain the status of the Georgian primate along with that of the king. This request was granted immediately and it remained in force for about a decade.

Russian diplomacy attempted to make the conditions for its supervision of Georgia as flexible as possible. A strong and growing empire, Russia was aware that the political status quo in Europe was subject to change and that much of the state's foreign policy in fact depended on these changes. The fluctuation of power in Persia and the Ottoman

Anthony II

The Caucasus at the end of the 18th century

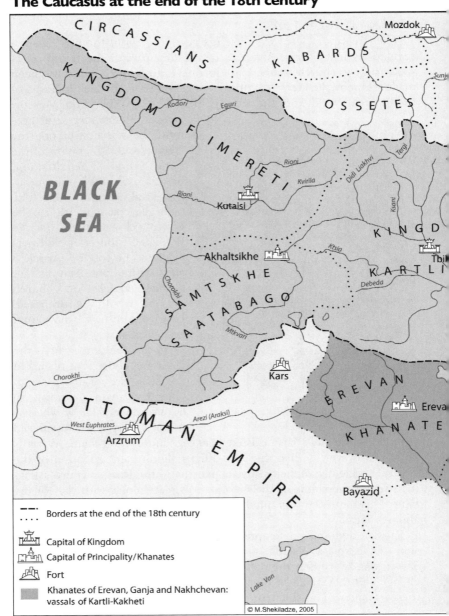

CIRCASSIANS

Mozdok

KABARDS

Sunj

KINGDOM

Kodori

Eguri

OSSETES

OF

Rioni

IMERETI

Kvirila

Didi Liakhvi

Terg

BLACK
SEA

Rioni

Kutaisi

KINGD

Ksia

Akhaltsikhe

KARTLI

Tbi

Debeda

SAMTSKHE

Chorokhi

SAATABAGO

Mtkvari

Chorokhi

Kars

EREVAN

OTTOMAN

West Euphrates

Arezi (Araksi)

Ereva

Arzrum

KHANATE

EMPIRE

Bayazid

Lake Van

© M.Shekiladze, 2005

- - - Borders at the end of the 18th century
. . . .

Capital of Kingdom

Capital of Principality/Khanates

Fort

Khanates of Erevan, Ganja and Nakhchevan:
vassals of Kartli-Kakheti

Empire determined the changes in Russian foreign policy with respect to the Georgian question, and Georgia may have never become a matter of interest *per se* except for its role in the greater plans of Russia for hegemony in the entire Caucasus and beyond to the Balkans.

On July 24, 1783, after prolonged diplomatic negotiations, Eastern Georgia (Kartli-Kakheti) and Russia signed the treaty in the North Caucasian fortress of Georgievsk. The signatories were General Pavel Potemkin on Russia's behalf and Ivan Mukhranbatoni and Prince Garsevan Chavchavadze on the Georgian side. King Erekle ratified it on January 24, 1784.

According to the terms of this treaty, Eastern Georgia officially came under the protectorate of Russia. The Georgian royal family recognised the supreme protectorate of the Russian Empire, eschewed any kind of dependence from Persia or any other state, undertook to serve Russia with its armed forces and not to establish any relations with other countries without consulting the command of the Russian Army in the northern Caucasus. Georgian kings were to receive the insignia of royal investiture from the Russian emperors and with it were to swear allegiance to Russia. The coronation of Georgian kings would be held in accordance with local traditions. In its turn, Russia undertook to retain the throne for Georgia's royal Bagrationi family and to protect it. Russia committed itself to restore Eastern Georgia by force of arms into the country's borders by regaining territories annexed by Ottoman Turkey and Persia. The Russian Empire also undertook not to interfere in the domestic affairs of Kartli-Kakheti, to regard Georgia's enemies as its own enemies, to deploy two infantry battalions and four cannon in Kartli-Kakheti, and to recover by force of arms ancient Georgian territory now in the hands of the Ottomans.

Moreover, Georgian noblemen who settled in Russia would enjoy equal rights with Russian noblemen. Georgian merchants would enjoy in Russia the same privileges and freedoms as granted to Russian merchants while the same would apply to Russian merchants in Kartli and Kakheti. As mentioned above, a special article of the treaty stated that the problem of the structure of the Georgian church would be the subject of a special agreement but that the Catholicos-Patriarch of Eastern Georgia would become a member of the Holy Synod of the Russian Church. Georgia's consent to this last provision was a terrible mistake, for it undeniably violated the rights of the Orthodox Church of Georgia as an autocephalous and independent Church.

The 1783 treaty was an act of voluntary acceptance by a small kingdom, surrounded by enemies, of a strong and vast empire's protection. Georgia's rulers wished to receive from great Russia judicial guarantees of security and the maintenance of Georgia's integrity as a state. The treaty was accordingly declared to be a "friendly agreement" concluded "forever". It could only be amended by mutual agreement on both sides.

By the 1790s, Russia had defeated the Ottoman Empire but did not take action to hand over its part of the lost Georgian territories. No less important was the fact that Leopold II of Austria reached an agreement in 1790 with King Frederick William II of Prussia to halt Austrian expansion into the western territories of the Ottoman Empire. Leopold therefore abandoned the alliance his predecessor Joeseph had made with Catherine. In August 1791, Austria signed a formal peace treaty with Turkey (at Sistova). Russian foreign policy was increasingly preoccupied with unrest in Poland, Sweden's invasion of Finland, and the French Revolution of 1789 (especially in the light of the rebellion by the Russian peasants under Emelian Pugachov a few years earlier).

These developments, along with the death in 1791 of the protagonist of the "Greek Project", Count Potemkin, and the resurgence of Persia (Iran) under the Qajar Agha Muhammad in the same period, completely changed the circumstances of the Russian protectorate in Georgia. Around this time, two Russian regiments were recalled to Russia never to return. The Treaty of 1783, though not formally abandoned by the Russian-Ottoman truce of 1791, was never mentioned again. The old plans for hegemony in the Caucasus were discarded and a new plan was set in motion. And so the hopes of Georgia's royalty to maintain and strengthen their state with the assistance of Russia were dashed. Georgia was to be without statehood or independence for a long time to come.

The 19th and early 20th centuries

Establishing Russian imperial rule

The Eastern Georgian kingdom of Kartli-Kakheti faced the year 1801 and the new 19th century without its king, Giorgi XII, who died on December 28, 1800. In the New Year, Eastern Georgia lost its national independence — and so Giorgi XII entered history as the last king of Kartli-Kakheti.

Having broken the terms of the 1783 Treaty of Georgievsk by abolishing Kartli-Kakheti as a kingdom, Russia declared Georgia to be one of the provinces of its empire. In fact, all of this had already taken place during Giorgi's lifetime. When the Russian tsar Pavel I (1796-1801) learned of the king's final illness and of the prevailing struggle among numerous claimants to his throne, he wrote on November 15, 1800 to the commander of the Russian army's Caucasian line, General Karl Knorring:

> The illness of the king gives all of us grounds to think that his demise is imminent. For this reason, when it occurs, immediately despatch on our behalf the command not to announce the heir to the throne without our permission" (Butkov, 1869, pp 463f).

On December 18, ten days before Giorgi's death, Pavel I signed a manifesto by which the kingdom of Kartli-Kakheti ceased to exist and its territory proclaimed a part of the Russian Empire.

In March 1801, Pavel was assassinated by conspirators. The new tsar, Alexander I (1801-1825) submitted the matter of Russia's annexation of Eastern Georgia for consideration by the State Council, which, on August 8, confirmed the advantages of such an action. No thought, however, was given as to its legitimacy. The State Council's decision was followed by a new Manifesto signed by Alexander on September 12, 1801 and officially announced in Tbilisi at Sioni cathedral on April 12, 1802.

The 19th and early 20th centuries

In it the Georgian question was finally settled: Eastern Georgia was declared a constituent part of the Russian Empire.

Russian troops, "who had a secret order to use weapons in case of any resistance" (Surguladze, 1991, p12), surrounded the cathedral. On the same day a supreme body headed by the "commander-in-chief of Georgia" was established to govern the country. General Knorring was appointed as the first commander-in-chief while General P. Kovalensky became the first "ruler" of Georgia and the second in command in the administrative hierarchy.

The Georgian administration was divided into four departments: executive (the principal, headed by the ruler himself), civil, criminal and treasury. Eastern Georgia was divided into five districts: Tbilisi, Gori, Dusheti, Telavi and Sighnaghi, each of which was headed by Russian bureaucrats — so-called *kapitan-ispravniks* ("captain-regulators" or district officers; Berdzenishvili *et al.*, 1958, p398). This system, adopted from Russian law, reiterated the principles of the Russian province laws of 1775.

After the complete annexation of Eastern Georgia, Russia now gradually began to occupy the west, where at the time there existed several independent and semi-independent political units: the kingdom of Imereti and the principalities of Guria, Odishi (Samegrelo/Mingrelia), Abkhazia and Svaneti.

General Pavel Tsitsianov, a Georgian prince brought up in Russia and later appointed commander-in-chief of Georgia, achieved considerable success in integrating Western Georgia into the Russian empire. The situation he found was a complex one. The king of Imereti, Solomon II, had been a long-time sympathiser with the Russians, but he realised that the same fate was in store for his realm following the events in the east. For this reason, he soon adopted an anti-Russian position, but the move came too late — Russia was set on laying its hands on Western Georgia. Solomon made every effort to resist the annexation of Imereti and even led a rebellion against the Russian intruders, but in 1810, defeated, he was forced to flee to Turkey where he died in exile in 1815.

Of the western principalities, the first to fall into Russian hands was Odishi (Samegrelo). In July 1803, its prince or *mtavari*, Grigol Dadiani, assumed the patronage of Russia, as did his counterpart in the neighbouring principality of Guria. Tsitsianov then began to meddle with Abkhazia but since it was under control of the Ottoman Empire, Russia could not lay claims to the territory. However, during the

Russian-Ottoman war of 1805-1815, Russia finally managed to gain a foothold in Abkhazia and placed Prince Giorgi Shervashidze under its patronage.

Soon after the appropriation of Eastern Georgia, Russian imperialist policies of assimilation began. These had their origin in the well-known formula expressed by Catherine II: "Georgian in body, Russian in spirit" (Khutsishvili, 1987, p36) — in other words, the gradual but total russification of all Georgians and the annihilation of Georgia's culture, traditions and language. It was a policy that infected every sphere of life throughout Tsarist Russia's sovereignty that lasted 116 years, from 1801 to 1917. All official state business correspondence, as well as communications in the military, and in every kind of court had to be conducted in Russian, of which most Georgians unsurprisingly were ignorant.

Autocephaly of the Georgian church was terminated and it now fell under the authority of Holy Synod of Russia. As a result, most of the cathedrals and churches began celebrating the liturgy in Church Slavonic, the old Slavic language used in the Russian church liturgy. Ultimately, Georgian was eliminated in many areas. There were villages, for example, where Russian troops were located and church services were conducted in Russian in spite of the fact that the local population did not understand the language. The same process was introduced in the larger towns and the capital Tbilisi. Russian rule inevitably brought Russian migrants and the creation of a gateway for other nationals into Georgia. In 1817, for example, more than 500 German families entered Georgia from Russia and, from 1829 to 1830, 6,000 Greeks and Armenians crossed over from the Ottoman Turkish border.

In addition, from the end of the 1830s the Russian government began to establish in Georgia special military settlements for retired soldiers (i.e. those who had served for a minimum of 15 years). It also systematically populated regions of Georgia, that were otherwise regarded as uninhabitable, with Christian sects persecuted by the Russian authorities. These included Dukhobors, Molokans, Khlysts, Skopts (who practised castration) and Old Believers.[1] By the middle of the 1840s their total number had exceeded 10,000 (Surguladze, 1991, pp 23-26).

---

1.   Known in Russian as the *Starovieri*, who split from the Russian Orthodox Church in opposition to church reforms introduced in 1653-1666 .

Uprisings against Russian domination

From the very onset of foreign rule in Georgia the struggle of the people against the Russian regime took effect. Once it had annexed the kingdom of Kartli-Kakheti, the Russian government saw its prime task as being the removal of the royal line of the Bagrationis from all official affairs and sending them as exiles to Russia. As early as 1802, members of the royal family instigated a revolt to overthrow the occupiers, but luck was not on their side and it was aborted.

The inspirer of this plot was Queen Darejan (1726-1807). She had been the wife of King Erekle II since 1750 but was never able to enjoy independent rule as the king's widow. The plot was hatched at her palace in Tbilisi, and she and Bagrationis had the full support of the majority of the nobility of Eastern Georgia. In a letter addressed to General Kovalensky, the Georgian nobles demanded firstly the restoration of the kingdom of Georgia, and secondly that all of the terms of 1783's Treaty of Georgievsk be observed (Kikvidze, 1977, pp 31f). The Russian authorities promptly detained the Georgian princes who delivered the letter and started investigating the other plotters. Such behaviour provoked an instant reaction from the Kakheti nobility, who gathered at the village of Magaro on July 24, 1802 with the intention of enthroning Erekle's son Julon. Russian troops managed to disperse the meeting and later to arrest all the instigators and leaders of the plot. In 1803, Darejan was sent into exile to the Russian capital of St Petersburg along with the other members of the Georgian royal family. She died in 1807 and is buried in the city's Alexander Nevsky Lavra.

Meanwhile, Georgian peasants from the highlands of Mtiuleti, who had been subjected to intolerable duress by the Russian military, began a fresh large-scale revolt in 1804. At the time, Georgia was connected with Russia by a single highway that led through the Daryal Gorge. This road was in constant need of repair and the entire burden of restorative work weighed heavily on the shoulders of the local people. If this were not enough, the peasants were also obliged to provide the Russian army with provisions and transport.

The Russian officers and soldiers were in the habit of mocking the village folk aggressively. Very often they harnessed men — even women — into bulls' yokes, and in Mtiuleti it was reported that Russian soldiers had whipped 23 peasants to death. Brutal punishment was meted out not only for disobedience but even if a civilian made a simple complaint to a senior officer. The soldiers burnt houses, raped women and took away everything the peasants still possessed. In one account a peasant wrote:

"If before we prayed to God to send Russian soldiers here to help us, now we long for death in order not to witness the degradation of our wives' and daughters' honour, and not to die from torture and the lash" (Gogoladze, 1973, p917). The cup was filled to overflowing, and so in May 1804, the peasants, supported by a number of noblemen, rebelled. This was an uprising that spread to many regions of Eastern Georgia.

The revolt which had begun principally on social grounds developed into a cause for the restoration of the Georgian state. Many other Georgians, however, supported the new regime and promoted the side of the Russian troops and rallied round the authorities. Tsitsianov, who at that time had besieged the Yerevan fortress, wrote to the eristavi of Ksani: "Ruthlessly slash and slaughter the rebels, ruin their villages. To put it bluntly, when entering their homes, forget mercy and make no allowance. You must treat them as malefactors" (Kikvidze, 1977, pp 48-49). Only by the end of October 1804 and with great difficulty and many losses did the Russian occupying troops manage to suppress this national armed revolt.

Again, on January 31, 1812, owing to the extraordinary excesses of the foreign regime, another uprising broke out in historic Kakheti and in some districts of Kartli. Prince Grigol Bagrationi was declared king of Kakheti, although Prince Alexander Bagrationi played a greater role in the uprising. The Russian forces, however, took energetic measures and by the end of 1812 succeeded once more in suppressing the insurgents. In the course of the hostilities thousands of peasants were killed and dozens of villages burnt (Kikvidze, 1977, p81).

With their elimination of the Patriarchate of Eastern Georgia and the subsequent reform of church administration, Russian civil and church authorities also put into effect a re-ordering in Western Georgia, where, unhindered, the church had retained control over its affairs. Now that the Western Georgian church was under Russian control, each and every item of church property (including land holdings and property) was itemised and the number of clergy and eparchies reduced (Dumbadze, 1957, p232). The inventory, which began in June 1819, met with fierce resistance from the Georgian clergy and the faithful. It did not take long before isolated skirmishes blossomed into a national rebellion which, under the slogan "Freedom for the Motherland", lasted for two years (Gogoladze, 1973, p932).[2]

Resistance spread as far as Imereti, Guria and Samegrelo. It assumed a threatening character for the Russian authorities owing to the fact that

2. See Part II, Chapter 1, 'Abolition of Autocephaly and Formation of the Exarchate'.

a very broad spectrum of the population — peasants, craftsmen, and nobility — was involved. By the end of July 1820, Russian troops suppressed the revolt and arrested its leaders, but at the same time concessions had to be made and the authorities were obliged to handle church reform with greater discretion. This was a clear lesson for the Russians: Georgia was not prepared to tolerate oppression.

After 1825 there appeared, among members of the Georgian royal family and other nobles forced to relocate to Russia, new groups whose aim was to liberate Georgia from Russian rule. In 1829, when a core group of conspirators returned to Georgia, they devised a plot to overthrow the occupiers. Key members of the group were Prince Okropir Bagrationi, Elizbar Eristavi, Alexander Chavchavadze, Grigol Orbeliani, Solomon Dodashvili, and the hieromonk Philadelphos Kiknadzde.

They had modelled their aspirations on the Polish rebellion of 1830-1831, and so the Poles' defeat came as a severe disappointment. But while many of the Georgian patriots lost all hopes of victory, some continued to be active for the cause. One plan arranged for November 20, 1832 was delayed by a month. The Georgian nobility had arranged a grand banquet in Tbilisi for members of Russian high society — both military and civil — who would have been summarily murdered. Simultaneous actions by the general population, but supported by the conspirators' military detachment, would then have been staged in the city.

The conspirators had hoped first that a knock-on effect would take place all over Georgia, and that support would then be provided by the Muslim and Armenian populations (Kikvidze, 1977, p149). In the event of success, a provisional government would be formed, which later would defer to the establishment of a constitutional monarchy. A sovereign would rule in collaboration with a two-chamber parliament: the upper for ministers under the monarch and the lower for deputies (5, 150).

The whole strategy, however, was aborted on December 9 as a result of the betrayal of Iase Palavandishvili, the brother of Niko, the governor of Tbilisi, who reported the plot to the police. All of the conspirators were arrested and exiled to remote Russian provinces. And yet, in spite of this failure, the struggle for national independence did not falter. Year after year in different parts of Georgia peasant revolts broke out. The aristocracy, the intelligentsia and the working classes worked and fought side by side in the struggle for freedom from colonial oppression.

Positive effects of occupation

Irrespective of the loss of state independence and the accompanying repression, there were some positive results stemming from the Russian occupation. Foremost was the fact that Georgia was finally relieved of the constant fear of invasion by Persian, Ottoman or Dagestani feudal lords. This alone had positive effects on the development of the country's economy. Of major significance was the fact that Georgians were now working together with Russian soldiers in the struggle for the return of those historic Georgian provinces that had earlier been seized by foreign powers.

In 1809, a joint Russian-Georgian army drove Ottoman occupiers from the Black Sea port of Poti, and again, in 1811, Ottoman troops were also driven from Akhalkalaki (though here the joint army proved itself unable to consolidate its position). Of singular importance for Georgia were the consequences of the Russian-Ottoman war of 1828-1829. At its end the ancient territories of Samtskhe-Javakheti (Akhaltsikhe, Atskuri, Artaani) were re-united with Georgia. Of course, it is true to say that in retrieving these regions the Russian government was less concerned with Georgia's past and the restoration of historical justice than with expanding its borders to the south. On the other hand, it must also be conceded that without the assistance afforded by Russian arms, none of these ancient Georgian territories would have been recovered.

With the cessation of Ottoman-led hostilities and the establishment of peace, Georgian culture received a new impetus for development and growth. Moreover, the opening of schools, gymnasiums, parish-based teaching and so on — despite their colonial bent — constituted a highly positive initiative. Many Georgians, having completed their high school education at home, were able to continue their studies at universities in Russia. A large number of these graduates were responsible for laying the bases for the future progress of Georgian sciences and the arts.

The former palaces and mansions of Georgia's princes and nobility now became centres of learning and exchange for the Georgian and Russian intelligentsia. Literary saloons were also created for gatherings of foreign nationals. These undertakings, and many others, contributed to the wider dissemination of Georgian culture in general and of its ancient literary heritage in particular.

Georgia received not only the worst bureaucrats and the most inconsiderate officials from Russia, but also its best intellectuals and scholars, all of whom expressed admiration for Georgia and its society.

"At different times Georgia was visited by famous poets and writers, such as Griboedov, Pushkin, Lermontov, Tolstoy and many Decembrists,[3] who in their turn, introduced the Caucasus and Georgia to Russia" (Berdzenishvili *et al.*, 1958, p478).

In these ways, the Georgian people, who had continually struggled against Russian domination and, despite the severity of the imperial authorities, managed to preserve their original traditions, language, and culture not only through their own unceasing efforts but also through the efforts of the Russian intelligentsia. Seen in a broader perspective, these events provided an appropriate milieu for the restoration of Georgia's religious independence in 1917 and state independence in 1918.

Reorganisation and liberalisation

The period between 1835 and 1840 was marked by restrictions placed on the local population's responsibilities in administrative structures, local self-government, and courts. Moreover, when the idea was raised to replace the administrative system established in the early 19th century, high-ranking Russian officials considered the prospect of the complete suppression of the local elements from administration. Earlier in the late 1820s, Field Marshal General Ivan Paskevich had initiated discussion along these lines. He demanded a "speedy [and] immediate" institution of a purely Russian system free of local elements but "with one joint decree" (Antelava, 1970, p127).

A reorganisation of the Russian administration that had existed in Georgia for 40 years was carried out in 1841 based on the regulations of "the officially confirmed supreme government of Transcaucasus" compiled by Baron Gan. In accordance with this law, the Transcaucasus was divided into two large entities, the Georgia-Imereti District and the Caspian District. The administration of the entire Caucasus operated at three levels — executive, provincial and district. The first level, exercising its powers over the entire Transcaucasus, consisted of the commander-in-chief of the Transcaucasus, Tbilisi's military governor, and the Council of the Supreme Administration.

3. The Decembrists, members of the Russian aristocracy, were revolutionaries who rebelled in 1825 against the tsarist regime and the feudal system. They dreamt of a constitutional monarchy while one faction, headed by P. Pestel, demanded the abolition of the monarchy. On December 14, 1814, the Decembrists led a huge protest in Senate Square in St Petersburg but it was broken up by the authorities. Five of the organisers — Pestel, Rileev, Kakhovsky, Muravyov and Bestuzhev-Ryumin — were hanged, 121 supporters were exiled to Siberia, and 2,000 citizens, officers and soldiers were despatched to the Caucasus.

The commander-in-chief was in charge of all secular and ecclesiastic affairs. Simultaneously, he headed the Council of the Supreme Administration and was the Commander of the Special Caucasus Corps. His powers were equal to those of the governor generals of the provinces of Russia proper. The military governor of Tbilisi was the commander-in-chief's deputy for all issues (Antelava, 1970, p129).

One more important change took place in 1845. Military rule and martial law gave way to civil rule. The post of commander-in-chief was abolished and a viceroy arrived to head the Caucasus administration. The viceroy had extremely broad powers when compared with those of the previous commander-in-chief, and he reported personally to the tsar and not to a central department of the Russian imperial administration. Furthermore, he was authorised to resolve all issues on the spot, whereas the commander-in-chief would in such cases have to consult with St Petersburg (Kikvidze, 1977, p180).

It was its viceroy policy that helped the Russian empire to annex the North Caucasus via Georgia. The first to hold the office was Mikhail Vorontsov (viceroy from 1844-1854), who decided to pursue a fairly liberal policy and build up good relations with the Georgian nobility. His course of action was more flexible than Russia's early policies towards Georgia, as evidenced by the fact that he helped found the periodical *Tsiskari* ("Daybreak") in Georgian and to establish Georgian theatre; on his initiative too a public library was opened in Tbilisi in 1846.

Incentives such as these aroused the sympathy of Georgian nobility towards Russian rule, though it did not entirely replace anti-Russian sentiments. Vorontsov also gave a number of concessions to the Georgian aristocracy. Many children of noble ancestry were sent for studies to universities in Moscow and St Petersburg. It is unsurprising, therefore, that the viceroy's policies stimulated some feelings of reconciliation with Russian rule on the part of the majority of Georgia's noble class.

Since the early 1830s, the Russian imperial court had been deliberating about who in Georgia might be recognised by Russian imperial protocol as princes and *aznaurs*. Owing to the difficulties of the times, many were negligent in presenting the appropriate documents to confirm their noble position. Hence, the matter turned out to be protracted and ineffective. Vorontsov ended the procedure promptly by conferring the title "nobleman" on around 30,000 individuals (Antelava, 1970, p134). At the same time, he relieved landowners of their obligation to submit documents to courts confirming their ownership of serfs. The upper classes of Imereti and Guria were empowered to elect their own leader, or

The 19th and early 20th centuries

"marshal". Through these measures Vorontsov almost completely won over the Georgian aristocracy, making most of them faithful subjects of the empire (Vachnadze & Guruli, 2001, p32).

At the same time, Russian demographic expansion continued both under Vorontsov and his successor A. Baryatinski (1856-1862). Settlements of the Russian military were founded — 21 were in existence by 1856 — and the imperial administration continued to encourage Russian sects and other non-Georgians to settle in Georgia.

A further change occurred in the 1846 administrative division of the Caucasus. Four provinces — Tbilisi, Kutaisi, Shemakha and Derbent — were created to replace those of Georgia-Imereti and Caspian. The Yerevan Province was added to this number in 1849 (Antelava, 1970, p135). The institution of the viceroy meant a certain administrative autonomy. But this came to an end in 1882, when the position was temporarily abolished and that of commander-in-chief restored. In 1905 the position of viceroy was reintroduced and lasted until the February Revolution of 1917.

Tightening of centralized rule

In the second half of the 19th century, with the final consolidation of Russia's military control over the Caucasus, the coloniser's oppression of the nation became harsher. Russia gradually removed the limited autonomy enjoyed by the Western Georgian provinces of Mingrelia (Samegrelo, also known as Megrelia), Abkhazia (Apkhazeti) and Svaneti — the province of Guria had been abolished earlier in 1829.

There were good reasons why Russian authorities had tolerated the existence of these provinces for so long. Firstly, by granting a level of independence to the provinces, Russia won over the princes and diminished the possibility of unification around Solomon II of Imereti. Secondly, Russia could, of course, have annexed all of Western Georgia by force in the early 19th century. But such a move could have aggravated the international situation, since the Ottomans, then in control of the Black Sea coast, could have interfered in Georgia's internal affairs by starting a new war (Vachnadze & Guruli, 2001, p35). In fact, Russia managed to avert the creation of a joint anti-Russian front in Western Georgia and gradually eliminated all of the provinces once its positions in Eastern Georgia and Imereti became consolidated. The province of Samegrelo met its end in 1857, Svaneti in 1858, and finally Apkhazeti in 1864.

In the economic sphere the principle aim of Russia's colonial policy was not only the transformation of Georgia into a market for Russian goods, but also the utilisation of Georgia as a base of raw materials for Russia's factories and plants. The country continued to be populated on an even larger scale by non-Georgians. The newcomers were given the best lands and granted particular privileges and rights never enjoyed by the Georgian population.

This period is also marked by absolute limitations on the degree to which Georgians were permitted to participate in the local ministries of government, such as, the police, courts, schools and churches. From the early 1860s the teaching of the Georgian language was first restricted and then totally excluded from state school curricula. The Russian authorities limited the distribution of Georgian newspapers and magazines and whatever was still being published had to pass the strictest censorship. The Russian administration even forbade mention of the word "Sakartvelo" (Georgia) — it had instead to be replaced in the press by "Tbilisi province" or "Kutaisi province" (Berdzenishvili et al., 1958, p528).

Towards national liberation

Concurrent with the strengthening of the colonial regime in Georgia, a new stage in the national-liberation movement began. As in the first half of the 19th century, this movement received its impetus from the Georgian people's desire for state independence and self-determination. The movement was led by a group called the "Tergdaleulebi" (literally "those who have drunk from the Terek river"), a name given to young Georgians who, in order to receive an education, were obliged to cross into Russia over the Terek (Tergi) river at Georgia's northern border. Since the Tergdaleulebi began their activities between 1860 and 1870, they are often referred to as "the Sixties Generation". Renowned Georgian writers and poets such as Ilia Chavchavadze, Akaki Tsereteli, Iakob Gogebashvili, Giorgi Tsereteli and Niko Nikoladze were prominent members of the group.

It was under Chavchavadze's leadership that the Tergdaleulebi developed and implemented the programme of the nationalist movement whose ultimate aim was the establishment of an independent Georgian state. Previous movements, especially the 1832 conspiracy, formed the basis of the nationalist agenda. Experiences of other oppressed peoples were also taken into account.

From the beginning, it was paramount to revive and strengthen Georgian self-consciousness and to consolidate the people. The

St Ilia the Righteous (1837-1907)

Ilia Chavchavadze was born into a family of a nobleman in Kvareli (Kakheti/Eastern Georgia). After receiving an elementary education at home, he entered a private boarding school in Tbilisi.

He went on to study law at the University of St Petersburg where he was introduced to modern philosophical and socio-political thought in Russia and Europe. After returning home in 1861, he became a leader of the Tergdaleulebi and of the national-liberation movement.

His activities embraced almost all spheres of social life. He contributed to the modernisation of the Georgian literary language. A writer of poetry and prose, he paid much attention to the national and social problems of the country. His ideal was to see a liberated Georgia with a society based on social justice.

In 1863, he edited the periodical *Sakartvelos Moambe* ("The Herald of Georgia"), around which the Tergdaleulebi gathered. In 1877-1901, he edited the daily paper *Iveria* ("Iberia"). After the abolition of serfdom (1864-1873), he worked in Dusheti in Eastern Georgia as a lawyer and was among the founders of the Georgian Estate Bank over which he presided from 1873 until his death. The profits of the bank were used for public schools, museums, and scholarships. Together with Dimitri Kipiani, he founded the Society for Dissemination of Literacy among the Georgians and helped to revive the country's Drama Society.

As a result of his active political life, he was elected as a member of the Russian State Council in 1906. He criticised the existing political regime, protested against capital punishment, and worked to protect the rights of the Orthodox Church of Georgia. He also exposed the anti-ecclesiastical policy of the tsarist regime as well as anti-Georgian policies of the state's theological schools. From the turn of the century he was actively involved in the movement favouring autocephaly.

For almost 50 years he was the spiritual leader of Georgia's national movement, a poet, writer, and public figure — the country's "uncrowned king". He was assassinated near the village of Tsitsamuri (20 km from Tbilisi) in August, 1907. The circumstances of his death remain obscure to this day.

country's economic revival was given prominence: the economy was to serve the interests of the population. The Tergdaleulebi's agenda was not oriented towards an individual class or social stratum but the entire nation. Chavchavadze had the greatest confidence that Georgia could only be saved and revived through reconciling the conflicting classes and through the co-operative efforts of the nation's varied social elements. In other words, this was intended to be an effort that encompassed the entire Georgian nation. It was Chavchavadze's belief that social confrontation and class struggle would only undermine the country's spirit, shatter its unity and weaken the new nationalist movement.

The Tergdaleulebi stressed the importance of organising purely Georgian schools as a means of reviving the national spirit, a move that would involve resistance to the policies of russification within the educational system. In 1879, they founded the Society for the Dissemination of Literacy for Georgians, whose most notable figure (*samotsianelebi*), Dimitri Kipiani, became its first chairman. In time, he was replaced by Ilia Chavchavadze. Although the Georgian language continued to be repressed, the society was successful in opening numerous elementary schools and libraries both in Georgia as well as in towns elsewhere in the Russian empire where significant numbers of Georgians were settled, including Vladikavkaz and Baku.

The Tergdaleulebi were also involved in publishing periodicals and books in Georgian. Noteworthy examples were *Sakartvelos Moambe* ("The Herald of Georgia"), a magazine founded by Ilia Chavchavadze in 1868, and his *Iveria* ("Iberia", 1877-1906).

Close to the hearts of the Tergdaleulebi was Georgian theatre, and they founded a dramatic society in 1880 that staged patriotic plays. One episode linked with the theatre is worthy of report where a play entitled *Samshoblo* ("Motherland", translated from the French by David Eristavi) proved to be such a success in Tbilisi that at one point, when the Georgian national flag was raised high onstage, the entire audience got to their feet. M. Katkov, editor of the Russian newspaper *Moskovskie Vedomosti* ("Moscow News") and a prominent reactionary, indignantly responded by referring to the Georgian flag as a "rag". He added that Georgians should "sell their flag to a circus", an expression meaning that it was an utter mockery. In response to these insults, Chavchavadze wrote a widely-acclaimed letter "In Response to Katkov" challenging negative attitudes to Georgian sovereignty.

The credo of the Tergdaleulebi could be summarised in the words of Ilia Chavchavadze, words that for many generations epitomised the national-liberation movement: "We have inherited three divine treasures from our ancestors — motherland, language and faith. Were we not to honour them, who should we be? What response shall we give to our descendants?"

Reforms and the peasant movement

As part of the empire, any legal decree that pertained to Russia applied also to Georgia — and this included the Great Reforms introduced by Alexander II (1855-1881) concerning the abolition of serfdom in 1861. In Georgia this came into effect some years later and in stages: first in the Tbilisi region (October, 1864), then in Kutaisi province (November 1865), and finally in Samegrelo (1867). Reforms of town and city administration implemented in Russia in 1820 also took place in Georgia much later: Tbilisi in 1874, Kutaisi and Batumi in 1888, and other towns between 1892 and 1894.

Each of these reforms provoked violent reactions from the Georgian peasantry. In 1856, four years before the abolition of serfdom, a major revolt broke out in Samegrelo that involved thousands of peasants. Other noteworthy insurgencies took place in Imereti (1857), Guria (1862), Kartli (1863) and Abkhazia (1866). In 1865, representatives of the poor and craftsmen in Tbilisi stirred up a rebellion in which petty tradesmen also became involved. Alexander's reforms were ultimately flawed and their implementation failed to quell unrest in Georgia. It was clear that the peasants continued to be dissatisfied.

Throughout the 1870s several uprisings occurred. A large peasant insurrection broke out in Svaneti in 1875/1876, and another in Samegrelo in 1876 that began in Zugdidi in Samegrelo district but soon spread to Senaki district as well. The 20,000 who were involved were quelled by Russian forces, resulting in a great number being killed or wounded, while many others were sentenced to long years of hard labour. When the peasants of Kakheti rose in rebellion in 1878, the authorities once more employed armed forces to quell the insurgence and, again, many rebels were later exiled to Siberia (Vachnadze & Guruli, 2001, pp 65-66).

It was at this precise time that Narodnik ("People") ideas began to circulate in Georgia. The Narodnik movement had emerged in Russia as an off-shoot of socialism. Its members campaigned for a society where all were equal in every respect; they also believed that all land should be taken from private hands and equally distributed among the peasants and the working classes (Vachnadze & Guruli, 2001, p65). One of the principal aims of the Russian Narodniks was to organise an all-Russian peasant rebellion, but in this they failed — some took the path of terror after the collapse of the organisation.

Young people returning from Russia began disseminating Narodnik ideas in Georgia and actively participated in the Russian Narodnik organisation Zemlya i Volya ("Land and Freedom"). Prominent Georgian Narodniks were intellectuals such as Ivane Jabadari, Egnate Ioseliani and Mikheil Kipiani; the main centres of their activity in Georgia were Tbilisi, Kutaisi, Gori and Telavi. Like their Russian counterparts, the Georgian Narodniks sought to organise a broadly-based peasant rebellion. To this end they had pinned great hopes on the peasant insurgences in Svaneti and, especially, Samegrelo and Kakheti. However, the authorities subdued the revolts and arrested most of the Narodniks. The two most active of their number, Ioseliani and Kipiani, were sentenced to lifelong exile in eastern Siberia.

In contrast with Russia, however, Georgian Narodnik ideals were limited and failed to influence the broader population. The movement failed to become either a social or political force of note, and by the 1880s most of the Georgian Narodniks had joined the nationalist movement (Vachnadze & Guruli, 2001, p67).

Political perspectives during the 1890s

A split occurred in the Tergdaleulebi group in the early 1890s, resulting in the emergence of three new groups in the political and nationalist movements of Georgia. The first group, led by Ilia Chavchavadze, was consolidated around the *Iveria* newspaper which he himself published. They remained faithful to the nationalist principles expounded in the 1860s and held a firm conviction that the political, economic, social, and cultural progress of the Georgian nation could only be realised through implementation of their programme.

The second group, led by the well-known economist and publicist Niko Nikoladze, united around the publication *Moambe* ("Herald"). Nikoladze's agenda was a democratic one: he and his supporters held that only the political, economic, and social systems that existed in western European countries could save Georgia (Vachnadze & Guruli, 2001, p77).

Giorgi Tsereteli, publisher of the *Kvali* newspaper, and his supporters formed the third group. They pursued the nationalist programme of the 1860s, but at the same time were devoted to socialist ideas. Linking the resolution of the nationalist problem with socialism, Tsereteli's ideology appeared as a form of national socialism. Tsereteli, however, stressed that he was not in favour of cosmopolitan socialism that ignored the interests of individual nations and states but instead he stood for national socialism as a superior path to resolving national issues through socialism.

All three political groups were legal entities; in reality, they represented the entire political spectrum within Georgia. Abroad, a secret organisation called the League of Independence for Georgia had emerged in Warsaw in the early 1890s. Though it existed a mere three years, it had considerable impact on the Georgian public and on the Georgian political movements. Well-known figures such as Archil Jorjadze, Tedo Sakhokia, Noe Zhordania, Giorgi Gvazava and Mikheil Kheltuplishvili, among others, figured among the league's members. Its manifesto stated that the following steps were essential to develop the Georgian nation:

1. Support for the Russian people in their struggle against the monarchy (the league believed that by eliminating the monarchy in Russia favourable conditions could be created for the liberation of Georgia).
2. Winning support from the European countries by arousing western interest in Georgia as a nation with a strategic geographic position between powerful countries.
3. Establishing links with the peoples conquered by the Russian imperialists (such as the Poles, Finns and Baltic populations).
4. Intellectual development of the Georgian people (Vachnadze & Guruli, 2001, p79).

It is equally noteworthy that this programme laid special emphasis on the common interests of the Caucasian peoples in their struggle for independence. In general, the league believed that the peoples of the Caucasus could become liberated from the Russian yoke only through a joint effort.

Politics at the turn of the century

The 1890s in Russia were marked by rapid industrial development and technical progress. This process also embraced Georgia although, understandably, the pace of production lagged behind. Notable success, however, was achieved in mining and metallurgy, oil-refining, tobacco and food production.

In spite of this progress Georgia remained an agricultural country. Most people lived in villages with farming as their principal occupation,

Georgia at the end of the 19th century

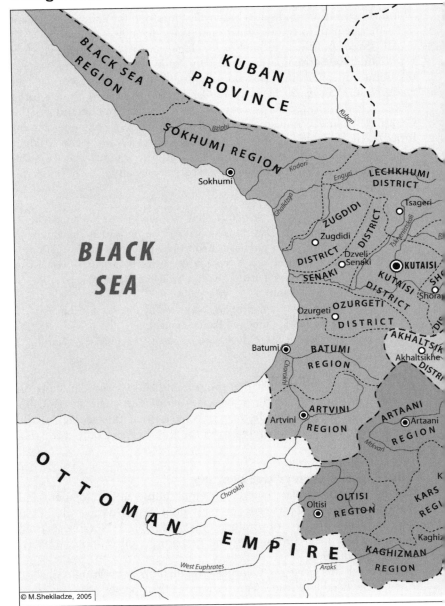

BLACK SEA REGION

KUBAN PROVINCE

Kuban

SOKHUMI REGION

Bziphi

Kodori

Sokhumi

Enguri

LECHKHUMI DISTRICT

Tsageri

Ghalitzga

ZUGDIDI DISTRICT

Zugdidi

Tskhenitstskali

BLACK SEA

SENAKI DISTRICT

Dzveli Senaki

KUTAISI

KUTAISI DISTRICT

SH

Shora

Ozurgeti

OZURGETI DISTRICT

Batumi

BATUMI REGION

AKHALTSIK

Akhaltsikhe

DISTRI

DIS

Chorokhi

Artvini

ARTVINI REGION

ARTAANI

Artaani

REGION

Mtkvari

OTTOMAN

Chorokhi

Oltisi

OLTISI REGION

KARS REGI

EMPIRE

West Euphrates

Araks

KAGHIZMAN REGION

Kaghiz

K

© M.Shekiladze, 2005

66

The 19th and early 20th centuries

Legend:
- ─ · ─ Border of Russian Empire
- ─ ─ ─ Borders of Provinces
- ········ Borders of Districts
- Province (Governership) of Tbilisi
- Province (Governership) of Kutaisi
- Region of Karsi

TERGI PROVINCE

Tergi

TIANETI DISTRICT

DAGHESTAN PROVINCE

GORI

DUSHETI DISTRICT

Gori

Dusheti

Tianeti

TELAVI DISTRICT

Telavi

ZAKATALA REGION

DISTRICT

TBILISI

TBILISI DISTRICT

Zakatala

SIGHNAGHI DISTRICT

Sighnaghi

Alazani

Shulaveri

BORCHALO DISTRICT

Debeda

Iori

Mtkvari

ELISAVETOPOL PROVINCE (GOVERNORSHIP)

ELISAVETOPOL (Ganja)

EREVAN PROVINCE (GOVERNORSHIP)

Lake Sevan

EREVAN

Araks

HA CT

Oni

NI

Didi Liakhvi

Ksani

Aragvi

Ktsia

ALKALAKI

STRICT

lkalaki

producing mainly cereals, wine, vegetables and fruit. By the turn of the century, silkworm breeding and tobacco-growing had also taken off.

During this same period, social inequality throughout all of the Russian empire was brought into sharp relief. Peasant disturbances and worker action became increasingly commonplace. Following the reforms of 1861 and semi-reforms of the 1860s and 1870s no single convincing social reorganisation had taken root, and it was patently obvious that absolute monarchy hindered the development of the country and blocked paths for the bourgeoisie to political power. Cumulatively, these issues resulted in discontent in all strata of the population. All over Russia new political parties and organisations promoted different kinds of agendas for the country's further development.

The social movement extended to Russia's borderlands, where, alongside with the demands for social reform were also national and anti-colonial problems. In Georgia as well new political organisations also appeared which attempted to rally round the cause of social reorganisation. The first to appear on the political horizon was the Social Democratic Party, whose ideology had spread to Georgia from Europe and Russia. It became a legal entity (ideologically and organisationally) at the Zestaponi and Tbilisi conferences (1892 and 1893 respectively). Leading the Georgian Social Democrats was Noe Zhordania while Georgian Social Democrats Akaki Chkhenkeli, Konstantine Chkheidze and Irakli Tsereteli played prominent roles in Russia's political life.

In 1903, at the second Congress of the Russian Social Democratic Party, a split occurred and two opposing factions, the Mensheviks and Bolsheviks, came into being. The Georgian Social Democrats found themselves involved in this struggle and also split up into Menshevik and Bolshevik camps.

The next significant step in political life was the Georgian Socialist Federalist Party under Archil Jorjadze, formed at the beginning of the 20th century. It declared it had two aims: the establishment of a socialist system in society, and for Georgia to become part of a federation headed by Russia. For this to be successful, Russia had first to become socialist and then be converted from a central into a federal state. A few years later, in 1905, an attempt was made to found a National Democratic Party of Georgia under the leadership of Ilia Chavchavadze. But this proved to be impossible even though the party's agenda had been fully worked out. The national question, of course, occupied a special place in its manifesto where it was stipulated that Georgia should acquire autonomy within the Russian state and that the autonomous state would have its own parliament to solve its domestic affairs. The party also envisioned the foundation of a Georgian university and the restoration of the autocephaly of the Georgian church (Vachnadze & Guruli, 2001, p91).

The revolution of 1905-1907

In the early years of the 20th century, the Russian tsarist regime, the Holy Synod of the Russian Orthodox Church, and the Exarchate of Georgia were in danger. Russia appeared to be on the brink of revolution as almost every class within society expressed their discontent with Russian imperialism, especially the workers and peasants who were nourished on the new ideas emanating from social democracy and Marxist ideology.

To redress this undesirable and negative situation and to divert the attention of the people to other problems, the Russian government declared war on Japan in 1904 on the grounds of the latter's annexation of Korea and Manchuria. As the tsar's interior minister Vyacheslav von Plehve (soon to be assassinated by a Socialist-Revolutionary bomber) announced, "in order to halt the revolution, a small victorious war is necessary" (Kacharava *et al.*, 1973, vol. ii, p35).

Almost every sector of Georgia's political and social movements took part in the Russian revolution of 1905-1907, whose beginning was hastened by Russia's humiliating defeat in the Russian-Japanese war of 1904-1905. The Russian bourgeoisie was finally convinced of the monarchy's inability to defend the interests of the state — this was a failing that infringed on the economic interests of the middle classes. Moreover, the war had worsened the economic situation of the peasants and trade had also fallen into dire economic straits. All these factors combined to pave the way for a revolutionary explosion. A Russian victory over Japan may have delayed this, but a year after the beginning of the war it was obvious that Russia was struggling.

The spark that ignited the revolution was struck on "Bloody Sunday" (January 9, 1905), when a peaceful procession of workers in St Petersburg was shot down by the order of the government. A string of mass demonstrations against the tsarist authorities followed and all corners of Russia fell under the weight of protests and strikes. The waves of revolution reached as far as the peripheries of the empire, Georgia included. Its people hoped to restore their independence as well as to become free from social oppression.

The revolution shook Tsar Nicholas II, who swiftly issued a decree on February 18, 1905 to his interior minister, A. Buligin, to give all citizens the right to express openly their opinion about the measures taken to improve the country's situation. There followed from this point an unprecedented flurry of activity by political parties and organisations as one and all expressed their ideas and attitudes. Led by the Georgians Mikheil Tskhakaia, Pilipe Makharadze and Ioseb Jughashvili (Stalin), the Bolshevik wing of the Social Democratic Party became more and more prominent in the revolutionary movement. In Georgia, the most progressive patriots, both clergy and lay, realized they had little time to waste and set to work for the political autonomy of Georgia within the framework of the Russian empire, as well as for the restoration of the autocephaly of the Georgian church.

However, by the second half of 1906, the tsarist government had recovered from the shock of popular insurrection and proceeded to eliminate the key nerve centres of the revolutionary movement. By 1907 the revolution was suppressed outright. On June 3, 1907 — regarded as the end of the first Russian revolution — Nicholas dissolved the Second State Duma, or Parliament.

For Georgia, the 1905-1907 revolutionary period was marked by increased activity in the nationalist movement. There were continuous demands for the granting of national autonomy as well as for the restoration of the Church's autocephaly. The Synod of the Russian Church was categorically opposed to the latter and, with the backing of the military, Nikon, exarch of Georgia, dispersed a gathering in 1907 of autocephalists, ordering the soldiers to beat them up.

A landmark for the nationalist movement was reached with the 1907 petition of the Georgian people which was sent to the Second Hague International Peace Conference, which was held to expand upon the original Hague Convention of 1899. In it, the signatories, representatives of the Georgian people, demanded national autonomy for their country in the Russian State. Though Georgia was not to receive the autonomy it sought, the national question was now elevated to such a point that all Georgians recognised its supreme importance. The matter had now moved from theoretical arguments and discussions to exploring practical ways for its realisation.

The era of repression — 1907 to the First World War

Large-scale political repression became the order of the day in Russia after the collapse of the first revolution. Several thousand people were tried and sentenced to death for their part in the uprising. Court martials were established in every region of Georgia and, in 1907, thousands

the point of taking Tbilisi. Acknowledging the volatile military and political situation, the executive committee adopted a historic decision on May 25, 1918, to call a meeting of the Transcaucasus Commissariat on the following day and to declare the dissolution of the Transcaucasus Democratic Federative Republic. On the same day the National Council of Georgia unanimously declared independence for the nation, which was now to be called the Democratic Republic of Georgia.

Aftermath of the
October 1917 Revolution

Acts of independence

The Act of Independence of May 26, 1918 was signed under complex international circumstances where the newly born Georgian Democratic Republic faced challenges from a variety of directions. In a separate peace deal, for example, the Treaty of Brest-Litovsk brokered between the new Bolshevik regime in Russia and Germany in March of the same year had stipulated that all Russian forces had to withdraw from Batumi, Kars and the surrounding areas and that the local population had the right to determine their own future. In practice, the deal meant that these territories were handed over to Germany's ally, Turkey. Moreover, German troops were stationed in Georgia, acting as "protectors and guarantors" of Georgia's independence.

But the situation was not long in changing. The German empire surrendered to the Allies in November 1918, thus ending the First World War, and its army was forced to quit Georgia. The country was declared a British-occupied zone and British military forces remained from December 1918 until July 1920. At this stage it was still unclear how the opposing territorial claims of Georgia, Turkey and Russia would ultimately be settled. Now an independent republic, Georgia placed its hopes on the solidarity of the Allied nations.

Independence was officially declared by the National Council of Georgia, which acted as the supreme law-making body of the republic. It elected Nikoloz Chkheidze as chairman after which government ministers were named. The first prime minister, Noe Ramishvili, was replaced in June 1918 by Noe Zhordania. In the same year, on October 8, the title "National Council" was changed to "Parliament of Georgia". There were also representatives of various nationalities in the parliament: ten Armenians, four Azerbaijanis, three Abkhazians, two Russians, two Ossetians, three Jews, one Greek, a German (Surguladze, 1991, p205).

Aftermath of the October Revolution

In 1919, parliamentary elections were conducted in which more than 60 per cent of the population voted. A range of political parties entered the arena and out of 130 seats, the Social Democratic Party won 109, the National Democratic Party eight, the Socialist Federalists eight, and the Socialist Revolutionaries five (Surguladze, 1991, p206).

The first session of the Constituent Assembly was held on March 12, 1919. Chkheidze continued as chairman, and the newly-formed government was again chaired by Zhordania. At its first meeting, the assembly affirmed the Act of Independence adopted by the National Council the previous May.

The final phase of state-building was to make the constitution more comprehensive. Adopted by the Constituent Assembly on February 21, 1921, it was in essence democratic and clearly distinguished between legislative, executive and judicial bodies. Democratic structures were introduced at all levels, including that of local administration, whose duties were conducted by elected bodies, the *erobas*. The constitution placed strong emphasis on the unity of the Georgian nation and, in a special article, Georgian was declared to be the official language of the country.

Social and cultural orientation

While social policies were determined by the middle classes, who held the most influence in this period, the government took care to protect the interests of all social ranks and sought to maintain public stability. It ensured the right to property for all as well as popular consultation in industrial development, both in towns and in rural areas. Agrarian reform was undertaken in such a way that neither peasants nor traditional landowners (gentry and bourgeoisie) remained without property.

These policies helped to avoid major social tensions or class struggles in the rural areas. At the same time, conditions for economic progress were created (Vachnadze & Guruli, 2001, p131). A balance was also sought between state and private ownership of industry. These procedures acted as a basis for social peace in the towns and laid the foundations for industrial development.

With the declaration of independence there surfaced a significant cultural and intellectual renewal and a sense of confidence. Several important steps were taken, including the founding of a Georgian university, an event that came to have special meaning for the Georgian people. On January 26, 1918, well before the Act of Independence, Tbilisi University had already been set up. This initiative had come from a number of Georgian academics, such as the well-known historian,

Ivane Javakhishvili, who led the university movement, Ekvtime Takaishvili, Shalva Nutsubidze, Giorgi Akhvlediani and Andria Razmadze. Petre Melikishvili, a professor of chemistry, who was elected first rector of the university, insisted that the development of science and the arts be one of the main priorities of the government.

The Tbilisi Conservatoire, established in 1917, became Georgia's centre of musical education. In 1919, the Caucasian Museum was transformed into the Georgian State Museum, and in 1920 the National Gallery of Georgia came into being.

Regional autonomy and national minorities

Though Georgia was declared to be a single state covering a single territory, regions such as Abkhazia, Ajara and Saingilo were granted a degree of autonomy in local affairs. The constitution also protected the privileges of national minorities, who enjoyed equal rights with Georgians, and attention was paid to their social and cultural needs.

For example, there were at that time 81 Armenian, 60 Russian and 31 Azerbaijani schools in Georgia. Material was also prepared for elementary education in the Ossetian language. Every ethnic group had its national council whose decisions had to be taken into account by the local and central authorities (Surguladze, 1991, p207).

Abkhazia

Immediately after Georgian independence, a delegation of the People's Council of Abkhazia, consisting of R. Kakuba (head), G. Tumanov, V. Gurjua and G. Ajalov, visited Tbilisi to hold talks with the new Georgian government on the future of their province.

At a meeting on June 6, 1918, Kakuba, emphasising the historic unity and spiritual affinity between the Georgians and the Abkhazians, insisted that close relations between them should be maintained and asked for the support of the Georgian government. He noted that there were several political groups of differing orientation in Abkhazia, some of them sympathising with Turkey and others with the newly created North Caucasian Republic of Mountain Peoples. For this reason the delegation urged the Georgian government not to withdraw its units from Abkhazia.

Two days later, an agreement was concluded by the two parties. The Abkhazians affirmed the indivisibility of Georgia while the Georgian government promised to grant rights of autonomy to Abkhazia within the boundaries of the country (Surguladze, 1991, p208). Later, in 1920, the Constitutional Commission of the Georgian Constituent Assembly elaborated a draft bill for the formation of an autonomous government for Abkhazia; this was approved by the assembly on February 21, 1921. Abkhazia was thus declared an integral part of Georgia but autonomous in its internal affairs.

Ajara

Relations between Georgia and Turkey had become particularly troublesome. In connection with the peace deal of March 1918, the new Russian government made extensive territorial concessions to Turkey. Three months later, Georgia and Turkey signed an agreement confirming Turkish ownership of the entire province of Meskheti with the exception of the villages of Atskuri and Abastumani.

Ajara, one of the ancient regions of Georgia that had been conquered by the Ottomans in the 16th century, presented particular problems. As a consequence of the Russian-Ottoman war it had been reunited with Georgia in 1878, but in recognition of the fact that there was a large Muslim population in Ajara, the region was granted autonomous status. Georgia and the Ottomans also agreed that the future of Ajara should be decided by referendum, and indeed one was organised some months later, but it was manipulated by the Ottoman occupying forces and Ajara returned to Ottoman Turkey.

This situation, however, soon changed again. Turkey's forces were forced to leave Ajara following the defeat of Germany and its allies and, by virtue of the Mudros Armistice, the region became part of the British occupied zone. Consequently, by December 1918, the Turkish presence had been replaced by the British army.

Whether under Turkish or British occupation, pro-Georgian forces in Ajara found themselves under constant pressure. In contrast to Germany, Britain had adopted an anti-Georgian line. According to the historian M. Vachnadze, "the English did not stop the activities of Turkish agents in Ajara and openly protected the government of Armenia which was known for its anti-Georgian positions" (Vachnadze & Guruli, 2001, p132). To give expression to the aspirations of the pro-Georgian part of the population, a counter movement came into existence under the leadership of Memed-beg Abashidze, Aslan-beg Abashidze, Zia-beg Abashidze and others, who sought to bring together those who favoured union with Georgia. On August 21, 1919, a congress of representatives of Georgian Muslims was held in Batumi, where a demand was made for the unification of Ajara with Georgia. Finally, when the British army left the region in July, 1920, Ajara once again became part of the Georgian state.

Turkey, nevertheless, did not so easily abandon its claims. Despite the withdrawal of its armed forces from Ajara as well as Samtskhe-Javakheti, Turkey continued to destabilise the region. It supported secession movements and incited Samtskhe-Javakheti to break away from Georgia. However, the Georgian army succeeded in defeating the insurgents and retained sovereignty over the region (Surguladze, 1991, p130).

International recognition

Since the most pressing issue facing the new republic of Georgia was international recognition, the Paris Peace Conference that opened in January 1919 at the Palace of Versailles was to be decisive. The intention was to draft a general peace treaty to end the state of war and to redraw the map of Europe. The attitude of the victors, i.e. the Entente led by Great Britain, however, was clearly anti-Georgian and desperate efforts were made by the Georgian delegation before they succeeded in obtaining recognition for the "Democratic Republic of Georgia" from the Supreme Council of the Allies (Britain, France and Italy) on January 20, 1920. This substantial step forward was followed shortly thereafter by serious failure: the attempt, in December 1920, to gain admission to the League of Nations failed.

In order to substantiate on historic grounds its claim for independence, the Georgian delegation submitted a detailed memorandum to the League of Nations and requested assistance in the event of aggression by external forces. The document was laid before a special commission under the chairmanship of the Norwegian representative, Dr Nansen. Following its consideration by the commission, the text was discussed at a plenary session of the League on December 16, 1920. Nansen and Lord Cecil (the representative of South Africa) supported the requests for admission and protection, arguing that the Bolshevik threat was quite real. But Britain spoke against it — holding the opinion that the League of Nations was hardly in a position to offer any help "to this little, courageous state situated on the Russian border", and advised the assembly to vote against Georgia's admission (Surguladze, 1991, p226).

Reinvasion by Russia

Relations with Russia were, obviously, of the greatest significance. Soviet Russia did not at first recognize Georgia's independence and yet, for

Ioseb Jughashvili (Iosef Stalin)

Stalin's revolutionary activities started in the early years of the 20th century when he joined the underground radical group Mesame Dasi ("Third Group"). He soon began to play a leading role, being involved in terrorist attacks against the Russian government. Between 1902 and 1913 he was arrested seven times. Although he was tried and sent into exile on six separate occasions, he invariably made a successful escape.

Over the course of the following decade he gradually rose up through the ranks of the Bolshevik (later Communist) Party, in the process becoming a national figure after the toppling of the tsar in the Revolution of 1917. After Lenin's death he finally became the undisputed leader of the Communist Party and of the USSR, which, as Commissar for Nationalities, he had been so instrumental in creating.

Though he has gone down in history as a merciless dictator, he nevertheless took his adopted country into the modern world. As Winston Churchill once told the House of Lords in Great Britain: "Stalin created and subordinated to himself a huge empire ... no one could compete with him. He received a Russia working with the plough and left it with the nuclear bomb ... history and nations never forget such persons."

Stalin was born into an Orthodox family in Georgia on December 6, 1878, and baptised soon after. His father, a worker in a shoe factory, had moved from Didi Lilo, a village close to Tbilisi, westwards to Gori. There he met and married the 16-year-old Ekaterie (Keke) Geladze. They had three sons, two of whom died at an early age. When Stalin was nine years old, he caught smallpox which left his face scarred for the rest of his life.

His parents had little understanding of his revolutionary commitment. His mother had always wanted him to become a priest and made no secret of this even when he had become the General Secretary of the Communist Party. In fact, in 1888 Stalin entered the theological school in Gori where he graduated in 1894 with distinction. He then won a scholarship enabling him to continue his studies at the theological seminary in Tbilisi.

He sang in the choir and had the reputation of being a good student, and was widely read both in Georgian and world literature. At the seminary he showed particular interest in the Old Testament, at that time taught by Archimandrite Dimitri Abashidze, who later became the Bishop of Simferopol in Russia and a leader in the anti-Soviet movement in the south of Russia during the Civil War.

After five years, he was forced to leave the seminary, reportedly because he had been studying Marx. In fact, the church authorities had simply cut his scholarship and Stalin had no means of his own to continue his studies. And so he turned himself, instead, to the path of revolution that would lead him to change world events and the lives of his fellow men.

political reasons, it soon consented to holding talks with the Georgian government. This led to an agreement which the two countries signed on May 7, 1920. Russia recognised Georgia's independence, in line with the members of the Entente and with Germany, Austria, Belgium, Romania, Turkey, Ukraine, Japan, Argentina, Mexico, Armenia and Azerbaijan.

The Soviet command, however, decided in January 1921 to invade Georgia once more. For political reasons the Soviets chose not to declare war but rather to mask their aggressive move. On the pretext that rebelling workers in Georgia had appealed for help, the Russian army felt "obliged" to intervene.

Lori, a territory that since 1918 had been disputed between Armenia and Georgia, was chosen as the site of the uprising. On February 11, 1921, Russian colonists there rose in revolt. On February 16, the Georgian Bolsheviks set up a revolutionary committee (Revkom) consisting of Pilipe Makharadze (chairman), Mamia Orakhelashvili, Shalva Eliava, Alexandre Gegechkori and others. This committee would lead the rebellion of the "Georgian workers" with Russia's assistance, which was requested on same day. Noteworthy is the fact that none of the members of this committee was anywhere near Lori at the time of the insurgence. Makharadze was in Moscow, holding consultations with members of the Soviet government, including Lenin and Stalin.

Stalin had left Georgia in 1907, and by the time of the invasion of his homeland, he had already held two posts in the Soviet government. In 1917 he had become the people's commissar (or minister) for nationalities, then in 1919 he was named people's commissar for state control. Moreover, as soon as he arrived in St Petersburg in 1917 from Siberia (where he had been exiled since 1913), he was elected a member of the ruling Politbureau of the Central Committee of the Bolshevik Party and was also made a member of the Military Revolutionary Committee of Petrograd. It was Stalin who initiated the decision to oust the government of the Democratic Republic of Georgia, and he charged a fellow Georgian Bolshevik, Sergo Orjonikidze, with the mission to carry out the mandate.

On February 15, Orjonikidze, who was in Armenia at the time, received a coded telegram in Georgian from Stalin: "There is consent. Attack and take the city" (Toidze, 1991, p99). Orjonikidze accomplished the task to the satisfaction of the Party. The same day the Soviet army crossed the Georgian border — one day *before* the workers' request for help was made — and simultaneously launched attacks from various sides. Units of the 11th Army entered the country from Armenia, while other troops deployed in Azerbaijan came in from the East Divisions also moved in from two other directions — from Sochi into Abkhazia and from the Northern Caucasus to Kutaisi through the Mamisoni mountain pass. Soviet military superiority over the Georgian forces was soon made evident and the situation was further aggravated by the movement of Turkish forces into south-western Georgia (Artaani and Artvini districts), which finally had to be given up. Though military action escalated, Soviet Russia continued to maintain the fiction of an insurrection. Soviet diplomats claimed that it was the Bolshevik Revolutionary Committee (Revkom) of Georgia that was in fact leading the struggle against the disloyal workers and that the 11th Army was therefore acting at the request of the committee.

Following battles at the frontier, the Georgian Army began its retreat on February 15-16, 1921. Two days later, the 11th Red Army Regiment initiated attacks against Tbilisi but was forced to retreat on February 20 owing to fierce resistance from Georgian defence forces, the National Guard and volunteer units. Above all, the cadets of Tbilisi's Military School distinguished themselves in the field of battle. The enemy again attacked Tbilisi on February 22 but was held at bay once more.

In a passionate speech, Noe Zhordania addressed Georgia's Constituent Assembly in connection with the Soviet attacks, saying:

> It has turned out that the Soviet government decided long ago to organise an insurrection in Georgia and declare Soviet rule here. Until now, however, it failed to carry this out since it had no valid reason to invade. Ten days ago an excuse was fabricated for the Lori district where a secret plot was organised under the guise of "the people's action against the Georgian government". A local Soviet leadership has been proclaimed and now the Russian Army has come, allegedly to offer assistance. Pilipe Makharadze, Mamia Orakhelashvili, Budu Mdivani, Shalva Eliava, Misha Okujava, Lado (also known as Vladimer) Dumbadze, Omar Nazaretyan and Alexandre Gegechkori are those who have chosen to lead the enemy in an attempt to exterminate the Georgian people and army by fire and the sword, and to become Georgia's tyrants. But the Georgian people will never follow them in their scheme. They will by no means accept this shame. Upon discovering what kinds of ruffians intend to trample them down, the Georgian spirit will become even firmer, and the people will cry out: "Victory or death!" (Vachnadze & Guruli, 2001, p142).

The Georgians fought selflessly, especially on the outskirts of Tbilisi.

Occupation of Georgia by Soviet Russia in 1921

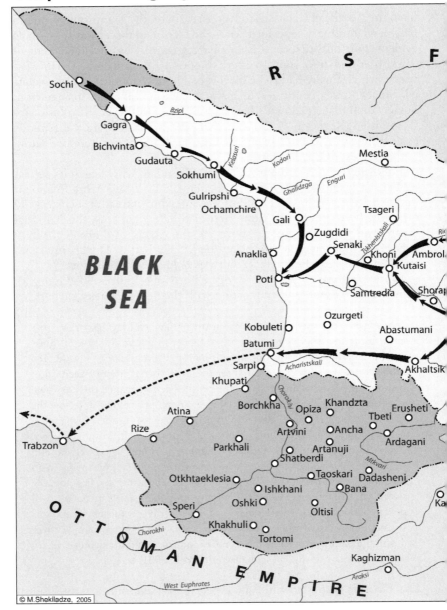

© M.Shekiladze, 2005

Aftermath of the October Revolution

Invasion by Soviet Russia, February 1921

◀━━ Advance of the Red Army

◀- - - Flight of Georgian Democratic Republic government from Batumi, March 17, 1921

◻ Territorial claims made by Georgia at the League of Nations, 1918

☐ Territory of Present-Day Georgia

S

R

Tergi

Tergi

Oni

Roka

Didi Liakhvi

Tergi

Tskhinvali

Pasanauri

Ksani

Akhalgori

Dusheti

Grozny

Vladikavkaz

...la

...hashuri

Gori

Tianeti

Mtskheta

Tbilisi

Telavi

Lagodekhi

Alazani

Algeti

Kojori

Iori

Belaqani

Zakatala

Ktsia

Tabakhmela

Tetritskaro

Sighnaghi

Kakhi

...alkalaki

Shulaveri

Qebeda

Mtkvari

Vorontsovka

Jalal-ogli

A Z E R B A I J A N   S S R

S

A R M E N I A N   S S R

Lake Sevan

Ganja

85

But on February 24 the situation became critical. While units of the Red Army received reinforcements, the Georgian army was faced with no reserves. The government and its commander-in-chief, General Kvinitadze, were forced to abandon the capital. When the 11th Red Army entered on February 25, 1921 it encountered no resistance. Meanwhile the government of the Democratic Republic of Georgia had fled to Batumi (Vachnadze & Guruli, 2001, p139).

On February 25, 1921, Orjonikidze was able to send the following telegram to Moscow: "Moscow, Kremlin. Attention: Lenin and Stalin. The red flag of Soviet power streams over Tbilisi. Long live Soviet Georgia!" (Surguladze, 1972, p693).

New political structures

From the very first day of the occupation, a Revolutionary Committee established itself as the highest lawmaking body in Georgia. In March 1921, it chose to dissolve the Constituent Assembly — an act both arbitrary and devoid of legality since the new committee had no right to revoke the powers of the country's supreme and democratically elected legislative authority. Moreover, the Revkom abolished all executive, parliamentary and judicial bodies as well as every ministry of local self-government. The Georgian army and the National Guard were also disbanded.

The leadership in Soviet Russia, seeking to legalise the occupation of Georgia, transferred the power usurped by the Revkom to the Soviets. In this way, Georgia's political system began to resemble that of Russia's, both in the urban and non-urban regions (provinces, districts, towns and rural settlements). All authority was to be exercised by the Soviets of the Deputies of Workers and Peasants.

Elections to the soviets were held under conditions of severe repression. Anyone who opposed the occupying forces was deprived of the right to participate in the voting. Under these circumstances, the Communist Party easily won most of the seats. Congress opened precisely one year after the day of the takeover of Georgia — February 25, 1922. It adopted the "Constitution of the Georgian Soviet Socialist Republic", according to which the Congress of Soviets was the highest governmental body of the new Georgian Socialist Republic. Between congress sittings, authority was delegated to the Central Executive Committee (elected by the congress). The Council of the People's Commissars was made the highest executive body in Georgia and the system of the soviets was also applied in the provinces.

Creation of autonomous entities

For political reasons, Soviet Russia created autonomous entities in the territory of Georgia. Before the invasion, Abkhazians and Ossetians, at Russia's instigation, had attempted to dismember the territorial integrity of the Georgian Democratic Republic but failed. Following the military operations of 1921, it became clear that Soviet Russia had been behind the Abkhazian and Ossetian separatists. In March 1921, instructions were received from Moscow that Abkhazia should declare itself a separate Soviet Socialist Republic. In May of the same year, the Russian authorities forced Georgia's Revolutionary Committee to recognise Abkhazia as a new political entity (Guruli *et al.*, 2003, p113). By December, however, the Georgian Soviet Socialist Republic and the Abkhazian Soviet Socialist Republic signed an agreement according to which Abkhazia agreed to reunite with Georgia, keeping the status of an "autonomous Soviet Socialist Republic". This was a move that was to have negative consequences for Georgia: though it had Abkhazia back within its borders, the special status of Abkhazia as a soviet socialist republic posed a serious threat to the territorial integrity of the nation.

Soviet Russia also supported the Ossetian separatists. Pressed by Moscow, Georgia's Revolutionary Committee created, within its borders, the South Ossetian Autonomous District in 1921 — including part of the district of Shida Kartli. But there was neither a historical nor a geographical rationale for transforming it into a separate district. This was clearly a measure taken to deliberately undermine Georgian identity since by this logic Armenians, Azeris and Greeks could have made similar claims to the South Ossetians in other parts of Georgia.

At the same time, Soviet Russia was also seeking to create larger political units. In December 1922, the First Congress of the Transcaucasian Soviets set up the Transcaucasian Soviet Federative Socialist Republic, and on December 30, the Union of Soviet Socialist Republics was solemnly established in Moscow. This union consisted of Russia, Ukraine, Belarus and the Transcaucasian Federation. Adopted in 1924, the constitution of the USSR recognised that all republics within its territory remained sovereign states and had the right to withdraw freely from the union. This right was again upheld in the USSR Constitution of 1936 — no republic, however, ever succeeded in exercising it.

Loss of statehood and resistance

The Russian occupation had severely dented the aspirations of the Georgian people but the nation proved unable to reconcile itself with this new loss of statehood and independence. And so it was not long before the population revived itself and began its struggle against the foreign regime. In due course, a new national movement of resistance was born. Already in 1921, Kakutsa Cholokashvili had formed partisan units and set about organising a rebellion in Kakheti and Khevsureti (Eastern Georgia). Mikheil Lashkarashvili, recruiting armed units in Kartli, did the same.

A significant moment in the history of this new nationalist movement is connected to the memorandum sent by Catholicos-Patriarch Ambrosi (Khelaia) to the Genoa Peace Conference. This summit was attended by all European countries with the aim of regularizing economic and political relations between Europe and Soviet Russia and to work out a plan (ultimately unsuccessful) for international economic reconstruction. This gathering, which took place in April 1922, had the objective of addressing important problems in international relations. Soviet Russia participated in the conference but representation from the Georgian government-in-exile was not permitted. In an open letter, Catholicos Ambrosi presented the conference with twin demands: the immediate withdrawal of Russian occupying forces from Georgia, and freedom for the Georgian nation to determine its own political future. The Bolshevik regime took measures to silence the patriarch and his action had no sign of any tangible impact on the delegates.

Meanwhile, the various Georgian political organisations (including Social Democrats, National Democrats, Socialist Federalists) united in a bid to restore independence. In spring 1922, they established the Committee for Independence, a multi-party body whose object was to organise a rebellion against the Bolsheviks. Georgian political figures in exile also lent their support. A military centre was established to provide direct leadership for the rebellion but late in 1923 it was exposed by the Bolsheviks, who executed all active members of the centre, including Generals Alexandre Andronikashvili, Rostom Muskhelishvili, Varden Tsulukidze and Konstantine Abkhazi.

Despite these setbacks, resistance continued and a wave of rebellions against Soviet rule — among the most significant actions during the entire Bolshevik hegemony — began on August 28, 1924. The uprising started in Chiatura (Western Georgia) and soon spread to other Georgian provinces. Unfortunately, the Bolsheviks succeeded in capturing Konstantine Andronikashvili, a relative of Alexandre, and Iason Javakhishvili, leaders of the Committee for Independence, and eventually suppressed the rebellion by means of punitive operations. In the course of events, about 4,000 people fell victim to the repression of the authorities (Vachnadze & Guruli, 2001, p151).

Industrialisation in the 1920s and 1930s

Because the Communist Party regarded industrialisation as a basic requirement for the successful development of socialist society, programmes of commercial production were launched in the 1920s and continued into the following decade. The plenary of the Central Committee of the Georgian Communist (Bolshevik) Party set targets in April 1926 for socialist manufacturing in Georgia. It demanded that priority be given to the development of industries that would ensure the economic independence of the Soviet Union from capitalist countries.

It is interesting to note how, in general, Georgian communists and Soviet propaganda alike assessed the importance of industrialisation. Unlike capitalist industrialisation, socialist industrialisation is centrally planned and organised. The Soviet state is the main political body in the working class's struggle for socialist industrialisation; it has to provide and to strengthen its foundations and to take the lead in assuring its implementation through the organs of state. All expenses arising from the new development must be co-ordinated with the general industrial plan (Kochlavashvili, 1976, p254).

In December 1925, the 14th Congress of the Communist Party assembled and developed policies of industrialisation that were regarded as vital for the growth of the country's socialist ideology. According to common wisdom, it was considered that the pace of development should be highest in the machine-building division. Consequently, 78 per cent of all capital investment in industry was devoted to this sector.

In Georgia, many considered that these plans of forced industrialisation were unrealistic. They felt that the balance of the targets had to be changed in favour of light manufacturing rather than heavy industry. According to some Communist Party functionaries, Georgia was not able to become an industrialised country at all, while others were even of the opinion that the goal set by the Party was undesirable. For example, Besarion Chichinadze, a prominent Georgian engineer who built the great Zemo Avchala hydroelectric power station (1927), maintained that it made no sense to develop metallurgy and a coal industry in Georgia. He observed that "it is impossible to pin hopes onto the development of heavy industry in the near future. This option would entail an unnatural pattern of development and result in serious economic disadvantages. The priorities for industrialisation in Georgia should be in the areas of

the timber industry, silk production, mining and electrical chemistry"
(Surguladze, 1991, p262).

Georgian Communist Party leaders, however, failed to take into
account local conditions and instead followed the model of Russia
and other nations which, from the viewpoint of industrial development,
were far ahead of Georgia. Those who opposed the hasty transformation
of agrarian Georgia into an agrarian/industrial republic were denounced
as opponents of socialism and agents of a "right-wing opportunistic
ideology".

The damage of collectivisation

The swift course of industrialisation caused irreparable damage to
agriculture. Huge numbers of peasants abandoned their villages in order
to take up work in urban factories and plants, encouraged by the government to take up jobs in industrial production. The initiative resulted
in the gradual emptying of rural areas as the artificial migration of the
population created a demographic imbalance.

Mass collectivisation of farms, initiated everywhere in the Soviet
Union, caused even more damage to agriculture. The Bolshevik policies
directed against peasants knew no ethnic boundaries: it was implemented with equal cruelty in Russia, Belarus, Ukraine and Central Asia as
well as in the Caucasus. Peasant farms were forcefully merged into
collective farms (kolkhozes), and the slogan "Those who do not join
collective farms are enemies of the Soviet authorities!" prevailed
throughout the Union.

The process of enforced collectivisation, perhaps inevitably, turned
into undisguised violence. The authorities' attacks on the well-off
and moderately wealthy peasant farmers (kulaks) were especially
fierce. Local Communist Party functionaries eventually refused to take
into account the local conditions but instead forced all peasants into
collective farms and confiscated people's property and livestock, even
their hen-coops. Lists of "class enemies" were created which were
topped by kulak families, who were exiled or, as was often the case,
executed by firing squads as "enemies of the people". Acts such as these
reduced the rural areas throughout the USSR to ruins. Repression,
confiscation of property and the deportation of tens if not hundreds of
thousands of farmers resulted in famine in Georgia and all over the rest
of the Soviet Union.

While the Soviet government may have achieved its political goals
through collectivisation, the damage to agriculture was calamitous.

Private ownership of land was deemed to be illegal, prosperous peasant farms were destroyed, and agricultural production and cattle breeding were diminished drastically (Vachnadze & Guruli, 2001, p156).

Impact of Communist ideology

In spite of the self-evident nature of these negative results, the first Five Year Plan was celebrated with great enthusiasm all over the Soviet Union and Georgia was no exception. Ordinary people suffered real material privation, but being assured that the future would bring a better life, they worked tirelessly, sometimes from 14 to 16 hours each day.

The communist authorities had long forgotten that, at the time of their struggle against the bourgeoisie (only a few years before), salary increases and an eight-hour working day were among their basic demands. Indeed, anchored in this enthusiasm, new factories, plants, and hydroelectric power stations were built all over the USSR. Outstanding achievements were also evident in Georgia. Several new factories were built and old ones reconstructed. For example, seven tea plants were constructed in the 1930s, as well as the Kutaisi Glass Factory, the Enguri Paper Works, the Tbilisi Automobile Repair Unit, amongst others (Surguladze, 1991, p273). In short, there was an unprecedented enthusiasm generated that was based on the belief that rigorous efforts would lead to a happy socialist society.

The government spared no effort in getting young people involved in the political system. From early school age they were inculcated with a fanatic loyalty for the official ideology. To this end, young "pioneers" and the Komsomol (the communist youth organisation) helped mould young communists according to the Russian model. The propaganda machine of the Soviet system was focused on fortifying belief in the victory of socialism. Any individual who was sceptical, or whose faith in the scheme was deemed lacking, was immediately labelled an "enemy of the people".

And yet the vision was not a perfect one since, with such blind faith came the belief of many that "the socialist cause had enemies always alert and committed to undermine — in league with the capitalist world — the country's strength" (Surguladze, 1991, p273). Reprisals by the Communist Party and security services against such enemies were therefore regarded as a natural consequence. Indeed, measures of repression were characteristic of the Communist Party from the very start, becoming more frequent and violent in the 1930s.

The Great Terror (1934-1938) commenced after the assassination in December 1934 of Sergei Kirov, a top-ranking Bolshevik who was leader of the Leningrad Communist Party organisation, and a former initiator and active participant in the Sovietisation of Georgia. From 1935, several show trials were held in Moscow where the courts sentenced to death members of the so-called "Leninist nucleus" of the Communist Party — Zinovyev, Kamenev, Bukharin, Rykov, Pyatakov and others. Party leaders especially faithful to Stalin such as L. Kaganovich, V. Molotov, A. Mikoyan, N. Yezhov, N. Khrushchev, Lavrenti Beria and A. Vyshinski played an active role in these trials.

Mass reprisals were also carried out in Stalin's home republic. In the 1930s, when Beria, formerly in charge of secret services, joined the leadership of the Georgian Communist Party, almost all the party leaders who had originally established the Bolshevik regime in Georgia found themselves objects of retaliation. Communist leaders who were executed or exiled included Mamia Orakhelashvili, Shalva Eliava, Mikheil Kakhiani, Vladimer (previously Lado) Dumbadze, Levan Gogoberidze, Samson Mamulia, Ephrem Eshba, Nestor Lakoba and Sergo Kavtaradze.

Also targeted were intellectuals, such as writers, actors, teachers and engineers, who had fallen out of favour with the Soviet government and were now regarded as "enemies of the people". Among them mention may be made of the following: the outstanding writer Mikheil Javakhishvili, the poets Titsian Tabidze and Nikolo Mitsishvili, the theatre directors Sandro Akhmeteli and Vakhtang Abashidze, the actors Elguja Lortkipanidze, Platon Korisheli, Ivane Abashidze, Buzhuzha Shavishvili, Ia Kantaria and Vano Lagidze, the conductor Evgeni Mikeladze, the writer/scholar Vakhtang Kotetishvili, and the theatre critic Sergo Amaglobeli.

The 1936 constitution

Stalin's new constitution for the USSR, adopted on December 5, 1936, had important consequences for Georgia. Ignoring the fact that the Great Terror continued unabated, the Soviets officially praised it as the most "democratic" of all constitutions in the world. An anthem, composed and disseminated at this time throughout the entire Soviet Union, contained the following line: "I know no other country in the entire world, where people can breathe so freely." To the millions of oppressed suffering in the gulags as a result of Stalin's purges it must have sounded like bitter mockery.

The 8th Special Congress of the Soviets that adopted the new Constitution abolished the Transcaucasian Federation that had been set up in 1922, which meant that Georgia, Armenia, and Azerbaijan now entered the Soviet Union as separate republics. Shortly thereafter, in March 1937, a new constitution for the Georgian Soviet Socialist Republic was adopted.

Twenty years of socialism

In February 1941, the Central Committee of the Communist Party of Georgia celebrated the country's 20th anniversary of sovietisation. The Georgian Communists proudly declared that Georgia had become a powerful industrial and agrarian state under the wise leadership of the Communist Party and so had relegated its backwardness to the past. The figures published in the press of the day did indeed give the impression of immense progress. Three hundred and fifteen new industrial enterprises were declared to be functioning in the republic and new fields of industry had been developed. As a result, the region now produced ferro-alloys, oils, cement, tins, tea, chemical and pharmaceutical products, and champagne. The amount of goods produced in 1940 was eighteen times as much as in 1928 (Surguladze, 1991, p279).

In the later 1930s, industrial development in the Soviet Union in general, including Georgia, became increasingly directed towards preparations for war against Nazi Germany. Production plants linked to military industry now started to work at full capacity, including the Zestaponi ferro-alloy factory, the Chiatura manganese mines and the Tkvarcheli and Tkibuli collieries. When war broke out, all industrial enterprises without exception entered the service of the military machine.

Georgia during the Second World War

In June 1941, Georgia, in line with all other Soviet republics, entered the theatre of the Great Patriotic War against Germany. Her machine-building and tool- and metal-processing factories began production of arms and ammunition. Light industry and food factories turned out clothing and supplies for the front. The Black Sea fleet was also fully involved in activities both at the front and in the rear, and the republic's civil aviation carried out 20,000 flights during the war to fulfil special combat assignments.

Although its population barely exceeded three million, Georgia sent 700,000 soldiers into battle. Her sons fought on all fronts: in Belarus and Ukraine, near Moscow, Leningrad, Kursk, Stalingrad and the Kerch peninsula. The death toll was high — in total, more than 300,000 Georgians were killed while many more were wounded and permanently disabled. Around 70,000 died in Kerch alone.

In response to a decree issued on November 13, 1941 by the State Committee for Defence, national armed divisions were created. These troops contributed greatly to the final victory, while Georgia's six divisions played a key role in the defence of the Caucasus. Many Georgians participated in the partisan groups operating against the Nazis in Belarus, Romania, Bulgaria, France and Italy. The Georgian generals P. Chanchibadze, K. Leselidze, M. Mikeladze, E. Koberidze, G. Naneishvili, A. Inauri, N. Tavartkiladze and others were responsible for leading important military operations during the hostilities. The highest wartime honour of Hero of the Soviet Union was bestowed on 164 Georgian soldiers, including Sergeant Meliton Kantaria, who hoisted the Soviet banner over Hitler's Reichstag in Berlin together with his Russian comrade in arms Sergeant Mikhail Yegorov.

The impact of the war on the USSR was severe and the economy suffered considerably. Georgia alone had unceasingly produced enormous quantities of arms and ammunition for the front. Six million sets of clothes and shoes were despatched between 1941 and 1943 alone (Surguladze, 1991, p282). Due to lack of manpower, agriculture also suffered considerably and it was mostly women and children who worked in the fields. Now Georgian industry lacked manpower in the aftermath of the war since more than 40,000 workers had been killed between 1941 and 1944. As a consequence, gross industrial product and, in particular, the production of manganese, cement, building materials, knitted fabrics, and other goods, significantly diminished. However, the sectors relating to machine-building, machine-tool and metal processing continued to grow.

Under Soviet rule the deportation of entire peoples was not uncommon. During the war the Chechens in the North Caucasus and the Kalmyks had been accused of links with Nazi Germany and deported en masse to Central Asia. In Georgia, a similar fate was suffered by the Meskhetian Turks, Muslims who lived near Georgia's southern border: they too were deported to Central Asia after being accused of links with Turkey.

During the Second World War there were large numbers of Georgians, both abroad as well as in underground groups within the republic, who entertained the hope that the USSR would be defeated and that Georgian independence would ensue. In Paris, Noe Zhordania, head of the Georgian government-in-exile, openly stated his belief that German victory over the Soviets would be a gain for Georgia. At the same time, he clearly disapproved of the Third Reich for its aggression against other nations and its agenda to establish German domination over Europe. In his eyes both political systems were equally dangerous and he had little love for either Hitler or Stalin.

In fact, Zhordania and his Social Democratic friends had condemned the war from the outset and refused to entertain any relations with Germany (Guruli *et al.*, 2003, p154). But their rivals the National Democrats took a different line: they actively sympathized with Nazi Germany and felt that a German victory was the only means by which the liberation of their country could be achieved (Guruli *et al.*, 2003, p155).

By the end of 1941, Germany had begun to recruit Georgian emigrants or war hostages who, for military purposes, were forced to join two battalions, known as Tamar I and Tamar II. Shortly afterwards, a change in policy brought about the creation of a new form of territorial militia that incorporated the Tamar II battalion: the Bergmann (i.e. Mountaineer) Groups, which consisted of foreigners and prisoners-of-war but were commanded by Germans. By 1943 three such contingents had been formed — one Georgian, another North Caucasian and the third Azeri. The Soviet authorities easily learned about the battalions and sought to take counter-measures. As a consequence, hundreds of German families were deported to Soviet Central Asia in the early 1940s and the German *Kirche* in Tbilisi was demolished.

Aftermath of war

The post-war period in the Soviet Union commenced with massive reconstruction in the manufacturing industries. Because Georgian territory had not been occupied during the war, the extent of destruction to industry was not as significant as in the western USSR although other consequences of the war were clearly visible. It was now imperative to reconvert industry into the service of peace and to close the imbalances in the various industries. To achieve these objectives a Five Year Plan was launched in 1946 throughout the USSR. New projects undertaken in Georgia during this period included the Kutaisi automobile factory, the Rustavi metal works, the Tbilisi locomotive plant, the Gori textile complex (Surguladze, 1991, p288).

The construction of such gigantic industrial ventures as the Kutaisi and Rustavi works in reality was not in the best interests of the republic's economy. These initiatives were in fact part of a masterplan that aimed to destroy the economic independence of each Soviet republic. Production was now designed to be interdependent.

For example, whereas trucks had been previously built from scratch in Kutaisi, the necessary components for assembly were now brought in from other Soviet republics. Materials for the Rustavi metal works were similarly delivered from production centres in other republics. Almost every area of business and industry was reduced to a mere cog in the united Soviet production system. It was soon obvious that, in the event of Soviet territorial disintegration — which eventually took place — this united industrial infrastructure would inevitably collapse. In short, the Georgian economic system had virtually all the features of a colonial economy (Surguladze, 1991, p288).

One might have expected that the people of Georgia, who had contributed so much to wartime victory and who had endured great suffering throughout the 1930s, could now be trusted and given fairer treatment. Quite the contrary: what followed was a period characterised by extreme political suspicion with new reprisals and recriminations. A considerable number of the ex-prisoners of war who had returned were sent into exile, including partisans who had previously been praised as heroes. Georgian families with relatives abroad were victimised and several thousand were deported.

At about the same time, the so-called "Mingrelian Affair" was instigated where innocent people from Mingrelia (Samegrelo), including many party functionaries, were accused of plotting to break Georgia away from the Soviet Union and to make it a part of Turkey (Surguladze, 1991, p292). This was probably a political manouevre directed against the Mingrelian Beria, then deputy prime minister of the Soviet Union, who, as a result of his unsuccessful attempts to gain power, had provoked Stalin's displeasure. This shameful campaign ended only after Stalin's death in 1953.

Khrushchev, Malenkov and Beria

In March 1953 Stalin, the "great teacher, father, and leader" who had ruled the Soviet Union and Communist Party for almost 30 years, died and, almost immediately, much-needed changes in state and society followed. A triumvirate rose to power where Nikita Khrushchev became chief of the Communist Party's Central Committee, Georgi Malenkov headed the government, and Lavrenti Beria maintained his post of deputy prime minister. For the second time, Beria was appointed to the post of the Soviet Union's Minister of Internal Affairs.

The alliance did not survive for very long. Beria was arrested and shot in the same year, Malenkov was first removed from his post and then expelled from the Communist Party, while Khrushchev became first secretary of the Central Committee and then head of government. It is to his name that the so-called "thaw" in the politics of the Soviet Union is linked.

It is clear today, however, that this thaw was little more than Khrushchev's condemnation of Stalin's personality cult, in the rehabilitation of innocent victims of repression, and in a limited easing of the restraints on intellectuals and artists. Internationally, the Soviet leader launched the concept of the "peaceful co-existence of systems", that the great powers, instead of threatening each other, should co-exist in peace.

Within the Soviet Union, however, the system continued to operate unchanged. The dictate of the Communist Party remained unflinching. Indeed, efforts to strengthen communist ideology and to promote the "new human being", the builder of communism, resumed with doubled force. This manifested itself, for instance, in renewed attacks against the Church. Thousands of churches and almost all theological seminaries and academies that had experienced a degree of freedom as a result of the war were once again closed.

Ironically, it was Beria who, in the short period of authority he held after Stalin's death, proposed to change the structure of the Soviet Union by calling for major reforms. Indeed, confidential documents recently published in Russia make clear that his plans went even further than Mikhail Gorbachev's later perestroika in the first years of his presidency. According to Beria's proposals, the Communist Party was to be relieved of its leading role in industry, agriculture, science and education. The cabinet of ministers, as the executive branch of the state apparatus, would take these over. The Party would remain as the guardian of the state's ideology but its Central Committee would not interfere in lawmaking, a responsibility that would be assigned solely to the Supreme Council (or parliament). Beria's reforms also envisioned the unification of Germany and the resumption of relations with Yugoslavia, which had been broken off in 1948 when its leader Josip Tito refused to toe Stalin's line.

It is also of interest that Beria required the removal of the portraits of Soviet and Communist party leaders from parades and that no monuments were to be erected in their honour for people to revere. In short, Beria intended to initiate reforms similar to Gorbachev's perestroika. Thus, in the wider perspective, it can be seen that the role of Georgian political leaders in the history of the Soviet Union is significant: Stalin was one of its creators, Beria was an inadvertent architect of perestroika, and Eduard Shevardnadze became a principal agent in its dismantling.

Nikita Khrushchev

The Khrushchev period came to be known as "the great ideal of communist construction" in the Soviet Union. Together with other soviet republics, Georgia participated in this cause under the leadership of the retired general Vasil Mzhavanadze, who led the Communist Party of Georgia for almost 20 years from 1953.

In March 1956, the anniversary of Stalin's death provided the occasion for large pro-Stalin meetings and demonstrations in Tbilisi at which young people were especially active. What they demanded was not the preservation of a personality cult — theirs was an expression of discontent because criticism of Stalin and the subsequent condemnation of Beria as enemies of the people had acquired the traits of an anti-Georgian campaign. In a defiant act of patriotism, they went into the streets to defend a man they still considered a great Georgian. The authorities in Moscow, fearing that the movement could spread, decided to teach Georgia a lesson. On March 9, 1956 Soviet troops in military vehicles machine-gunned a peaceful demonstration in Tbilisi and dozens of young people were shot and killed.

A commission from Moscow attempted to prove that the victims had attacked the Red Army, but it turned out that all of the slain demonstrators were shot in the back while fleeing. But Khrushchev was still not satisfied: and the Politbureau proceeded to accuse the Georgians of chauvinism and an "unhealthy inclination" towards "national exclusivity" (Surguladze, 1991, p297).

Industrial development

The period that followed Stalin's death was remarkable for the quantitative growth of the republic's industrial potential. Several dozen large industrial complexes opened in Georgia in the 1950s and 1960s, including concrete production, the Rustavi synthetic fibre plant, the Avchala silicate brickworks, the Sokhumi canning factory, and so forth.

Agricultural production also increased: Georgia's share in subtropical cultivation in the Soviet Union was in the region of 90-100 per cent depending on the product, and the republic was also responsible for more than 50 per cent of the wine and 95 per cent of the tea in the entire Soviet Union. In addition, Georgia produced locomotives, planes, lorries, motorboats, steel, cast iron and precision instruments. Most of these goods were exported to other Soviet republics or went abroad, and so the profits went to Moscow — Georgia's share in these revenues was insignificant (Surguladze, 1991, p198).

Although the USSR continued to promote a façade of power and authority, the crisis of "socialist economics" and the Soviet system in general began to show their cracks by the 1960s. The power of the USSR in reality was actually based on military force and production of armaments.

A change of leadership in Georgia

After Khrushchev's ousting in 1964, Leonid Brezhnev took his place at the head of the Communist Party of the Soviet Union. During his rule, the slogan "building up communism" was replaced by "developed socialism" — today, Brezhnev's era has been labelled as one of "stagnation".

A change in leadership of the Georgian Communist Party took place eight years later when, in 1972, Eduard Shevardnadze replaced the long-serving Mzhavanadze in the post of First Secretary of the Central Committee of Communist Party of Georgia. Previously, Shevardnadze had worked for years as the Georgian minister of internal affairs and his new party leadership now undertook to eradicate the "shortcomings and mistakes" allegedly caused by his predecessor.

It was expected that the Georgian Communist Party would struggle for the eradication of deeply-rooted nationalist tendencies and guarantee "universal" education for everyone. Efforts made to rectify the republic's industrial shortcomings created the impression of success and progress but the reality was that the Georgian administration provided misleading indicators of its fulfilment of the Soviet five-year plans while measures of repression imposed by Shevardnadze failed to eradicate corruption at any level within the party. But, by virtue of his labours, Shevardnadze achieved the reputation of a "firm and pure" party leader, committed to "Leninist principles of party leadership".

Early signs of resistance

Communist Party ideology failed to completely suppress nationalist sentiments. As in other parts of the Soviet Union, dissident groups were now starting to emerge again in Georgia. When caught, their leaders were usually sent to prison or to psychiatric hospitals. Two dissidents who rose to prominence in the late 1970s were Zviad Gamsakhurdia and Merab Kostava.

The former was the son of Konstantine Gamsakhurdia, a prominent Georgian writer who had studied philology before working as a researcher and translator. He and Kostava were students when they became involved in the national-liberation movement and were responsible for underground publications such as *Okros Satsmisi* ("The Golden Fleece"), *Sakartvelos Moambe* ("The Herald of Georgia") and *Matiane* ("Annals"). These disseminated ideas of national sovereignty and condemned both the communist creed and the activities of Party functionaries. Ultimately, both dissidents were punished for being traitors against the system. Gamsakhurdia was forced into making a public apology on television for his anti-Soviet activity and then sent into exile for a short period. Kostava, however, remained resolute and was sentenced to several years imprisonment.

In the late 1970s a cohesive national-liberation movement began to take shape in Georgia. A new constitution for the republic, intended to be introduced in 1978, made no reference to the official status of the Georgian language in the republic — Russian was to replace it. The draft sparked indignation, especially in the younger generation, and a few days before its adoption, high school and university students organised mass demonstrations and sit-ins in the centre of Tbilisi. The Georgian Communist Party leaders were forced to contact their superiors in Moscow in order to secure their consent for the re-inclusion of the appropriate article in the Constitution. Georgian was no longer to be removed as the republic's language. The incident was a clear demonstration that the Georgian people were hardly quiescent and that their national feeling was still alive (Surguladze, 1991, p303).

Collapse of the Soviet Union

In the late seventies, the entire Soviet system and, more pertinently, its economy were in deep crisis. After Brezhnev's death in 1982, his successor Yuri Andropov attempted to improve the situation by enforcing ideals of work and discipline, but his attempts turned out to be futile.

Since all spheres of life were in a mess, more radical changes were required. After the short leadership of Constantine Chernenko, Mikhail Gorbachev became the new General Secretary of Communist Party of the Soviet Union, and he swiftly proved himself to be the radical leader the nation needed. Perestroika and glasnost — policies aimed at democratising the system — are linked to his name and he wasted no time in appointing Eduard Shevardnadze as foreign minister to help get his policies over to the international community. Gorbachev and his supporters, however, were ultimately to realise that democracy and communism are incompatible.

It was only to be expected, therefore, that the processes of democratisation opened up by Grobachev would be followed by the rise of nationalist movements all over the Soviet Union. Initially, these occurred in the Georgia, Ukraine and the Baltic republics. In Georgia itself, new political parties sprang up such as the Ilia Chavchavadze Society, the National-Democratic Party, the National Independence Party, the Green Party, the Rustaveli Society and the People's Front.

Rise of the nationalist movement

As the USSR's political and economic crisis deepened in the 1980s, the nationalist movement in Georgia gained in strength. Organisations such as the Helsinki Union of Georgia were created and anti-Soviet meetings and demonstrations in the latter part of the decade became more frequent. Public demands were made for the withdrawal of Georgia from the Soviet empire and the restoration of its national independence.

In early 1989 the tension increased. Abkhazian and Ossetian separatists, instigated by Moscow, added to an already complicated situation. Their demands for territorial separation from Georgia and their incorporation into Russia caused great disturbance in Tbilisi.

On April 4, a group of young people started a hunger strike in front of the government building and, as protests immediately broke out all over Tbilisi demanding independence, Moscow took the decision to suppress these by force on the grounds that they were anti-Soviet. Early in the morning of April 9, 1989, special units dispatched from Soviet Russia used poison gas and sharpened spades to brutally disperse the peaceful demonstrators in front of the government building. Twenty people were killed, mainly women, while hundreds were injured and poisoned by gas.

Independence

Moscow failed, however, to stop the nationalist movement, and May 26, 1989, the day of the restoration of Georgia's independence, saw jubilant celebrations throughout the republic. On October 28, 1990, the Supreme Council of Georgia was forced to announce multi-party elections, a decision that was hailed by the nationalist movement as a great victory. These were won by the seven-party Round Table-Free Georgia alliance and their leader Zviad Gamsakhurdia became chairman of the Supreme Council.

The Act of Restoration of Independence of Georgia was adopted on April 9, 1991, exactly two years after the massacre in Tbilisi by the Soviet authorities in Moscow. The proclamation was preceded by a referendum held on March 31, 1991, in which a reported 99 per cent of the Georgian people voted for their country's independence. On May 26,

Gamsakhurdia was elected with 87 per cent of the vote as first president of the republic of Georgia — and the first to be directly elected in the republics of the crumbling USSR.

Gamsakhurdia's presidency

Owing to the fact that the USSR continued to maintain military bases in Georgia and that the Soviet army guarded the country's borders, the new government faced numerous problems. Crucially, Moscow refused to recognise Georgia's independence and made all possible efforts to undermine the new status quo. Indeed, the Soviet Union went to great lengths to destabilise the entire country.

For example, incited by Moscow, the Supreme Council of the Autonomous District of South Ossetia declared itself in November 1990 to be an independent republic. By way of response, a month later the Supreme Council of Georgia had pronounced the decision to be illegal and had the new territory abolished. In his turn, Gorbachev, as president of the USSR, in January 1991, issued a decree reinstating the South Ossetian Soviet Republic. The situation had also become tense in Abkhazia. When, in August 1990, the Supreme Council of the Abkhazian Autonomous Republic adopted a motion to proclaim Abkhazia a sovereign state, the Georgian authorities also declared this act of secession legally null and void.

But because the rival political parties and nationalist forces in Georgia had failed to unite — the ruling Round Table-Free Georgia bloc had disintegrated — the country found itself in a state of political disarray. Conflict had already begun in the Georgian national-liberation movement before the first multi-party elections, and tensions heightened after Gamsakhurdia was voted in as president.

In his election campaign, Gamsakhurdia had concentrated almost exclusively on the issue of independence, but now he was under fire for his authoritarian concept of rule. Partly due to his inflexible character and partly to conflicts between the various political parties, popular support for him began to fade. Between December 1991 and January 1992, the democratically elected government was forcefully overthrown by members of the national guard under the command of the former minister of defence, Tengiz Kitovani, and paramilitary forces such as the Mkhedrioni ("warrior-horsemen") led by Jaba Ioseliani. Gamsakhurdia found refuge in Chechnya but in December 1993 he died in uncertain circumstances in Western Georgia. His remains were subsequently transported to Grozny, Chechnya, where they were buried.

Conflict broke out in almost every corner of Georgia following the crises of 1991-1992. An illegal Military Council seized power and called on Shevardnadze, then in Moscow, to return and take control in March 1992. The council was replaced by an equally illegitimate State Council. This *de facto* situation was legalised however by parliamentary elections which took place in October 1992. Shevardnadze became Chairman of Parliament and was given the powers of head of state.

Continuing conflicts

Discord in the country continued even after these latest parliamentary elections. The separatist government of Abkhazia, urged on by the Russians, was determined to secede from Georgia. In August 1992, Georgian forces, having entered Abkhazia to protect transportation lines, found themselves engaged in hostilities in response to armed provocation. Eventually a full-scale war for Abkhazia erupted. The Abkhazians were supported by Russian military units and North Caucasian militias. In late September 1993, the Abkhazians fixed a border along the Inguri (Enguri) river and around 300,000 Georgians and other nationalities were forced to leave.

In order to establish some semblance of stability, it was necessary for Georgia to adopt a constitution. The one finally adopted by parliament on August 24, 1995 was used as a basis for the presidential and parliamentary elections held in autumn 1995, in which Shevardnadze was elected president. The subsequent parliamentary elections, held four years later, in 1999, brought Shevardnadze again to power in 2000. But during Shevardnadze's tenure, the republic faced acute economic, social and political problems which refused to go away. Most of its citizens still lived in dire poverty and not even state-sponsored anti-corruption policies succeeded in producing satisfactory results.

The disintegration of the Soviet Union in December 1991 opened the way for international recognition of the independence of the former Soviet republics. This included Georgia, which joined the United Nations in July 1992. In December 1993, Georgia entered the Commonwealth of Independent States, an alliance created on Moscow's initiative after the formal dissolution of the USSR. Georgia's principal objective here has been to work on resolving the conflict in Abkhazia. Georgia also became a member of the Council of Europe in April 1999, and in July 2000 it became fully affiliated with the World Trade Organisation.

Parliamentary elections held on November 2, 2003 saw the majority votes cast for Shevardnadze's bloc, but both the opposition parties and international observers condemned the result as blatantly rigged. Although faced with mounting unrest across the country, the government refused to back down. And so, on November 23 the opposition masterminded the unforgettable "Rose Revolution" when protesters peacefully stormed the Parliament Building as Shevardnadze was addressing the assembly. Shevardnadze resigned and Mikhail Saakashvili, the leader of the National-Democratic Party, was voted president, at the age of 36, in a landslide victory on January 4, 2004. His party swept the board in elections for the new parliament in March.

Georgians are now working hard for the peaceful restoration of their territorial integrity, to resolve the ongoing energy and economic crises as well as to end the pervasive corruption hindering progress at every level. And yet, in the long run, Georgians clearly have much to celebrate: their centuries-long struggle to regain their lost nationhood is over and they have already begun the task of restoring their national and cultural institutions. Despite the traumas of its new birth, Georgia is working hard for a future in the world arena and to become integrated both politically and economically as a part of Europe.

Part II

The Orthodox Church of Georgia in the 19th and 20th centuries

Abolition of autocephaly and formation of the exarchate, 1801-1840s

The issue of autocephaly

Autocephaly was one of the issues that dominated the history of the Orthodox Church of Georgia. Following the Russian Empire's annexation of Georgia, the independent status of the country's Orthodox Christian Church was abolished little by little until it became an exarchate of the Russian Orthodox Church.

As the movement towards independence expanded in Georgia, the hope for restoration of self-rule became a central issue for both church and nation. In order to understand the significance of the recurring debates throughout the 19th-20th centuries, some general knowledge of the underlying issues is necessary. Hence, this history of the Orthodox Church of Georgia during the previous two centuries begins with a short survey on autocephaly in general, and on the autocephaly of the Orthodox Church of Georgia in particular.

"Autocephalous" is taken from the Greek term (deriving from *auto* "self" and *kephalos* "head") meaning "oneself at the head" and indicating an independent Church. In the early Church, bishops with governing rights resided in the main cities of provinces (*eparchies* in Greek) and metropolises. For this reason they were often called "metropolitans". From the 4th century, the number of such autocephalous bishops gradually diminished and metropolitans and bishops became subordinated to senior bishops in the capital cities.

From the 5th century there were five patriarchs in the Christian world. These were the patriarch of the West (or the "Bishop of Rome"), the patriarch of Constantinople, and the patriarchs of Alexandria, Antioch and Jerusalem. Their churches were autocephalous. There was also one other independent church, that of Cyprus, headed by an archbishop.

New autocephalous churches began to emerge at a later time.[1] To grant autocephaly to a part of one's own church, or to a new church, was a complicated process. The so-called "Mother Churches" granted autocephalous rights to territories under their jurisdiction. In this way, different peoples could establish their own independent national churches under local ecclesiastic governance.

The autocephalous status of the Orthodox Church of Georgia was linked to the Patriarchate of Antioch — the Antiochian bishop Eustathios is believed to have consecrated the first bishop of Kartli. In the first half of the fourth century, when Christianity was declared to be the official religion of the Roman Empire and the earliest ecclesiastic structures were created, Kartli (Iberia)[2] was already a strong, independent state. Hence, from the very moment of its emergence, the Church in Kartli fell under the jurisdiction of the Bishop of the Great City of Antioch and of All the East. From the outset, the bishops of Kartli were consecrated in Antioch and sent to Mtskheta (the capital of Kartli). This situation continued until the 480s, when ecclesiastic structures were reorganised at the initiative of the king of Kartli, Vakhtang I Gorgasali.[3]

Between 480-490, Vakhtang addressed the imperial court of the Byzantine emperor Zeno (476-491) and the patriarch of Constantinople (Akakios, 471-489) with the request to send a catholicos to Georgia. Vakhtang asked for one particular cleric, a Greek priest, Petre, with whom he had become acquainted during his campaign with the Persian army against Byzantium (the Georgian king had had to side with Persia during a period of increased Persian aggression against the Southern Caucasus).

Through the mediation of the patriarch of Constantinople, the patriarch of Antioch fulfilled the request of Vakhtang and consecrated Petre as catholicos[4] of Kartli. He also consecrated thirteen other bishops,

1. Today there are 15 (Eastern) Orthodox Christian autocephalous churches. These are the Churches of Constantinople (the Ecumenical Patriarchate), Alexandria, Antioch, Jerusalem, Russia, Georgia, Serbia, Romania, Bulgaria, Cyprus, Greece, Albania, Poland, the Czech Lands and Slovakia, and the Orthodox Church in America (although its autocephaly is not recognised by all the Orthodox churches).
2. "Iberia" was the Greek name for Kartli (Eastern Georgia) while "Kolkheti" was used for Egrisi (Western Georgia).
3. See p23.
4. In the East, independent and semi-independent Church hierarchs were given the title of "catholicos".

who had jurisdiction over different eparchies, on their return to Kartli. Henceforth Mtskheta became the residence of a Georgian catholicos.

Vakhtang's ecclesiastic policies advanced significant changes in the Church's administrative system: a) the number of eparchies grew; b) a local church assembly (synod) was established; c) an archbishop, having the title catholicos, was appointed as head of the synod — it was his responsibility to consecrate bishops and appoint them to sees; d) the synod had the right to bring bishops to trial and to elect a new catholicos in case of death.

None of these developments were intended to suggest that the Church in Kartli maintained complete independence from that of Antioch; rather, it continued to have obligations to the Mother Church. The name of the Antiochian patriarch was commemorated during prayers and the Church of Antioch continued to confirm and to consecrate the locally-elected catholicos in Mtskheta. The latter obligation was abolished in the late 740s.

According to Ephrem Mtsire, an 11th-century Georgian theologian, the Church of Georgia continued to make annual payments to Antioch of 1,000 drahkans — a sizeable sum — even after that time. Moreover, in case "any heresy" were to be found among the Georgians, the patriarch of Antioch had the right to send an exarch to Georgia in order to correct the state of affairs and to eradicate the heresy. Until the 9th century, Holy Chrism was also received from the Mother Church. Only in the time of St Gregory of Khandzta did the Georgian church proceed to make its own Holy Chrism, and thus the independent Church acquired a new dimension.[5]

Discussion on the issue of the autocephalous status of the Church of Kartli broadened after the Great Schism. Theodore Balsamon (1140-1195), the well-known canonist and patriarch of Antioch, provides the following unambiguous testimony:

> When Lord Peter was the Holy Patriarch of the great, divine city of Antioch, the Synod decided to make the Church of Iberia (Kartli) autocephalous. Until that time it had been subordinate to the Patriarch of Antioch (Percival, 1899, p17).

Historians rightly believe that this "Patriarch Peter" had to be Peter the Fuller (†488) who was Patriarch of Antioch exactly at the time of

5.   See p28.

Vakhtang Gorgasali's reign in Georgia. According to the 14th-century canonist Matthew Blastares (†1335):

> If you find other churches which are autocephalous as the Church of Bulgaria, of Cyprus, of Iberia, you need not be astonished. For the Emperor Justinian gave this honour to the Archbishop of Bulgaria, the third Synod gave this honour to the Archbishop of Cyprus . . . the judgment of the Synod of Antioch is annulled and this honour is granted to the Bishop of Iberia (*Georgica*, 1970, pp 119-120).

The situation changed entirely in the first half of the 11th century when all of the Georgian kingdoms and principalities were united into a single state. The catholicos of Mtskheta (Kartli) spread his jurisdiction over Western Georgia (until the 9th century it had been under the control of Byzantium) and named patriarch. The name Melkisedek I (1010-1033) is mentioned in the sources as the first catholicos to be made "patriarch". Since that time the head of the Orthodox Church of Georgia has been known as "Catholicos-Patriarch of All Georgia" and the Church has been completely independent in its domestic and foreign affairs.

Opinions diverge about the status of the Orthodox Church of Georgia between the 5th and 10th centuries. It was variously considered to be "independent" (Lominadze, 1981, p71), "semi-independent" (Nikoladze, 1918, p59), "autonomous" (Faris, 1992, p31) or "dependent upon Antioch" (Nikandr, 1905, pp 21-22). Indeed, its partial dependence on the Church of Antioch both from the time of Vakhtang Gorgasali and in the 8th century suggests a state of "autonomy" or "semi-independence" rather than autocephaly. However, the real issue at stake is: what was actually meant at that time for a church to be deemed "autocephalous"? In spite of the fact that the term "autocephaly" has always been understood as a principle of self-government for a local church, the practical application of that principle differed in the first centuries of Christianity from that in the Byzantine era and again from the present time.

Currently, the autocephaly for a church means its full and unconditional independence in domestic and foreign affairs, administrative and judicial matters, the local production of Holy Chrism, the canonisation of its own saints by the local Synod, the inscription in the diptychs of the head of the church together with the heads of the other autocephalous Orthodox churches and, above all, the election and enthronement of the head and of all hierarchs without interference from any other church. In the Middle Ages, however, the term autocephaly did not necessarily imply complete self-rule; full autocephaly was a privilege of only the aforementioned five patriarchates (the Pentarchy).

On the basis of evidence drawn also from other churches, it would appear that from the time of the creation of the Pentarchy until the 19th century, autocephaly denoted any form of self-government for any church (the term "autonomy" was introduced to denote a particular ecclesial status only from the late 19th century).

In 1811, after the Russian empire annexed the kingdoms of Kartli-Kakheti and Imereti, the autocephaly of the Orthodox Church of Georgia was dissolved. It was made subject, illegally and in violation of eighth canon of the Third Ecumenical Council, to the Holy Synod of the Russian Orthodox Church. In March 1917, after more than a century's subordination to the Russian Synod, the Georgian hierarchs convoked an assembly of ecclesiastic and secular figures and restored the autocephaly of the Georgian church. However, the Russian Patriarchate did not recognise this restored autocephaly until 1943. For its part, the Ecumenical Patriarchate did not recognise it until 1990. On 23 January 1990, the Synod of the Church of Constantinople made a decision to recognise the ancient autocephaly of the Church and to rank its head as Catholicos-Patriarch of the Church of Georgia.

In 1900s, when Georgian clergy and historians began the struggle to restore the Church's autocephaly, the matter was raised in St Petersburg before the Russian church and the secular authorities. Certain Russian hierarchs attempted to prove that up until 1811 the Orthodox Church of Georgia had been subordinate to the Antiochian Patriarchate and had never been autocephalous. At the same time, Archimandrite Nikandr, rector of Tbilisi's Theological Seminary, wrote: "Emperor Alexandr Pavlovich found it necessary to subordinate the Georgian church to the Holy Synod and this was his right — a right indisputable, even by the canons of the Ecumenical Councils — a right which had always been exercised by the Byzantine emperors" (Nikandr, 1905, pp 20-21).[6] It is

6.   Canon XII of the Fourth Ecumenical Council states the following: "It has come to our knowledge that certain persons, contrary to the laws of the Church, having had recourse to the secular powers, have by means of imperial rescripts divided one province into two, so that there are consequently two metropolitans in the one province. Metropolitans in one province decreed that for the future, no such thing shall be implemented by a bishop, since he who shall undertake it shall be degraded from his rank. But the cities that have already been honoured by means of imperial letters with the name of metropolis, and the bishops in charge of them, shall take the bare title, all metropolitan rights being preserved to the true Metropolis." This canon does not give power to the emperor to divide one church province into two,

significant that Nikandr was a theologian and therefore would have been only too aware of the fact that in the past several autonomous churches had already coexisted within the borders of the Christian Byzantine Empire.

Within the Russian church, however, there was an alternative opinion on the subject of church independence. The canon lawyer I. Berdnikov wrote in his study *The State Position of the Church in the Roman — Byzantine Empire*: "Whatever the civil government — whether secular or Christian — it has no right to interfere with Church affairs. Above all it must not pass any laws or make other governmental decisions on any aspect of Church life including its administration" (Berdmikov, 1881, pp 493-4). Even if the Russian claims were accurate — that the Church of Georgia was under the aegis of the Church of Antioch until 1811 — it remains that the church and the civil authorities in Russia did indeed violate canon law, specifically the ruling of the Third Ecumenical Council, by annexing a province over which it had never held rights.

Russian troops enter Georgia

By virtue of the Manifesto of the Russian tsar Alexander I, dated September 12, 1801, the kingdom of Kartli-Kakheti (Eastern Georgia) was abolished and Georgia became a part of Russia possessing only the rights of a province.[7] Russian troops entered the capital of Eastern Georgia, Tbilisi, carrying before them the Cross of St Nino[8] —

nor can he completely abolish local church power. Interpreting this rule, a well-known expert on Orthodox canon law, Bishop Nikodim (Milash) notes that this canon, repeating the rule confirmed at the First, Second and Third Ecumenical Councils, affirms that no bishop shall dare resort to the emperor's power in order to seek or to receive the rights of metropolitans to the prejudice of a canonical metropolitan. Naturally, neither Archbishop Varlaam nor, more particularly, General Tormasov had any right to interfere in the affairs of the Georgian church. Neither did the emperor Alexander I nor the Russian church authorities. From the eighth canon of the Third Ecumenical Council, which preserved the independence of the Church of Cyprus, it is stated that: ". . . his fellow Bishops Zeno and Evagrius of the province of Cyprus, also beloved of God . . . have told us in writing and by word of mouth that the Bishop of Antioch has in this way held ordinations in Cyprus; therefore the Rulers of the Holy Churches in Cyprus shall enjoy, without dispute or injury, according to the Canons of the Blessed Fathers and to ancient custom, the right of performing for themselves the ordination of their excellent Bishops. The same rule shall be observed in other eparchies and provinces everywhere, so that none of the God-beloved Bishops shall assume control of any province which has not heretofore, from the very beginning, been under his own hand or that of his predecessors. But if any one has violently taken and subjected a Province, he shall give it up . . ."

7. See Part I, Chapter 2, 'The 19th and Early 20th Centuries'.
8. See the box on St Nino, p21.

one of the most important relics and holy items of the Georgian church.

This cross, made from vine stalks and held together by the hair of St Nino, the Enlightener of Georgia, was a major symbol of the christian-isation of Georgia and throughout the centuries it had been kept at Mtskheta's Svetitskhoveli cathedral (at present it is kept in Sioni cathe-dral, Tbilisi). In 1723, during a joint raid on Georgia by Turks and Lezgins, the cross was transferred for safe-keeping to the Ananuri church in the mountainous region of north-western Georgia. From there it was taken to Moscow by the Georgian bishop Timothy Gabashvili at the request of Prince Bakar Bagrationi. In 1801, Bakar's grandson, Giorgi, passed it over to Tsar Alexander I. Having signed the Manifesto of September 12 in that year, the Russian emperor was com-pelled to return the cross to its rightful home.

In bearing the cross at its head, the Russian army showed the Georgian population that Russian rule and sovereignty over their coun-try was an act of protection and of God's mercy. Indeed, many people, among them hierarchs of the Georgian church, interpreted the entry of the Russian army precisely in this manner. It was their hope that the mis-fortunes of the Georgian people would come to end and that the land would revive under the patronage of Russia. Archbishop Ambrosi of Nekresi, a renowned preacher, addressed his flock in this way:

> Our enemies will be crushed by His Majesty's power and we shall be for-ever saved from the Muslim yoke. Georgia shall be delivered from the bonds of hell. Weep not and grieve not, for Georgia is saved and our enemies, the Persians, have fallen! (Kirion, 1901, p15)

However, not all shared the same opinion. Many realised that Georgia's independence had come to an end and that a time of unknown dependence had arrived. And so, immediately after the abolition of the Georgian state, the new civil authorities began to interfere into the affairs of the Church.

Conflicting systems of Church governance

The administrative system of the Church in the Russian empire differed fundamentally from that of the Church in Georgia. Following the reforms of Tsar Peter I (1689-1725), the patriarchal seat was abol-ished in 1721 and collegial management was introduced through a governmental synod which, since 1722, had been led by a layman — the over-procurator. In 1784, Empress Catherine II subordinated the Church to the state apparatus even on a larger scale than it had been before. Under her rule all church and monastic property was confiscated. As a result the state inherited thousands of peasants and vast estates. Similar changes were intended to take place in Georgia.

However, the Georgian church resembled a large-scale feudal organization. It was regulated by the catholicos-patriarch, or occasionally by a member of the ruling royal dynasty, the Bagrationi, who had unlimited rights. The Orthodox Church of Georgia owned large arable lands and pastures, forests, mills, fishing areas, candle factories and other property, which gave it a significant independence. The secular authorities almost never interfered in the management of the Church — it was the patriarch who controlled all affairs at his own discretion.

While it is true that the first commander-in-chief of Eastern Georgia, General Karl Knorring, did not have time to do anything of substance with respect to church affairs during his rule, he did write to Catholicos-Patriarch Anthony II (1762-1827), head of the church hierarchy, in fulfilment of the tsar's will as early as February, 1801, i.e. before the total abolition of the Georgian kingdom:

On the occasion of the unification of Georgia with the Russian Empire, His Majesty wishes to have detailed information about the state of the Georgian clergy. In this connection I ask your Holiness to provide me with your benevolent testimony to the following items:

—How many and what kind of eparchies exist throughout the Georgian provinces? Which hierarchs administer them and by whom are the hierarchs themselves administered?

—How many monasteries and convents, cathedral and parish churches are there in each eparchy and how are the hierarchs, monasteries and priests supported and paid?

—Do the hierarchs have legal bodies, such as the dicasteria [Greek: *dikasterion* — "trial", "court"] or church offices, for managing their churches and monasteries?

—Do clergymen conduct their legal cases against civilians in the ecclesiastical or the civil courts?

—The representatives of which social classes are promoted to the rank of the clergy? Are they the representatives of a special estate, as it is in Russia, or of any estate?

—Are there in the eparchies any schools or colleges for the clergy? If so, what do they do? (*Acts*, 1866, vol. i, p529.)

Abolition of autocephaly

Aside from these questions, Knorring asked Anthony to touch upon other matters which the catholicos would find important and necessary. From this questionnaire it is clear that Russia, in requiring such detailed information, had serious intentions. Anthony himself passed on to Knorring the answers to his questions together with a short outline of the past history of the Georgian church. In his letter to the general, Anthony named nine eparchies in Kartli (Tbilisi, Samtavro, Tsilkani, Manglisi, Ruisi, Urbnisi, Nikozi and Samtavisi) and six in Kakheti (Bodbe, Alaverdi, Ninotsminda, Rustavi, Nekresi and Kharchasheni). In addition, there was the principle eparchy — Mtskheta — where the patriarchal throne was located. Kartli possessed eleven monasteries and there were twelve in Kakheti, though some were not functioning at that time. The Georgian patriarch mentioned that hierarchs, archimandrites and some clergy were paid through the Church, "monastic" peasants and the estates but the parish priests received remuneration from the parishes and through their personal labour.

In Georgia, unlike Russia, representatives from all ranks of society could be ordained to the clergy so long as they were considered to be worthy for the position. The patriarch made it clear in his letter that in every eparchy of Kartli and Kakheti, reading, writing, church singing and the fundamentals of the Christian faith were taught. Unfortunately, by that time, the theological seminaries in Tbilisi and Telavi that had been opened under King Erekle II (father of Patriarch Anthony), where theology, philosophy, history, rhetoric, hagiography and mathematics had been taught, were no longer functioning (*Acts*, vol. i, p530).

In the same letter to Knorring, Anthony also provided details about the landholdings of certain bishops. Metropolitan Arseny of Tbilisi, for example, owned 18 villages, Bishop Justin of Ruisi — 46 villages, Bishop Ioane of Tsilkani — also 46 villages. The bishop of Nikozi possessed eight villages, the bishop of Bodbe held 31 villages, and so on (*Acts*, 1866, vol. i, pp 530-531).

By the time of Russia's annexation of Eastern Georgia, it administered only 15 eparchies. Catholicos-Patriarch Anthony II turned out to be the last Georgian patriarch of the 19th century.

Interference by the Russian church

From the very beginning it became quite evident that the Russian authorities were interested in Georgian church affairs. With the signing in 1783 of the Treaty of Georgievsk between Russia and the kingdom of Kartli-Kakheti, Georgian political figures and diplomats themselves gave grounds for Russia to behave in this way. Article 8 of the treaty affirmed: "for the management of the Georgian church and for its attitude to the Russian Synod a separate article will be worked out" (Paichadze, 1983, p74), but this never occurred. Violating the terms of the treaty and abolishing the kingdom of Kartli-Kakheti, the Russian government intended to behave in the same manner with the Orthodox Church of Georgia. Nor was there any secrecy over the issue. In 1800, Tsar Pavel I wrote: "I want Georgia to be a province, so bring it directly into contact with the Senate; but with respect to religion — with the Synod" (Kirion, 1901, p13).

General Knorring was ordered to provide a complete study on the Georgian church and to collect all necessary data for "regulating the affairs on the management of the Georgian clergy (Kirion, 1901, p33). For the Russian authorities, this "regulating" meant introducing into Georgia a church management similar to that in the Russian empire, i.e. the complete submission of the church to the state authorities. Having submitted to the state, the church was obliged to convey Russian policies, such as training clergy devoted to the Russian empire and becoming a firm ideological support for the Russian dominion.

However, under the prevailing circumstances, the Russian government was not prepared to entrust to the Orthodox Church of Georgia responsibilities similar to those in Russia, since it considered the Church to be unreliable and unfit both in its structure and in its clergy (Khutsishvili, 1987, p16).

First steps in altering church structure

Because General Knorring was dismissed from his post of viceroy of Georgia in 1802, he did not have time to examine seriously any issues connected with the church in Georgia. Nor did the situation change during the supervision of Knorring's successor, General Pavel Tsitsianov. The latter was mainly involved in civil and military affairs, though it must be said that he occasionally intervened somewhat actively in church affairs. For example, when in 1803 Patriarch Anthony II appointed Archimandrite Dositheos to the Tsilkani eparchy rather than forcing him to retire, General Tsitsianov sent the patriarch a curt letter:

> To my utter astonishment I have heard (something which I do not wish to believe) that Your Holiness deigned to turn the Tsilkani eparchy over to Archimandrite Dositheos whereas you have been notified that His Majesty's sacred will is *not* to increase the number of high ranks among the

clergy. Furthermore, I have declared to you verbally that the dissolved eparchies must be united with those that are neighbouring (*Acts*, vol. ii, 1866, p264).

In this letter Tsitsianov threatens the patriarch: in case of disobedience he would have to report back to the tsar "concerning the disorder in the ecclesiastical affairs of this place" (*Acts*, vol. ii, 1866, p264). This correspondence bears witness to the fact that the Russian state authorities, in this case military authorities, actively intruded into the internal affairs of the Church.

Indeed, in his letter, Tsitsianov hints at the true "sacred will" of the tsar, namely the elimination of the autocephalous status of the Orthodox Church of Georgia and its complete subordination to the Russian Synod. The most effective way to execute this plan was by abolishing the eparchies progressively; to do so all at once would have been somewhat dangerous. As Tsitsianov, in his report to Tsar Alexander I on May 22, 1804, wrote:

Following the retirement of elderly bishops, the best way to dissolve the eparchies is to unite them to neighbouring ones . . . I put this rule into practice during my stay in Georgia (Kartli) where I eliminated three eparchies and left three, though I believe it was sufficient to have one eparchy in Kartli (*Acts*, vol. ii, 1866, p265).

The tsar himself was of the same opinion. On September 13, 1804 Count Kochubey, a member of the Senate of the Russian empire, wrote to Tsitsianov:

His Majesty has expressed his supreme will, namely, that the intended dissolution of the eparchies should be accomplished little by little — one could say, in a discreet way — taking all possible precautions . . ." (*Acts*, vol. ii, 1866, p270).

This evidence indicates that a policy on the Orthodox Church of Georgia had been settled and it was only a matter of time before it would be fully brought to fruition.

Changes in church management
Further steps in reorganizing the structure of the Orthodox Church of Georgia were undertaken by the Russian administration during the time

of General Alexander Tormasov's command in the country from 1808 to 1811. A decree from Tsar Alexander I stated that all Georgian priests and deacons were henceforth liberated from serfdom. His Majesty's order of July 7, 1808, addressed to the Transcaucasus commander-in-chief General Ivan Gudovich declared:

> Having learnt that many priests and deacons are appropriated by local princes and noblemen as serfs, and having considered that such a state of affairs is neither in agreement with the laws of the Russian Empire nor is it appropriate for the conduct of good order so highly respected by me, I command that from henceforth, as a general rule for Georgia, all clergy are free not only from bondage but also from all taxes and duties to their landlords (*Acts*, vol. iii, 1869, pp 77-78).

The liberation of the clergy from repression was a key event, and that proved to have positive consequences.

In the opinion of Tormasov, in order to establish new regulations in the Georgian church, it would be necessary to create a dicasteria in Georgia on the same principles as in Russia. The dicasteria was the Russian church's judicial and administrative body for its eparchies and was regulated by local bishops. This body was concerned with almost every kind of ecclesiastic affair, especially judicial. It covered issues such as divorce, unmarried church-member couples, adoption, property disputes between churches and monasteries, violations of ecclesiastical and secular laws by ecclesiastic figures, and so forth.[9] Tormasov expressed his views in a report of June 6, 1809 to the over-procurator of the Holy Governing Synod, Prince A. Golitsin. The ruler of the Transcaucasus urged the appointment of Catholicos-Patriarch Anthony II as head of this institution, "out of deference to his royal origin and for the general respect that he enjoys in Georgia" (*Acts*, vol iv, 1870, p140).

As assistant archbishop to the head of the dicasteria, Varlaam Eristavi should have been the logical appointment. At that time he was a member of the Russian Synod; he was also fluent in Russian and knowledgeable in the conventions of the Russian church. The dicasteria also required the appointment a president, a vice-president, three clergymen (nominated by the other clergy), a secretary, an interpreter and a certain number of clerks.

---

9. The first Dicasteria in Georgia was established by Catholicos-Patriarch Anthony I in the 1770s with the aim of fulfilling the functions of the collegial court of the Catholicosate. However, it was not destined to survive for long.

Removal of Catholicos-Patriarch Anthony II

General Tormasov hoped that the dicasteria would be established quickly but it soon became bogged down by delays. On one occasion, for example, a decision was made in St Petersburg in November 1809 to summon Anthony to the Russian Synod in order to discuss Georgian church affairs — evidently it would have been somewhat difficult and time-consuming to conduct these matters by correspondence. The patriarch accepted the invitation but tried to delay his departure as much as possible on the grounds of poor health. He seemed to have sensed that he would never come back to Georgia, and his foreboding was not without good reason: though the patriarch remained in Georgia, by this time nearly every member of the Bagrationi royal family had already been exiled to different corners of Russia.

Anthony's baptismal name was Teimuraz and he was the son of King Erekle II and brother of the last Georgian king Giorgi XII. He was so revered by the Georgian people that he had become a symbol both for the nation and for the independence of the Georgian church. This naturally created considerable anxiety among the Russian authorities. After delaying his departure for about a year, the patriarch finally left on November 3, 1810. On the way, he stopped at Georgia's main religious centre, Mtskheta, where, on November 9 at Svetitskhoveli cathedral, he served his last patriarchal liturgy. The next day he again set off with his entourage for Russia (Bubulashvili, 2002, p79).

In his report to Prince Golitsin, Tormasov commented on Anthony's personal qualities:

> In my opinion, Catholicos Anthony, who is generally accustomed to being in control of all things, is, owing to poor health, unable to apply sufficient energy into setting local church affairs in order. According to local practice, his royal origin gives him the right to act spontaneously. This is why I find it useful to appoint Archbishop Varlaam (as a member of the Holy Governing Synod and as someone experienced in church management), as exarch of Georgia and metropolitan of Bodbe Ioan as the ruling hierarch of Alaverdi and Kakheti (*Acts*, vol. iv, 1870, pp 164-165).

In the same report Tormasov also suggested that if Catholicos Anthony were to remain in Russia, in consideration of his annual income in Georgia, the church leader should be given as maintenance a pension of 6,000 silver roubles. It seems that the future of Anthony had been decided well in advance.

Anthony arrived in St Petersburg on March 19, 1811 after an arduous journey of four months, and was accommodated in a house that was rented on his behalf. On the very first day after his arrival, at a solemn reception in honour of the catholicos and Prince Golitsin, he was informed that the tsar had allocated a thousand roubles as his allowance (Zhmakin, 1905, p108).

What was said between the Catholicos and Over-Procurator Golitsin or during Anthony's conversation with the tsar at the reception remains unknown. However, it is clear that the results were disappointing for the church leader. On May 22, 1811 he pleaded with the tsar to allow him to retain the title of catholicos (Zhmakin, 1905, p110). On June 10, 1811, only twenty days before the adoption of the new managerial order for the Georgian church, Anthony received a letter from Alexander:

> Following the incorporation of Georgia into Russia, the Georgian church should also naturally come under the authority of the Holy Synod. It would be incompatible with the new administration to retain the post of catholicos. No doubt, having foreseen all of this, you addressed me with the request to settle your future and retain the title you have borne for so long. For these reasons, I graciously discharge you from overseeing the affairs of the Georgian church, yet charging you with the titles of a member of the Holy Synod and catholicos. You will retain all of the privileges in the holy services that you held have until now and will be addressed as "Your Beatitude" (Zhmakin, 1905, p111).

Moreover, the tsar assigned the catholicos an annual pension of 10,000 silver roubles. At the same time, Anthony was given the Award of the Holy Apostle Andrew. Later in June, he was presented with a green velvet mantle embroidered with gold crosses and initials that indicated his name and title. The tsar also presented the catholicos with a four-seated golden coach and seven horses from the court's stables that had been formerly owned by Empress Elisabeth (Zhmakin, 1905, p113).

Anthony resided in Moscow for some time and later in Tambov, further to the south. His health was believed to have deteriorated as a result of the northern climate. On March 1822, he petitioned the tsar with the request to allow him to return to Georgia. The tsar refused.

In 1823, Anthony finally settled in Nizhny Novgorod where he died on December 21, 1827 at the age of 65.

Varlaam Eristavi, the "Russified" hierarch

In his report to the Holy Synod, Tormasov enclosed an inventory of the Georgian churches as well as lists of hierarchs and lower clergy. These documents identify that at that time in Eastern Georgia there were 799 churches, 7 hierarchs, 746 priests and deacons and 661 lay employees (*Acts*, vol. iv, 1870, p163).

Following the departure of Catholicos-Patriarch Anthony II, the hierarch Varlaam Eristavi was given temporary management of the Orthodox Church of Georgia. Varlaam, the first exarch of Georgia to hold the title of Metropolitan of Mtskheta and Kartli, contributed greatly to the abolition of the Church of Georgia's autocephaly and to the establishment of the exarchate. He also headed the dicasteria.

Metropolitan Varlaam was born in 1762. The son of a well-known feudal lord, David Eristavi of Ksani, he rose to the rank of archbishop of Akhtala before his election to the post of metropolitan of Mtskheta. Between 1801 and 1808, he lived in St Petersburg where he was a member of the Holy Synod of the Russian Church. Varlaam studied all aspects of the internal affairs and of the administrative procedures of the Russian church, knowledge of which naturally drew his attention to the Russian government in its preparations to reorganise the Orthodox Church of Georgia.

In December, 1810 (a month after the Catholicos' departure for Russia) Tormasov wrote the following to Archbishop Varlaam:

> The over-procurator of the synod has drawn attention to the fact that to this point the synod has influence neither on Georgian church affairs nor on the Georgian clergy. It therefore commissions me (following consultations with you) to present a personal opinion on ways of arranging the administration of the Georgian clergy. On what bases and in what form these things ought to be done will depend upon decisions taken by the Holy Synod (*Acts*, vol. iv, 1870, p161).

General Tormasov questioned the archbishop about his views on these matters. In what situation, for example, did he find the Georgian clergy? Since Varlaam had lived in Russia, perhaps he had considered measures that could be taken for establishing the dicasteria. Finally Tormasov enquired whether Varlaam himself had received directions from the Russian synod since he was a member of it.

Eventually, Varlaam was commissioned to undertake strategies for the future organization of the Orthodox Church of Georgia and for the establishment of the dicasteria. In other words, this was tantamount to complete abolition of the Church's autocephaly. There were a number of issues that made his task a relatively difficult one, such as the fact that the number of churches and clergy could not be absolutely determined, and that information on income received by churches and monasteries from the known eparchies was incomplete. According to Varlaam, data on income was in the hands of the eparchial hierarchs and these were not prepared to proffer information to anyone other than the catholicos (*Acts*, vol. iv, 1870, p161).

Despite these difficulties and the clear delicacy of the situation, Archbishop Varlaam managed to fulfil his obligations in good time and to present his opinions to General Tormasov. On February 18, 1811 the latter, in turn, reported on everything to the over-procurator, Prince Golitsin. Varlaam had suggested permitting only two of the existing fourteen eparchies to remain in Eastern Georgia: one in Kartli under the name of the Mtskheta and Kartli eparchy, and the other the Kakheti-Alaverdi-Kakhetian eparchy. The same scheme envisaged only five of the nine monasteries to remain functioning.

Although Varlaam became exarch of Imereti in 1814, he failed to arrange church affairs there in the same way as those in Eastern Georgia. He was finally recalled to Russia where he remained a member of the Holy Synod until 1825, and from that time until his death in 1830, he held the post of abbot of St Daniel Monastery in Moscow (Bubulashvili, 2002, p76).

Long-term effect of reducing hierarch authority

In his letter to Prince Golitsin, Tormasov highlighted Archbishop Varlaam's suggestion that, were the dicasteria to be established, its elected members should not be made up of the hierarchs themselves but of archimandrites and archpriests. Furthermore, Varlaam's advice had been that the head of the dicasteria should be the ruling hierarch of Eastern Georgia. In his opinion, this ruling hierarch should be conferred the title Metropolitan of Mtskheta and Kartli, exarch of Georgia (parallel to the Moldavan and Valakhian exarchates) — confirmed by the tsar but acting under the authority of the Holy Synod (Kirion, 1901, p49). Such an administrative change would have had an impact on the entire life of the church. Bishops were intentionally not invited to the dicasteriain order to keep them in their own sees, while the number of eparchies was gradually reduced. The same counsel of Varlaam's also included the transfer of all church nobility and peasants together with their estates to the dicasteria, which meant subordination to the state. Tormasov also added the following suggestions:

—To open in Tbilisi (for the purpose of educating the future clergy) a high school for the children of clergymen, allocating 6100 roubles annually from the church's income for its upkeep.

—To open nine district schools in different areas of Kartli and Kakheti whose function would be to prepare children for entering the Tbilisi High School. For this purpose 3,800 silver roubles were to be allocated annually. An annual sum of money was also meant to be earmarked for supporting the widows and orphans of clergymen.

—To avoid financial malpractice, all church income and expenditure would be controlled by the dicasteria (Kirion, 1901, p49).

Having considered and approved the report from Varlaam and Tormasov at the beginning of June 1811, the governmental synod passed it almost without change[10] to the tsar for ratification on June 21. Alexander I signed this on June 30, 1811, which may be considered to be the official date when the autocephaly of the ancient Church of Georgia was dissolved by the power of the Russian ruler.

As a result of this, the first decade of the Russian protectorate saw the subjection of the autocephalous Orthodox Church of Georgia to the Russian Synod. Tokens of this subordination included:

—first and foremost, the election of the Georgian catholicos as a member of the Synod of the Russian Church;

—the eradication of the post and the title of catholicos-patriarch;

—the gradual dissolution of all eparchies of the Georgian church and the foundation only of two (which later were united to form a single eparchy);

—the institution of the position of exarch and his election not locally in Georgia, but by an appointing body in St Petersburg;

—the establishment of a bureaucratic organ: the Governmental Synod-Dicasteria (later the Georgia-Imereti Synodal Bureau);

—the abolition of the material independence of the Orthodox Church of Georgia by the transference of all church property and monastic estates by command of the Treasury (Gorgadze, 1905, p13).

These changes resulted in a gradual transformation of the Georgian

---

10. The proposal for the foundation of a high school had been substituted by one calling for the foundation of a seminary.

church. The long-term objectives were openly voiced by the Russian Archpriest Ioan Vostorgov several decades later: "The Georgian exarchs should remember that their foremost duty is to devote all their energy to the russification of the Georgians with respect to their religion" (Khutsishvili, 1987, p20).

As examined below, the majority of the exarchs contributed to this russification of the Georgian church, so much so that even certain Russians were obliged to admit that "if any Georgian were intending to write a true story about the commandeering actions of the Russian exarchs, we would have to blush for in shame have they protected the Russian clergy" (*From the History of Georgia*, 1907, p8).

Certainly, on canonical grounds, there is no defence for the actions either of the Russian secular authorities or of the Russian Synod in annulling the autocephaly of the Orthodox Church of Georgia or in replacing its patriarchate with an exarchate or in submitting the latter to the Russian Synod. However, attempts to refashion church life in Georgia following the model that existed in the governing state should not be viewed as an entirely unexpected course of action. For example, there are understandable grounds for the Russian empire not keeping its promises of "protection" as regulated by the treaty of 1783 — the strategy of the empire was one that changed according to the political situation and to the balance of power in the world at large.

At the same time, the bitterness of most Georgians for being deprived of their national dignity can also be justified. It was highly regrettable that the Russian church authorities were complicit (perhaps by force), in maintaining and supporting the political agenda of russification with respect to one of the ancient autocephalous churches. Initially this was done covertly, through cautious diplomacy, but later explicitly in the manifold guises and activities of the Russian Synod. It is not surprising that so obvious a violation of canon law created disquiet for a number of Russian theologians and church historians.

The Georgia-Imereti Synodal Bureau

In 1814, Metropolitan Varlaam energetically set about arranging the Exarchate of Georgia. Indeed, all reforms initiated in the church after the establishment of the exarchate were connected with him. However, the particular organ of church administration that he founded — the dicasteria — did not last for long. By an imperial decree dated August 30, 1814, the dicasteria was replaced by the Georgia-Imereti Synodal Kantora (or Bureau).

Abolition of autocephaly

The move was a well-reasoned decision since, by this time, the Russian authorities had not only brought the kingdom of Imereti (Western Georgia) under their full control but also established military and civil rule there. All that was left was to bring Imereti, Guria, Samegrelo and Abkhazia under Russian control also from the perspective of religion. Hence, at the initiative of Bishop Dositheos of Gori (the bishopric of Gori was established on July 30, 1811 to provide an assistant hierarch for the Mtskheta-Kartli eparchy), the Holy Synod of Russia acknowledged his undertaking to be an "arrangement of theological affairs in Georgia and other districts incorporated to the Russian power" (Kirion, 1901, p53).

Considering this action to be altogether acceptable and expedient, both the Holy Synod of the Russian Church and the tsar decided to reorganise the dicasteria and to create a synodal bureau similar that in Moscow. Following the establishment of the Georgia-Imereti Synodal Bureau, the authorities intended to establish a dicasteria in Kutaisi for the churches in Imereti, Guria and Samegrelo but this did not transpire; instead, an eparchial chancellery was established (Bishop Kirion, 1901, p54).

When the Georgia-Imereti Synodal Bureau opened officially in Tbilisi on May 8, 1815, the exarch, Metropolitan Varlaam, himself led a solemn divine liturgy in the capital's Sioni cathedral. In addition, a thanksgiving service for the health of the tsar and the imperial family was served after the liturgy. Varlaam invited guests to a formal luncheon for this occasion while, in honour of the bureau's first meeting, the commander-in-chief of Georgia, General Rtishchev, hosted an official dinner at which the exarch of Georgia and Imereti was appointed as the bureau's head.

The bishop of Telavi and Georgia-Caucasus,[11] two archimandrites and two archpriests were also made members of the board. These were appointed by the president and the second hierarch but these had to be approved by the Holy Synod in St Petersburg (Bishop Kirion, 1901, pp 54-55). The fifth-ranking prosecutor, also a member of the board, was obliged to know Russian and Georgian. It was his duty to supervise the proper conduct of affairs in the bureau and in the chancellery of the Kutaisi eparchy. Of the three chief officers chosen to assist him, one worked in Gori, the other in Telavi and the third in Kutaisi. Their chief tasks were to supervise the immovable property and estates of the church

---

11. From August 30, 1814 the Alaverdi-Kakheti Eparchy was renamed the Telavi and Georgia-Caucasus Eparchy, and was headed by Archbishop Dositheos.

and to report on their circumstances to the prosecutor, who, in turn, would give account to the bureau. For the conduct of written business, the bureau had two secretaries: one for the affairs of Eastern Georgia and the other for Imereti (Kirion, 1901, p57).

As for Imereti, it was decided at the time of the establishment of the Georgia-Imereti Synodal Bureau to allow the existing eparchies to remain in place, at least temporarily, until such time as the issue became the subject of special consideration (Kirion, 1901, p56). The Synodal Bureau was responsible for informing the Holy Synod about the deaths of hierarchs, the appointment of new bishops, the dissolution or merger of eparchies, and the evaluaion of the expediency of each eparchy.

By the end of each year the Synodal Bureau had to submit to the Holy Synod an annual report on work taken on, affairs resolved and unresolved, and justifications for incomplete undertakings. The Holy Synod decided to pay the following salaries in silver to all members and functionaries of the Synodal Bureau:

1. Exarch and head of the bureau: 5,000 roubles.[12]
2. Archbishop of Telavi and Georgia-Caucasus: 3,000 roubles.
3. Bishop of Sighnaghi and Kiziki: 2,500 roubles.
4. Bishop of Gori, assistant bishop of Kartli Eparchy: 1,500 roubles.
5. Prosecutor: 1,000 roubles.
6. Three officers: 250 roubles each.
7. Two secretaries: 400 roubles each (Kirion, 1901, pp 60-1).

Reorganisation by territory

Following the establishment of the Synodal Bureau, the Holy Synod of Russia decided to replace the two existing Eastern Georgian eparchies of Mtskheta-Kartli and Alaverdi-Kakheti by three new ones: in Kartli, Ossetia and Sighnaghi.

The first would be headed by an exarch holding the title Metropolitan of Mtskheta, Tbilisi and Kartli, the second by the archbishop of Telavi and Georgia-Caucasus, and the third by the bishop of Sighnaghi and Kiziki (a historical province in Kakheti whose centre was in Sighnaghi).

The former bishop of Alaverdi, Ioann (Makashvili), was appointed to lead the third eparchy and was given the title of metropolitan. As noted earlier, Archbishop Dositheos (Pitskhelauri) was given charge over the second eparchy while Exarch Varlaam (Eristavi) headed the

12.   Thirty roubles at the time would have been enough to buy two cows.

chief eparchy. Over and above these was the post of assistant bishop of Gori.

Impact of economic and social changes

One of the main objectives of church reform in Georgia was to cripple the Church's economy by confiscating its property. The principal method used was to convert church noblemen and church peasants into state noblemen and state peasants and to substitute the payment of tax in kind with a monetary excise, thus making the clergy financially dependent on the state.

This secularisation was conducted in three phases:

1. From 1811-1841, when all church noblemen were made subordinate to the state and their lands and peasants were handed over to the state;
2. between 1843 and 1852, when all of the Church's real estate became state-owned;
3. and finally, between 1853 and 1869, when all inhabited and uninhabited church lands, pastures, forests and other estates were sequestered by the civil authorities (Tadumadze, 1993, p12).

The commutation of church tax — i.e. the substitution of tax in kind with a monetary levy — was implemented in 1818. Naturally, as a result of this measure, the economic situation of the peasants deteriorated as they were forced to find the required sums of money, on the other hand, the state thrived on the large revenues. The exarch Theophilact (1817-1821) noted in his report to the Holy Synod that "church income doubled in 1819 and will increase even more in the future, but one must not stretch the strings now. Let us thank God for this totally unexpected increase" (Tadumadze, 1993, p13).

In the official documents, the exarchate attempted to justify the economic policies by referring first to "the noble purpose" of relieving clergymen of the "heavy burden" of economic management, which drew them away from their principal duties. To a certain extent this was true. Nevertheless, this action mainly served to subordinate Georgian clergymen to the holy synod and to give state ownership to the extensive land holdings of the church.

Following the establishment of the Georgia-Imereti Synodal Bureau, Metropolitan Varlaam was charged to implement in Western Georgia (i.e. Imereti) administrative and economic measures similar to those operating in Kartli and Kakheti.

Although, as exarch, Metropolitan Varlaam proved himself to be a staunch devotee to the Russian authorities in that he undertook with enthusiasm their church policies in Imereti, he failed to make any significant progress. Consequently, the churches in Imereti remained out of the control of the holy synod. It would seem that this contributed to his removal from the management of the exarchate and for his being sent to St Petersburg. The former archbishop of Ryazan, Theophilact Rusanov, was despatched from St Petersburg to replace Varlaam as exarch of Georgia and Imereti.

Historians view Theophilact as a good administrator: energetic, well educated and decisive, but also wayward. It should be noted here that every exarch, beginning with Theophilact up to the last, Metropolitan Platon (1916-1917), were ethnic Russians.

Tightening of Georgian language policy in the church

On November 9, 1817, several months after his arrival in Georgia, Metropolitan Theophilact gave orders to Archpriest Ioseb Palavandishvili at Sioni Synodal cathedral in Tbilisi to hold services in Church Slavonic not only on Sundays and feast days, but also on Tuesdays, Fridays and Saturdays. On the remaining three days the services could be in Georgian (Bishop Kiron, 1901, p20). Shortly thereafter, the Georgian language was almost entirely eradicated from the churches in the capital.

Rebellion in Imereti

Despite warnings by General Alexei Yermolov, commander-in-chief and viceroy of Georgia, who advised care in implementing changes indiscriminately, Metropolitan Theophilact decided to simultaneously introduce a number of sweeping church reforms in Imereti. In June 1819, he ordered employees of the Synodal Bureau to close down churches in the regions reduce the number of parishes, evict clergymen and announce to the people that the conventional tax in kind would be substituted by monetary payments. All of these actions occurred with neither explanation nor the blessing of the Imereti bishops. Theophilact himself went to Imereti to conduct the activities.

Naturally, these actions by the church officials and the exarch provoked such indignation on the part of the people that protests and, eventually, armed rebellion, spread throughout the provinces of Imereti and the principality of Guria. The governor of Imereti, General N. Kurnatovski, found himself in a difficult situation — so much so that he was forced to seek assistance from Georgia's ruler General A. Velyaminov (Yermolov was fighting in Daghestan at the time). Velyaminov, in turn, was obliged to communicate with the population of Imereti through leaflets. In these, he promised to stop inventories of ecclesiastical properties and estates, to re-open churches, to restore the powers of the former administration of the churches, and to recall Metropolitan Theophilact from Imereti. The general pleaded with the people to remain calm and to put an end to the revolt.

On June 9, Theophilact was forced to leave Imereti and return to Tbilisi. In spite of this, however, the population refused to stop the insurgence[13] — on the contrary, their uprising gained strength (Kikvidze, 1977, p95). Once in Tbilisi, the exarch made a full report about the developments to the government, declaring that popular unrest had been fired by the provocations of Metropolitan Dositheos of Kutaisi and Metropolitan Euphemios of Gelati. The two hierarchs were accused of heading the rebellion and their removal from Imereti was regarded as the only solution to peaceful settlement.

Seeing that hostilities were gaining more and more in strength, the Russian authorities decided to rekindle their efforts at maintaining order and, at the same time, to end their latest concessions in church reorganisation. Additional military forces were despatched to Imereti. Kurnatovski, whose reputation was that of an indecisive character, was replaced by Colonel P. Puzyrevski. The new governor was ordered to arrest at any price the leaders of the rebellion — which included Dositheos and Euphemios — and to quell the rebellion (Kikvidze, p96).

On March 4, 1820, the two metropolitans and several other Imeretian noblemen were arrested and delivered to Eastern Georgia that night. On the way to Tbilisi, Dositheos died — according to some reports he was strangled.

Yermolov appealed to the population through a special leaflet issued following the arrest of the metropolitans. It stated that the putting of church affairs in order, being the will of the tsar, had to be strictly observed. Furthermore, the leaflet noted, the former leaders of the eparchies, Dositheos and Euphemios, had only their own interests at heart and cared nothing about well-being of the people (Kikvidze, p97). The authorities managed to end the rebellion only late in the summer of 1820: almost every fortress lay in ruins, hundreds of houses were burned to the ground and many rebels were killed in Imereti, Racha and Guria.

As a consequence of this uprising, the government acted with greater

13. See Part I, Chapter 2, 'The 19th and Early 20th Centuries'.

care in church reform. The secularisation of church property continued for decades in the region whereas administrative reorganisation continued for about a year following the suppression of the rebellion. By an imperial decree dated November 19, 1821, only one eparchy was left in Imereti, namely, the Imereti eparchy. This was placed under Archbishop Sophrom (Tsulukidze) who was given the title Archbishop of Imereti. Following his death in 1843, Metropolitan David (Tsereteli), previously metropolitan of Chkondidi, assumed his position.

Church reforms in Samegrelo and Guria

When Exarch Theophilact died in 1821,[14] Archbishop Iona (Vasilevsky) of Astrakhan (1821-1832) was sent from St Petersburg to replace him. During the rule of Metropolitan Iona (starting on August 22, 1828), church reorganisation was carried out in the principality of Samegrelo.

By the 1820s, there were three eparchies: Chkondidi, in the charge of Metropolitan Besarion (Dadiani); Tsageri, in the charge of Metropolitan Ioann of Tsaishi; and Samegrelo in the charge of Bishop Grigol (Chikovani). Following the deaths of Iona and Grigol (both died in 1823), their eparchies were merged into the Chkondidi eparchy which, from June 23, 1829 was now named the Samegrelo eparchy. Metropolitan Besarion governed the eparchy until 1828 (Kirion, p74); subsequent hierarchs were Metropolitan David (1828-1834), Bishop George (Kukhalashvili) (1835-1842), and Bishop Anthony (Dadiani; 1843-1852).

Only one eparchy, Jumati, remained in the principality of Guria by that time. Metropolitan Nikoloz (Shervashidze) oversaw it until 1827. In 1833, the Jumati eparchy was merged with the Imereti eparchy, which was restored in 1844 as the Guria eparchy. Bishop Euphemios (Tsulukidze), the first bishop of the Guria eparchy, ruled until 1853.

The eparchy of Abkhazia

One more Georgian principality, Abkhazia, previously comprised several eparchies — Bichvinta, Mokvi, Dranda and Bedia — but these had been abolished under Ottoman rule. Under the Russians the Abkhazia eparchy merged first into the Tsageri eparchy early in the 19th century, and then into the Chkondidi eparchy where it remained until 1851, when the Abkhazia eparchy was re-established (Kiron, p79).

Thus the administrative and structural reorganisation of the

---

14.   He died on the morning of the day when, at his orders, the burial-vault of St Nino was to be opened.

Abolition of autocephaly

Orthodox Church of Georgia essentially was undertaken between 1820 and the 1840s. It should be noted here that the so-called *"blagochinny"* districts — the gathering of several parishes in an eparchy and supervised by senior priests (*blagochins*) — were established in Georgia in accordance with the Russian practice by the end of the 1830s. Bishops of eparchies appointed as heads of such districts were those who had become distinguished and possessed a good reputation. Priests assisted bishops in supervising parish churches and also oversaw the completion of churches, managed church finances and archives, and reported on the moral behaviour of ecclesiastical figures.

Missionary activity by the Holy Synod of Russia

During the preparation period and in the course of carrying out the re-organisation of Georgian church structures, the Russian government and the Holy Synod paid considerable attention to missionary activity both in the mountainous regions of Georgia as well as throughout the entire Caucasus — especially on those territories populated by various non-Christian peoples which had been devastated by the Russians.

Diverse historical records and the presence of ancient churches on the territory of the North Caucasus testify to the fact that some of the Ossetians and other peoples in the region — such as the Circassians (Kabardins and Adygeis) and Lezgins — had been Christian at various points in their long histories. Most, however, remained liberally pagan. Missionaries from the Orthodox Church of Georgia were reported as being active in some of these areas. Following the great Mongol invasions that began in the 13th century and after them the hordes of Timur Leng at the end of the 14th century, Christian missionary activity in the Caucasus came to an end.

Following these invasions, the mountain tribes of the Greater Caucasus slowly converted to Islam, especially after the intensification of Turkic influence. Mention, however, should be made of the fact that Georgian missionaries appeared in the Caucasus from time to time, and by the end of the 18th century there existed a missionary school attached to the Nekresi eparchy. In the 18th century, Bishop Ioan of Manglisi played a significant role in the christianization of Ossetia and in 1745, after the foundation of the Ossetian Commission, Georgian monks were sent to Ossetia as preachers.

In 1792 the Ossetian Commission ceased to exist, but after Georgia's annexation by Russia, it was decided to reactivate missionary activities in the Caucasus. The Ossetian Commission, restored in 1815 in Tbilisi, was put under the charge of the Telavi and Georgian-Caucasian Archbishop Dositheos (Pitskhelauri). The staff of the commission included one archimandrite, one father superior, four hieromonks, two priests and one deacon. Moreover, there were thirty peasant guards and a detachment of 100 Cossacks. During the two years of Archbishop Dositheos' residence, Georgian records state that 6,059 Ossetians were converted to Christianity.

In 1817, the commission, together with its staff and office, was transferred to the direct authority of the Georgian-Imeretian Synodal Office. Henceforth it would remain under the direct supervision of the exarch (Kirion, p97).

On December 28, 1818, following the advice of Exarch Theophilact and with the approval of the tsar, the commission was broadened and instructions were submitted on how to conduct missionary work. For the conversion of the mountain peoples to Christianity, motives more spiritual than temporal were to be used. The matter of preaching was not to be considered accomplished until those converted expressed the wish to have a church and a priest. Preachers, unescorted, should proclaim the good news avoiding publicity and should not show themselves as being sent by the government. Rather, they should appear as ordinary travellers, praying for the salvation of all. Where the Christian faith was not accepted they should leave in peace, but where it was accepted they should remain for further preaching, admonition and consolation in the faith. Baptism should not be conducted in haste; there had to be conviction of the sincerity of the conversion (Kirion, p97).

According to reports from Theophilact, missionary activity in the Caucasus progressed swiftly after 1818. This is evident from the fact that between 1817 and 1820, 28,512 males and females were received into Christianity from Islam and paganism. In addition, 130 families of Udins (descendants of the ancient Christian Albanians who had become islamicized under pressure from their Muslim Azerbaijani and Dagestani neighbours) returned to the bosom of the Orthodox Church. On the whole, in the period from 1815 to 1830, 60,895 Ossetians, Ingush, Adygeis, Lezgins as well as others were converted to Christianity. During the same period, 62 places of worship (both new and damaged) were built or restored. Parishes were formed from the settlements of the newly-converted mountain peoples. By January 1, 1825 there were 67 parishes under the control of the Ossetian Commission.

Particularly active in missionary work were the exarchs Ioann

Abolition of autocephaly

(1821-1832) and Moses (1832-1834). In spite of the relatively short period of his activity, the latter left fond memories of himself in Georgia, especially as one who cared for preserving the unique tradition of Georgian church choral music. He gathered around him the best practitioners of Georgian church music from Kartli, Imereti, Samegrelo and Abkhazia with himself as the choir master. Moses also established a bursary for clergymen in need that existed for some time after his death.

During the exarchate of Evgeny (Bazhenov; 1834-1844) and Isidor (Nikolsky; 1844-1858) the work of the Ossetian Commission and of missionary activity in general increased. In addition to new churches, parish schools were also built, where children were taught by local priests. Unfortunately, the priests did not always possess an acceptable level of education — nevertheless, these schools were of great significance for missionary work. The children of the mountain peoples studied in these schools, and while they may not have received a full education, they still achieved a rudimentary level that included some knowledge of Orthodox Christian doctrine. This certainly helped in spreading the faith among the mountain peoples.

By the end of the 1840s and beginning of the 1850s, there were six such schools under the aegis of the Ossetian Commission (Kirion, p105). In Vladikavkaz, the Commission opened a four-year theological seminary where, apart from Orthodox theology, students studied the history of religion (including paganism and Islam), elementary economics and business administration — necessary for the everyday life of the mountain peoples.

Theological education

Following the abolition of autocephaly, General Tormasov suggested opening a high school for the children of clergy in Tbilisi. The Holy Synod of the Russian Church, however, deemed it necessary to open, not a high school, but a theological seminary alongside the existing theological school.

The initiative was made possible through a grant of the holy synod to the Ossetian Commission in 1816. The seminary was provided with the house that had previously belonged to the chairman of the Ossetian Commission, Archbishop Dositheus of Telavi (before this, it had been the property of King Erekle II's wife, Darejan). The seminary was opened on October 1, 1817. After celebrating a special liturgy at Sioni cathedral, numerous clergy and laymen, led by the exarch of Georgia, Metropolitan Theophilact, made their way towards the future site of the seminary, where a thanksgiving service was held and speeches made by a number of laymen (Kirion, p171).

In its early years, the seminary consisted of two classes: literature, and general history and geography. It held sixteen students at a sitting and was open not only for Orthodox, but also for Catholics and Armenians. In 1818 theological schools were opened in Gori and Telavi. Students attended these reluctantly — not because of their alleged indiscipline and low morals, as officially reported to the Holy Synod — but for fear of corporal punishment and also because all of the teaching was conducted in Russian (Kirion, p173).

Church Slavonic plainchant was taught in the seminaries along with the principal theological subjects. The curriculum also included subjects such as algebra, geometry, physics, logic, Russian and world history, the history of Russian literature, Russian, Greek and Latin, as well as Western European languages (German, French). It was only in 1849, during Metropolitan Isidor's exarchate, that Georgian church music was introduced as well as the study of Georgian church service books (in place of those written in Greek and Latin).

By the 1840s, however, it had become almost impossible to find a priest who could read *nuskhuri*, the ancient Georgian alphabet traditionally used in the service books, or who could sing time-honoured Georgian chant. These priests found it arduous to serve in the Georgian parishes, and the rural population ceased to attend services because they did not understand Church Slavonic. Ultimately, Georgian was almost completely ousted in favour of Russian from the curricula both of the theological and the secular schools. This made sense, however, from the perspective of Russian imperial policy in annexed territories of the empire. The notion of educating the local population had always been closely connected by the occupiers with russification (Khutsishvili, p39).

The Georgian exarchate, 1850-1900

Consequences of Russian imperial policy

During the first half of the 19th century, Russia began to expand its authority over the Caucasus. In 1859, following many years of his war of resistance against the Russian armies, the North Caucasian leader Shamil[1] was finally captured. By that time Russia had annexed all of the Caucasus (in the same year one of the new squares in Tbilisi was named after Ghunib). As a symbol of the conquest of the Caucasus, foundations were laid in Tbilisi for an immense cathedral dedicated to St Alexander Nevsky: a Russian-style military temple, it was completed at the end of the century.

The second half of the 19th century gave birth to a new phase for the Georgian exarchate. By then the grave consequences of the dissolution of the Church's autocephaly had become quite evident: the earlier tendency to legitimize the Slav typikon in Church services and to eschew the old Georgian hymns had now become commonplace. However, in spite of the official Russian enforcement of Church Slavonic in the churches and monasteries, the clandestine use of Georgian persisted.

A colonial ecclesiastical policy arose. In a letter from the Russian imperial court written in 1867 and addressed to the viceroy of Georgia, it is stated: "We should conquer the Caucasus again, but this time by different means. Physical conquest will not endure without a spiritual victory. Such victory is indeed religious in form" (Paviliashvili, 1995, p33).

Naturally, in achieving these goals, great hopes were pinned on the Exarchate of Georgia. It is precisely for this reason (though there are others) that the Orthodox Church of Georgia was reorganised in such a way that it became one of the bureaucratic arms of the Russian Empire.

1. Shamil was the principal leader of the national-liberation movement amongst the North Caucasians of Chechnya and Daghestan. From the 1820s he led a campaign against the Russians, first declaring a jihad that later became an all-out war of resistance. After 1869 he lived in exile in St Petersburg and died in Mecca in 1871.

Structural changes in monastic and church life

According to the Russian system, Georgian churches and monasteries were divided into different hieratical ranks. None of the Georgian monasteries was ranked as belonging to the first rank. Some were consigned to the second, but most were relegated to the third. Many churches and monasteries were consequently abandoned and closed.

Some of the functioning monasteries were financed by the state and provided with a regular income. Others were not and had to survive on donations. Most were filled with Russian monks from the inner provinces of the empire whereas Georgian monks were moved from the monasteries of Sapara, Dranda, Bichvinta and Mamkoda (Durnovo, 1907, p10). Bodbe monastery, which houses the remains of St Nino, the Enlightener of the Georgians, was occupied by Russians and church services there were conducted in Russian. Such was the sad consequence of the symbolic entry of the Russian troops into Kartli in 1801 led by the cross of St Nino. The exarchate also cultivated a policy of secret reporting on day-to-day monastic affairs to the church authorities back in Russia.

Confiscation of church property, 1869, 1871, 1880

In order to obtain total subjection of the Georgian clergy, an initial decision was made to confiscate all church land. Although the Russian government had attempted to achieve this objective in the first half of the century, it failed to do so because of the stiff resistance of the Georgian people. In Eastern Georgia, the state seizure of church lands was permitted by a directive dated November 13, 1869, from Tsar Alexander II (1855-1881). All movable and immovable property of the Georgian church entered into the possession of the Treasury. Church peasants, moreover, were given the status of state peasants and now had to pay taxes to the state.

Similar measures were undertaken in Imereti and Guria (1871) and in Samegrelo (*Droeba*, no. 164, 1880; cf. Tadumadze, 1993, p15). This was a reform of considerable advantage for enhancing the Russian Imperial Treasury. According to incomplete data that has survived, annual income from the former properties of the Georgian church amounted to 68,205,125 roubles. The Exarchate of Georgia was now financed from income received following the seizure of the Church's land holdings: an annual amount of 1,060,000 roubles was given by the Treasury for this purpose (Kelenjeridze, 1905, p335).

According to the records, the state reaped a very considerable source of income through the appropriation of ecclesiastical property and real estate. The clergy, however, were deprived of the ability to acquire a personal income, which constituted their essential means of subsistence, and instead received state salaries. In taking this political step, the Russian policy-makers effectively transformed Georgian clergymen into obedient executors of the will of the Russian state authorities.

The territorial principle in action

The areas of the eparchies under the Exarchate of Georgia coincided with Russian administrative borders in the Caucasus. From the very beginning, Russian officials either abolished the eparchies or merged them into single units. Although Russian church officials had hoped to appoint non-ethnic Georgians (i.e. Slavs) as administrators in the eparchies, they were unable to do so because such action would have created serious discontent among the Georgian faithful. To avoid this, therefore, Georgian hierarchs were appointed as eparchial administrators with the exception of the Abkhazia eparchy.

The Abkhazia eparchy, previously a part of Imereti after the abolition of the Chkondidi eparchy, was established in 1851 but eliminated in 1869 when it again became subject to the Imereti eparchy. It was restored once more in 1885 as the Sokhumi eparchy, being ruled mostly by Russian bishops. The Samegrelo eparchy was abolished and incorporated into the Imereti eparchy following an order (dated May 16, 1874) of the Holy Synod of Russia. Another decision in 1885 united the Samegrelo and Guria eparchies. Baku (Azerbaijan), Yerevan (Armenia), Gori (Kartli, Eastern Georgia) and Alaverdi (Kakheti and Eastern Georgia) were amalgamated into a single administrative body and governed by the exarch himself. Bishops, regarded as assistants of the exarch of Georgia, were responsible for governing the local parishes. The exarch ruled over the subjected eparchies through the Georgia-Imereti Synodal Bureau.

At the turn of the century, the Exarchate of Georgia was divided into five eparchies:

1. Georgia (12 monasteries, 485 churches), consisting of the provinces of Tbilisi, Baku, Yerevan and Elizavetopol, Kars district, and the regions of Daghestan and the North Caucasus;
2. Imereti (8 monasteries, 478 churches), consisting of Kutaisi province and the districts of Shorapani and Racha;
3. Vladikavkaz (2 monasteries, 122 churches), consisting of the North Ossetia and Tergi districts;

4. Guria-Samegrelo (5 monasteries, 407 churches), consisting of the regions of Lechkhumi, Senaki, Zugdidi and Ozurgeti, and Batumi district;

5. Sokhumi (1 monastery, 46 churches) (Hierarchy of the All-Russian Church, pp 189-193).

Although it may seem as if the structure of the Georgian exarchate and its eparchies conformed to the Russian model, there were, in fact, significant differences. Firstly, the Russian ecclesiastical leadership viewed the four eparchies as being subordinate to the exarchate and considered the several local parishes as forming a single eparchy directly under the exarch. The eparchies in Russian inland provinces had consistories, while no such institution existed in Georgia. Secondly, each eparchy in Russia had its own journal, unlike their Georgian counterparts which were deprived of using the press. Only the Exarchate of Georgia launched a magazine (in the 1860s) but it was not issued on a regular basis. Thirdly, the rights of diocesan bishops were significantly restricted in Georgia. They could not ordain clergy in their eparchies without permission of the exarchate or of the Georgia-Imereti Synodal Bureau. Fourthly, unlike bishops in Russia, those in Imereti, Guria and Samegrelo could not send reports directly to the Holy Synod of Russia. It was the exarch who performed this task and what he sent to the synod was based on accounts given by eparchial managers who were under his supervision.

The division into five eparchies was instituted according to a territorial-administrative principle — no consideration was made of the traditional eparchial division.

Moral consequences of church reform

The annual salary of the Georgian clergy under the exarchate was to a certain degree lower than that of clergymen from the inland Russian provinces. Being commensurate with the number and the wealth of parishioners, the salaries of clergy in towns and rural areas differed. Urban priests received 150 to 300 roubles, archdeacons 100 to 150 roubles and chanters/readers 24 to 60 roubles (*Messenger of the Georgian Exarchate*, p10).

In order to compensate the low-salaried clergy, the government decreed that each of the several categories of peasant that existed had to pay different levels of taxation. At the same time, all the faithful paid a specific sum for baptisms, weddings, funerals and other necessary services of church life. The rate of pay was first negotiated on the basis of a contract between the priest and his parish; consequently different eparchies paid different sums. In the 1880s, the Exarchate of Georgia decided to fix an aggregate rate of pay. Some clergy frequently attempted to take money in excess of the amount sanctioned for self-gain, a circumstance that resulted in controversy between clergy and their congregations. There were those who, through dire poverty, were unable to pay the church tax. In such cases, the clergy collected the money by force. This, too, fuelled opposition between the clergy and their parishes.

Further estrangement between clergy and laity stemmed from the latter's perceptions of the former, who were recipients of state salaries. Under these conditions the clergy were often unable to meet the spiritual needs of the Georgian people. Indeed, in some regions of the country, people even gave up church attendance because of the cupidity of the clergy. Any mutual trust and love between the clergy and the faithful declined rapidly.

During the second half of the 19th century, Georgian periodicals regularly published articles unmasking dishonorable clergymen. Public figures ruthlessly criticized clerics who refused to conduct religious services without receiving a certain sum of money, noting possible serious consequences of such behaviour.

Demotion of Georgia's historical and religious heritage

Yet a further destructive effect of the Russian ecclesiastical policy in Georgia was the practice of renaming churches dedicated to local saints with the names of saints of Russian ethnic origin. For example, St Abo's church, located in one of the old districts of Tbilisi, was rededicated as St Michael Tverskoy and the latter's icon was mounted for veneration. In spite of the fact that the people of Tbilisi expressed their discontent, the exarchate ignored them. The exarchate also discontinued the tradition of holding services that commemorated such local saints as Queen Tamar, King David IV, Queen Ketevan, and David and Konstantine Mkheidze. An exception was the feast of St Nino the Enlightener of the Georgians, whose celebration — in Church Slavonic — took place at Sioni cathedral and the monastery of Bodbe.

In addition, Russian imperial policy influenced Georgian Christian architecture. From the second half of the 19th century, the Russians commenced reconstruction of the old Georgian cathedrals in the Russian style, an action that resulted in the disfigurement of many

Georgian Orthodox churches. At the same time, the Russians began to build new churches in their tradition with onion-shaped domes.

The repair and restoration of a number of ancient Georgian churches during the incumbency of the exarchs Evgeny (1834-1844) and Isidor (1844-1858) deserve comment. For example, it cost 30,000 roubles to clean the grounds and restore the façade of Svetitskhoveli cathedral. This otherwise honourable endeavour activity, however, took an unexpected turn: under the pretext of giving places of worship a proper cleaning they were completely whitewashed on the interior, so that in many places unique Georgian wall paintings were destroyed. Examples include Sioni and Alaverdi cathedrals and Samtavro and Martkopi churches.

Implementation of imperial policies by the exarchs

The title "Exarch of Georgia" received various interpretations. By a decision of the highest authorities in Russia, exarchs, from the first half of the 19th century until 1858, held the rank of metropolitan. Later they were demoted to that of archbishop. It was soon made clear that this policy aimed to have hierarchs of comparatively low rank serve as exarch. It was intentional that three of the four permanent members of the Holy Synod of Russia were metropolitans, while the fourth — the exarch of Georgia — was an archbishop. In exchange for "commendable service", the Russian authorities would elevate former exarchs to the office of metropolitan and then appoint them to high posts in Russia.

The Russian overlords implemented their ecclesiastical policies in Georgia through the Georgian exarchate to which, in turn, was subordinated the Georgia-Imereti Synodal Bureau, an agency staffed mainly by individuals sent on mission from Russia. Candidates appointed to the position of exarch were carefully selected by the Russian tsar in consultation with the Holy Synod. The person chosen was always fully reliable, experienced in ecclesiastical activities, and prepared to sacrifice himself in the interests of the empire. Guided by the interests of the state, the exarch, himself one of the representatives of Russia's ecclesiastical bureaucracy, carried out imperial policy.

For such a high-profile political assignment, the Exarchate of Georgia and its head — the exarch — could not pursue activities specifically in the interests of the Georgian people. As a rule, the exarchs could not speak Georgian and they knew little or nothing about the ancient culture and history of the country to which they had been sent to serve as its ecclesiastical primate and spiritual leader. In other words, the Georgian people viewed the Russian exarchs, whose activities were confined to visiting eparchies, churches and monasteries, as alien.

The highest secular authorities granted the exarchs huge administrative powers for the implementation the state's political objectives. They performed their activities in consultation with local secular bureaucrats in the Caucasus even though they were not officially of inferior rank to them. Exarchs were responsible only to the Holy Synod of Russia.

The activities of the Exarchate of Georgia were always concomitant with Russian state policy. From the late 1840s until the late 1850s, the exarchate and its head, Isidor Nikolski (1844-1858), pursued a tolerable policy, being influenced by Russian liberal tendencies towards the Caucasus.

There were only a few exarchs after 1850 who, such as Exarch Isidor, were not excessively anti-Georgian in their attitudes. From 1852-1857, Isidor used, on his own initiative, income from church lands to repair monasteries in Mtskheta, Alaverdi, Kvatakhevi and Martkopi. Moreover, he negotiated with the Holy Synod of Russia to provide salaries to the Georgian clergy. He also founded a women's school, in 1857, at the Mtskheta convent. Following Isidor's instructions, Platon Ioseliani brought from Mount Athos the 10th-century Georgian translation of the Bible, copied in a manuscript dated 978. Two copies were made and donated to the Samegrelo and Imereti eparchies and Sioni cathedral in Tbilisi (*Mogzauri*, 1901, p358).

It was also Isidor's intention to create a religious journal for the Exarchate of Georgia and made the necessary petitions to the Synod. Later, in 1864-1868, when recalled from his post and he left Georgia, the exarchate issued a monthly periodical titled *Spiritual Messages from Georgia* under the editorship of the priest Giorgi Khelidze. This publication provided official material from the Holy Synod of Russia and from the Exarchate of Georgia both in Georgian and in Russian. A special place was devoted to the lives of the Georgian saints and to documents on the history of the Georgian church. The subsequent exarch Yevsevi Ilyinski (1858-1877) suppressed the periodical, allegedly for financial reasons, and for a long time thereafter the exarchate produced no journals. From 1891 to 1917 the *Spiritual Messenger of the Exarchate of Georgia* was published (in Russian only) but this was notorious for its anti-Georgian stand and its colonial agenda.

Russian historians have described Ilyinski as being typical of the exarchs who "were in Georgia to rob the congregation of the Church of Ancient Iberia that had been entrusted to them by wasting its property, suppressing the language of its population and then returning to Russia together with stolen goods and money" (Durnovo, p20). Ilyinski, having been invested with unrestricted authority, victimized any manifestation of personal opinion among Georgian clergy and teachers. He frequently resorted to corporal punishment, not to mention spying and threats, all of which were commonplace in his day.

He expressed his particular disgust for Bishop Gabriel Kikodze (1825-1896). In his hostility towards the Georgian bishop, Ilyinski attempted to get rid of him by means of intrigue and other unacceptable means. For example, he endeavoured to convince the supreme ecclesiastic authority of Russia of the bishop's unreliability. The truth of the matter was that the exarch despised the fact that Gabriel was deeply respected throughout the country.

Fortunately, Ilyinski failed in his resistance against the bishop. The ecclesiastical establishment of Russia paid no attention to his denunciations, as Bishop Gabriel was too well known all over the empire. At the same time, Russian officials were well aware that any repressive measures against the Georgian hierarch would have laid the foundations for great discontent on the part of the Georgian people, a circumstance that would have developed as a source of disquiet for the Russian authorities.

Ilyinski was also notorious for his dishonesty. He misappropriated funds from the church treasury for personal gain, stole mitres and precious crosses belonging to the former Patriarchate of Georgia and, with the help of his agents, sold them to collectors. In 1869, he acted as an accomplice to Governor-General Levashov of Kutaisi, who stole the 10th-century Khakhuli triptych with its enamelled and gilded silver ornaments from Gelati monastery. In collaboration with the exarch, Levashov commissioned a Russian artist, Vasilyev, to design a new tryptich while another artist, Sazikov, was assigned to execute the chasing in imitation of the images of the Khakhuli original. Levashov then sold the original triptych to a collector by the name of Botkin, and installed the copy in the monastery of Gelati (Amiranishvili, 1972, p17; cf. *Jvari Vazisa*, 1988, & Nozadze, 1967).

The Georgian faithful became highly indignant at this sacreligious act and enormous efforts were made to have the ancient tryptich returned. It took almost a quarter of a century for this to happen when the original returned finally into Georgian hands in 1923. The Khakhuli triptych is now preserved in the Museum of Georgian Art in Tbilisi.

With Ilyinski's consent, Levashov also appropriated the 11th-century Georgian Gospel Book under the pretext of wanting to restore the gold cover with its enamel cloisonné decoration. The governor-general had the gold chasing removed and in its place Sazikov's cheap silver reproduction was fixed (Durnovo, p22). Levashov's stolen Gospel Book found its way to the Stroganov Museum in St Petersburg but was removed from Russia at a later date. Under the aegis of Exarch Ilyinski, icons from Sioni cathedral in the capital, and Mtskheta, Alaverdi, Bodbe, Jumati and other monasteries were robbed of their precious stones. He also assisted Count Bobrinskoy in the removal and sale of ancient Georgian manuscripts illuminated with miniatures from Sioni. Furthermore, several kilos of pearls, turquoise and other jewellery disappeared from the cathedral.

The next exarch, Ioannike Rudnev (1877-1882), was not particularly partial to the Georgians but he did have the interests of the empire at heart and so he did his best to restore to the exarchs the authority that had been undermined by his predecessor Levashov. He began by using the income from candle sales to pay the salaries of the clergy of Eastern Georgia, thus improving relatively their financial condition. He also founded St Andrew's Brotherhood to help poor students at the theological seminary in Tbilisi. Furthermore, Ioannike granted certain privileges to Georgian teachers who worked in theological schools and he paid serious attention to restoring and teaching Georgian hymns and church music. The common people, unaware of his true feelings towards them, respected Ioannike as a truthful and charitable hierarch. They expressed their goodwill towards him when in 1899 they sent him, now Metropolitan of Kiev, a telegram of congratulation on the occasion of the 50th anniversary of his ordination to the hierarchy (*Mogzauri*, p362).

The exarch Pavel Lebedev (1882-1887) caused considerable damage in the sacred sites of the Georgian church. In his day, the golden triptych of the Mother of God from Metekhi cathedral and St Nino's miracle-working icon from Sioni cathedral mysteriously disappeared. Lebedev even ordered the burning of several old Georgian manuscripts in the courtyard of Tbilisi's Theological Seminary (Durnovo, p25).

Lebedev's successor Palladi Rayev (1887-1892) came accompanied by a photographer, Sabin-Gus, who claimed to be an artist from St Petersburg but instead robbed Georgian churches and monasteries of more of their treasures. With the approval of the exarch, Sabin-Gus removed icons from churches and monasteries in Western Georgia (Jumati, Khobi, Martvili and Shemokmedi) supposedly for the purpose of restoration. None, however, was returned. With the support of certain of the exarchs, prominent Russian art collectors such as Botkin and

Zvenigorodski arranged for other Georgian pieces to be removed from the country.

Despite public outcry in opposition to these crimes against the Georgian churches and monasteries, Russian authorities remained silent and unyielding to the people's demands. The exarchs who organised these acts of theft were treated with deference and were appointed to high posts upon their return to Russia.

And so, as transmitters of imperial policy, the Russian exarchs in Georgia both limited and ignored the rightful demands of the Georgian people. In 1887, for example, nobles from Samegrelo and Guria petitioned the Holy Synod of Russia to restore the independent eparchies of Guria and Samegrelo, which had been merged in 1885. Rayev, however, not only rejected this reasonable request but also ordered them to acknowledge the right of the Synod of Russia to reduce the number of eparchies in Georgia and to act to the interests of the Georgians. As a result, the noblemen were forced to reconcile themselves to the fact that inconvenience needed to be tolerated (Brail, 1896, p101).

Far more liberal were the actions of the next exarch, Vladimir Bogoyavlenski (1892-1898). He set up and headed a committee charged with restoring Svetitskhoveli cathedral and granted pensions to the teachers of the Society for Restoration of Orthodox Christianity in the Caucasus. He was the only exarch to demand the reorganisation of Georgia's Department of Religion in order to intensify the activities of the exarchate. Moreover, Bogoyavlenski supported those Georgian public figures who in 1894 presented a report to the Holy Synod of Russia exposing the oppression of the Orthodox Church of Georgia by exarchs and the actions of certain church functionaries who regarded the Church and its property as a source of private income. In order to improve the situation, they demanded, among other things, the immediate abolition of the Georgia-Imereti Synodal Bureau and the appointment of a Georgian hierarch to the post of exarch (Brail, p92). Both secular and spiritual authorities in Russia responded with silence to these demands of the Georgian faithful.

Bogoyavlenski's successor, Exarch Flavian Gorodetski, in office between 1898 and 1901, made no impression in either direction. He neither promoted liberal policies nor misused his authority.

Missionary work within the exarchate

In the second half of the 19th century, Russian imperial policy seriously embraced missionary work in order to pursue religious strategies in the

Caucasus and, more especially, in Georgia. Although the Ossetian Religious Committee had served this goal in the first half of the century, it became evident, following the complete annexation of the Caucasus, that this body could no longer satisfy the colonial demands of the empire.

Russian officials were seriously concerned about the difficulties they were experiencing in bringing the conquered mountain peoples under control. They perceived that religious diversity was a significant impediment towards the subordination of the people in the region. In their opinion, religious unity would promote a trouble-free assimilation of the highlanders but, as we shall see, this was not to be the case.

The Exarchate of Georgia, together with the viceroy of the Caucasus, Alexander Baryatinski (1856-1862), established a missionary society in the 1850s to serve this objective. The viceroy was particularly interested in the future of the Caucasians in recently-annexed territories. In his reports to the ecclesiastical and secular officials in St Petersburg, he stressed the urgency of implementing ecclesiastical measures in the area. For Baryatinski, it was important to restore churches, monasteries, and church schools in order to spread Christianity among Georgians and non-Georgians residing along the military route leading to Georgia. "The establishment of such schools is the duty of an Orthodox state. This issue is one to which Russia cannot remain indifferent," he stated in his report to St Petersburg (Central State Archives of Georgia, Act 3).

Baryatinski's proposal aroused interest in St Petersburg and the matter was passed on for further investigation to the senior procurator of the Holy Synod of Russia. Both state and church officials regarded Baryatinski's tactical suggestion in a positive light — it was considered to be a shrewd political measure for Russia's imperial policy in the Caucasus.

Mistakes made by the earlier Ossetian Religious Committee were taken into account in forming the new missionary society and particular attention was paid to staff recruitment. A decision was finally made to send graduates of Russia's theological schools (mainly ethnic Russians) as missionaries. In some cases, it was possible to also include in the programme non-Russians who were educated in the theological schools of the Russian empire. The missionaries received instruction in the history and lifestyles of the local communities yet their principal directive was to make the Russian way of life familiar to the targeted groups, not only with respect to religion but in wider terms (Khutsishvili, 1987, p52).

Based as they were on the political interests of the empire, the statutes of the society were adopted in St Petersburg in 1857, and on June 9, 1860 Tsar Alexander II confirmed by decree the founding of the Society for the Restoration of Orthodox Christianity in the Caucasus, which would have its centre in Tbilisi. According to its statutes and by-laws, the society was responsible for a much more broadly-based network of activities. The missionaries would work not only among the Caucasian highlanders but also in regions of Georgia, such as Tusheti, Pshavi, Khevsureti and Svaneti, where Christianity had prevailed but had in later times returned to the pagan ways of old. The society was also charged with spreading Christianity among the populations of Abkhazia and Samtskhe-Javakheti, who had converted to Islam under Ottoman rule.

By virtue of its agenda, the Society for the Restoration of Orthodox Christianity in the Caucasus superseded the Ossetian Religious Committee, which now ceased to exist. The government took special measures to subsidise the new society; even the imperial court gave a donation of 119,738 roubles (*Review of the Activities...*, 1910, p17). In order to raise additional funds, donation boxes for the society were placed in all churches of the Russian empire. Furthermore, the Russian government, on an annual basis, allocated a considerable sum of money for the society from the state budget.

At the suggestion of Exarch Yevsevi, it was decided to raise the salaries of those clerics who served as missionaries to the mountain peoples. The committee also considered it necessary to open church schools in Abkhazia and Char-Belakani as well as to translate ecclesiastical literature into local languages. The committee even requested that a number of students at the theological seminary of Tbilisi be trained especially for missionary work. When the Provisional Committee was abolished in 1865, the viceroy of the Caucasus was appointed chairman of the society with the exarch of Georgia as his deputy. In 1885, the exarch became chairman following its reorganisation, and the viceroy was relieved from his duties in this field.

By the decision of Viceroy Mikhail Nikolayevich, the first missionary schools were opened by the committee in 1863. They were supervised by a chief inspector appointed by the society. The main objective of the schools was to russify the local population. In order to expand its activities, the society established branches in Vladikavkaz, Guria, Samegrelo, Abkhazia, Tusheti, Pshavi and Khevsureti.

*

Theological schools in the service of imperial policy

Theological schools in the Exarchate of Georgia were obliged to serve the colonial policy of the empire by assisting in the implementation of its policies. However, the Georgian schools, with regard to their teaching methods, goals and objectives, differed greatly from corresponding institutions in Russia. The latter aimed at developing the intellectual skills of the Russian younger generation, whereas in Georgia there existed a quite different, political agenda: the russification of local populations and to nurture future functionaries for the empire. Imperial officials attached great importance to the exploitation of the theological schools — here there was great potential and so no means were spared to broaden their scope.

During the second half of the 19th century, biennial theological schools were founded in Tbilisi, Kutaisi, Telavi, Ozurgeti, Gori and Samegrelo. In order to raise the educational level, preparatory courses were provided for each of them. Following graduation, students continued their studies at theological schools and their graduates could sit entrance examinations for the Tbilisi Theological Seminary — the only higher educational institution in Georgia. Later, in 1894, a theological seminary was opened in Kutaisi to train future clergy in Western Georgia. The children of clergy had preferential rights to study at the Tbilisi Theological Seminary and, together with them, representatives from a range of social classes were educated. The latter were of diverse ethnic origin: alongside the Georgian students were Russians, Tatars, Ossetes, Assyrians and others. Primarily, however, the seminary trained potential clergy for the Exarchate of Georgia. The more outstanding graduates were sent at the expense of the state to theological academies in St Petersburg, Kiev, Kazan and Moscow.

In addition to the aforementioned schools, there were also parish church schools. Parish priests were known to open these free schools with their own financial resources for poorer and less privileged children. They were given primary education in their mother tongue: religion, Georgian hymns, Russian language, elementary mathematics, needlework, church history and the history of Georgia. At the Congress of Non-Russian Hierarchs in 1869, the Holy Synod of Russia made a decision to expand the activities of the parish schools. The synod wanted to exploit them for their own purposes but ultimately failed to do so — patriotic teachers and priests of the parish church schools strengthened the Christian faith but also inspired nationalist feelings in the younger generation.

Russia also directed appropriate attention to the matter of women's education. It was assumed that women, the bearers of future citizens, could aptly play a decisive role in nurturing generations to be devoted to the empire. For this purpose, the exarchate in 1866 opened the Institute of Noble Young Ladies in a nunnery at Mtskheta. Two years later, Exarch Yevsevi approved a statute that promoted eparchial women's schools in which students studied religion, catechism, church history, the Georgian and Russian languages, geography, hymn-singing, the histories of Georgia and Russia, handiwork and embroidery. In 1879, after Ioannike became exarch, the school was transferred from Mtskheta to Tbilisi where it was financed by income from the candle plant, a small factory linked to the school. At the end of the 19th century, sixteen eparchial schools were placed under the authority of the exarchate (Khutsishvili, 1987, p32).

Functionaries were especially invited from Russia in order to manage and teach at the theological schools, as well as to ensure the implementation of objectives set by the state. Georgian teachers, themselves graduates of the seminary, were also invited to the schools, since, to begin with, some attention was given to Georgian language and history. They were carefully selected since they were intended to conduct their activities solely in accordance with the interests of the state. The teachers were under constant scrutiny and any of their number who was judged "unreliable" was dismissed. This was particularly true of those teachers who were seen to encourage students in studying their mother tongue.

Unsurprisingly, the salaries of teachers who worked at identical schools differed depending on whether they were Russian or Georgian. The former received higher salaries and enjoyed privileges in terms of promotion. Government officials, however, kept tight control over the Russian teachers, so much so that they had to receive permission from the Church authorities to arrange their personal lives (such as getting married, and so on). The rights of the Georgian teachers were even more restricted and their relations with their Russian colleagues — who represented the dominant nation — were always marked by an uneasy tension (Bakuradze, 1937, p113). Often the behaviour of the Russians was arrogant, humiliating and offensive towards the Georgians.

Students at the theological schools also lived under trying conditions. The Tbilisi Theological Seminary was the only one that had a boarding house where students from different regions of Georgia could live at the expense of the state. Since seminary graduates were to become state servants, the Russian administration in the Caucasus needed to have them under permanent supervision. Hence, the students were isolated from their natural, domestic environments. Russian teachers at the boarding house continued to deal with them even after their lessons were over, by following the same, strict routine. For example, house rules forbade students from leaving the building without permission and they were permitted to read only theological literature.

Student living quarters were generally in a poor condition because regional theological schools were located in unsuitable buildings. This often had a negative impact on the well-being of the students. And while conditions in the Tbilisi Theological Seminary were comparatively better, even there malnutrition frequently caused deterioration in student health.

The language of theological education

Throughout the second half of the 19th century, Russia was blatant in its policy towards Georgia's theological schools in getting them to cultivate a devotion to autocracy and to promote the russification of the younger generation. School curricula, developed in conformity with this strategy, laid emphasis on Russian language courses. Principal theological subjects, such as Church Slavonic hymnody, Russian church and national history and the humanities were taught in Russian. In the first half of the 19th century, Georgian was used as the language of instruction for lessons in local history and literature, but in the second half these subjects were removed from the programme. Pertinently, before the establishment of the exarchate, Russian teachers were obliged to learn Georgian. Although this new directive was hard to put into practice, it is a good example of how radically different Russia's policies were in the two halves of the century.

The Georgian language was the prime cultural element to be attacked by imperial policy. The Russian administration in the Caucasus ordered the administrators of the theological schools to prohibit the use of Georgian by students — even in private conversations after school hours — allegedly to help them master Russian. Though it was impossible to implement, an 1854 directive relegated the Georgian language to an inferior position among the subjects at the theological schools. It was a decision that would have negative consequences. The level of education deteriorated so considerably that the situation attracted the attention of Tsar Alexander.

In 1864, the independent educational administrators of the Caucasus was restored in order to raise the level of secular and theological learning. In the same year, the tsar ordered that lessons in elementary schools be given in the mother tongue. While this decision was approved for the regional theological schools, the exarchate made no effort to implement it. Once the teaching in Georgian was made official at the Tbilisi Theological Seminary, the number of Georgian teachers increased.

The well-known educator and public figure Iakob Gogebashvili was appointed in 1864 to teach geography and mathematics at the seminary. In due course he was promoted to the position of school inspector. Appropriate educational procedures were revived at the Tbilisi seminary. Unlike the Russian teachers, Gogebashvili took a new stand on the problems of educating the youth. First, he strongly opposed the current strict regime, corporal punishment and admonitions. Secondly, he established groups of young scholars at the seminary in order to raise educational standards.

Furthermore, in defiance of Russia's colonial policy, Gogebashvili attempted to develop progressive pedagogical procedures. He published a Georgian ABC entitled *Deda Ena* (*"Mother Tongue"*) in 1865, and *Bunebis Kari* (*"The Door to Nature"*), in 1868. Without seeking the permission of the seminary administration, Gogebashvili used these books to instruct his students.

On 14 May 1871, the imperial court decided to eliminate the Georgian language in all educational institutions in order to achieve full russification of the theological schools. In the preparatory courses for these institutions, Georgian could only be used for didactic purposes. This caused great indignation and several articles were published in the Georgian press condemned the ruling of the tsar, forcing the Russians to retreat temporarily.

In order to mollify the Georgian public, the imperial decision was reformulated in a slightly different manner: the Georgian language could now be used as a basis for teaching Russian. No separate hours, however, for teaching Georgian language and literature were allocated: instead, they were included with other subjects such as Russian literature and Russian history. The Russian language was still exclusively prescribed at the theological schools, although the Holy Synod of Russia allowed the students of the Tbilisi theological seminary to study Georgian theological literature after official lessons.

The local Russian administration of the Caucasus instantly expressed its outrage at these new moves, declaring that it was instead in favour of expunging Georgian completely from the theological schools in the exarchate. Officials in St Petersburg, however, rejected this option, with the following statement:

The Georgian exarchate

To leave the clergy without knowledge of the Georgian language would greatly harm the Church and Christianity in the country in general . . . This in itself would be dangerous in the long run, so the Synod has permitted the use of Georgian at theological schools, while it has also supported the development of teaching Russian exclusively (Khundadze, 1951, pp 65-66).

"Prayers in your mother tongue speak from the heart"

In 1872, on the basis of a report written by Inspector Zinchenko, a number of progressively-minded Georgian teachers were dismissed from the Tbilisi Theological Seminary. In order to fortify the regime of russification in the seminary, the ruthless Ivan Kuvshinski was appointed to the post of inspector. The students hated him.

Although opposed by church officials, Gogebashvili continued as a seminary teacher. Numerous reports slandered him: he was, for example, accused of propagating anti-state ideas. In 1874, the Holy Synod of Russia sent Inspector Kerski to Georgia to study Gogebashvili's activities. The teacher had the following to say about Kerski: "He accused us of being indifferent to religion and labelled us extreme 'Georgiaphiles'." In his denunciatory letter to the Russian Holy Synod, Kerski noted that the Georgian teachers had settled comfortably in the seminary and were opposed to expelling Georgian students over whom they exercised considerable authority. Students were even permitted to read literature otherwise banned by the school administration. Supported by the students, the Georgian teachers had demanded that the seminary administration re-instate the chair of Georgian language at the seminary in Tbilisi. They also spoke to and examined the Georgian students in Georgian.

Kerski further inflamed the situation by informing St Petersburg that the Georgian seminary teachers had "set up a party in the effort to secure every place at the seminary for their compatriots, and to evict the Russians". An indignant Gogebashvili responded: "Woe to us Georgians! The Tatars, Armenians and other nations of different religious orientation possess well-organised theological schools in the Russian empire. In these all subjects are taught in their mother tongue, the Russian language merely a independent subject. However, as soon as the Georgians raise their voices, we immediately hear accusations of separatism" (Gogebashvili, 1962, p132).

On the basis of Kerski's report, Gogebashvili, condemned as unreliable, was relieved of his post. He never again entered public service but spent all his efforts on developing his pedagogical views. His studies *Deda Ena, Bunebis Kari* and *Russkoye Slovo* (*"The Russian Word"*) gave significant prominence to Christianity and were published several times for use in Georgian schools, where the teaching of Christianity was given a worthy position. Gogebashvili attached great importance to theological education, not only because it promoted the formation of a "clear ethos" but also because it "enriched the intellect of students by offering diversity of knowledge". He made the point — especially for those who favoured the imperial policy of russification — that when a Georgian says the Lord's Prayer in his own language, the prayer comes from his heart — "it is sincere, passionate and pleasant for the Lord," he declared. And again, when the same Georgian says the very same prayer in a foreign language, his heart is cold and his feelings are dormant, only his memory works. Such prayers, he affirmed, have no value to the Lord, for they cannot even bring warmth to a person's heart:

> It was not without reason that the Lord gave the Apostles knowledge of different languages. They were to preach the Gospel to all nations in their mother tongue. They were taught to pray and beseech the Lord in their mother tongue, too. This is why all nations appreciate prayers in their native languages and consider the introduction of foreign languages in churches as a great misfortune . . . In any country where religious services are conducted and theology is taught in a foreign language, church services and the faith are in danger of subjection to waste, deterioration . . . Here a clergyman performs church regulations mechanically, indifferently . . . Church services are an object of ridicule, churches and monasteries are empty, and the whole nation is on the path of losing God (Gogebashvili, 1903, p17).

Here, Gogebashvili articulates a position held by the vast majority of the Georgian faithful in the late 19th century.

Following the expulsions of Gogebashvili and several other teachers from the theological schools, the Tbilisi Theological Seminary in particular — but also the other schools — came under considerable pressure from Kuvshinski. Students were forbidden to speak in Georgian even during breaks, books by modern or secular writers were removed from the seminary library, and, by explicit order of the administration, seminarians were only permitted to read works of religious content. The reading of contemporary Georgian newspapers was also banned. Students housed in seminaries were strictly supervised and soon began to develop mistrust for each other.

The Georgian exarchate

By the close of the 1870s, a number of students were expelled from the seminary because they had been caught in possession of prohibited literature. In defiance of the strict regime, many seminarians were now seeking spiritual guidance beyond the walls of the institution. In time they created an underground group that secretly started circulating a hand-written periodical. Hoping to broaden their knowledge, they became acquainted with banned literature at Tbilisi's Ivanov Library. Some even joined the populist movement. Eventually, the group was disbanded by the police force and its members were arrested.

The clergy's opposition to russification

A group of Georgian clergymen now appeared who raised their voices in protest against the colonial regime of imperial Russia. The hierarchs Gabriel Kikodze and Alexander Okropiridze, both of whom were canonised by the Orthodox Church of Georgia in 1995, were especially distinguished in this action. Their lives and activities confirmed the fact that imperial-sponsored russification was failing to achieve the desired objectives.

Despite the fact that both churchmen had been acquainted with Russian culture from their childhood and had received theological education in Russian, this had failed to suppress their boundless love for their motherland. They struggled actively against the intransigence of tsarist rule in order to protect the religious and ethnic rights of the Georgian people.

Bishop Gabriel, who was principally concerned with public education, founded a women's eparchial school in 1890 and a theological seminary in Kutaisi in 1894. During his life, he took the initiative to open at his own expense more thsn 100 parish schools and libraries. Many young people received a higher education thanks to the material assistance offered by the bishop and, on account of his endeavours in education, he was elected an honourable member of the Society for the Dissemination of Literacy among the Georgians.

Gabriel attended to the spiritual life of his flock both in word and in deed. Eighteen thousand people returned to the Christian faith in Abkhazia thanks to his activities. He also paid for the construction and restoration of dozens of churches and monasteries, and he never ceased to bestow charity on widows, orphans and the homeless.

At the political level, Gabriel criticised the decision of the exarch of Georgia (taken after Kerski's 1870s report) to dismiss Georgian teachers from theological schools. On this matter, he sent a letter to Yevsevi stating that the action was harmful to Russian interests. His criticism and candour left him open to accusations by the ecclesiastical and civil authorities in the Caucasus, and various scandalous and malicious rumours were subsequently spread with the aim of damaging his reputation. However, as befitted the dignity and fortitude of a hierarch, he patiently, faithfully and selflessly performed his duties in protecting the violated rights of the Georgian people.

Bishop Alexander, together with Gabriel, played a leading role in raising the spirit of the Georgian people. In his efforts to ensure the progress of the nation, he attached great importance to the education of its youth. Alexander spent his money unsparingly towards achieving this goal. On his initiative, an eparchial school was established in Tbilisi and others were founded at the Teklati nunnery and the Women's Eparchial School in Poti. As an incentive, he granted scholarships from his own income to distinguished and poor students.

Additionally, Alexander donated a significant sum for the restoration of abandoned or ruined churches and monasteries — the Shiomgvime and Zedazeni monasteries were repaired and maintained with his permanent assistance. He considered essential the publication of works such as old Georgian manuscripts, Sulkhan-Saba Orbeliani's *Dictionary*, works by Catholicos Anthony I and sermons by Metropolitan Ambrosi of Nekresi, all at his own expense. His contribution to the restoration and publication of old Georgian church hymns was of cardinal importance.

As a national figure, Alexander was able to confidently defend the Georgian language, long oppressed by the imperial regime. In order to evoke a national self-consciousness, he appealed to the Georgian people:

> It is time for you to open your eyes and to be made aware of our obligations. Words alone are not enough. We should require of wealthy Georgians to patronise, protect and sponsor the poor, otherwise we shall vanish, we shall disappear (Chichinadze, 1907, p29)

Positive reactions to imperial policies: the Tergdaleulebi

Together with the Georgian clergy, a new generation of political activists known as the "Tergdaleulebi" [2] stood up against the reactionary ecclesiastical policy of Russia. Young Russian-educated men, such as Ilia Chavchavadze, Akaki Tsereteli, Sergi Meskhi and Niko Nikoladze, appeared in the public arena during the 1860s. Their activities marked a new stage in the national-liberation movement headed by

2.   See p60.

Chavchavadze — canonised as St Ilia the Righteous by the Georgian church in 1987.

Their immediate attention turned to the problems facing an Orthodox Church of Georgia deprived of autocephaly. Their literary and public activities made crystal-clear the imperial anti-Georgian ecclesiastical policies that were threatening the spiritual demise of the Georgian people. In 1861, Ilia warned the Georgian public:

> We have inherited three divine treasures from our ancestors: motherland, language, and faith. If we fail to take care of them, what will happen to us? What answer shall we give to future generations? (Chavchavadze, 1965, p15)

The Tergdaleulebi also sympathised with the difficulties faced by Georgians of different religious orientation — Catholics and Muslims — and defended their rights. They were well aware that, owing to unfavourable historical circumstances, a great number of non-Orthodox Christians, whose ethnic identity was also threatened when Russia annexed Georgia, had appeared among the Georgians at different times. They began a concerted struggle to awaken national self-consciousness in all Georgian communities with the realisation that religious differences, if emphasised, could destroy the movement. It was imperative to unite Georgians of all faiths under a single national banner, and Chavchavadze's remarks proved to be prophetic when he declared: "Faith does not determine nationality — a Georgian always remains a Georgian whatever his religious orientation" (Chavchavadze, *Works*, p15).

The prudent national and religious policies of the Tergdaleulebi and of the Georgian clergy yielded positive results. They paid significant attention to teaching the Georgian language at the theological schools and raised their voices against the ecclesiastical powers in Russia in the 1870s when their mother tongue was in danger. Unlike the Georgian exarchate with its intransigent policies, the Society for the Dissemination of Literacy, headed by Chavchavadze, established in 1879 free schools in different regions of the country. Unlike the state educational institutions, students in the free schools were taught in Georgian.

Imperial ecclesiastical policy, 1880s to 1890s

In the early 1880s, besides stirring revolutionary movements into greater activity all over the empire, the Russian state reinforced its diehard, anti-Georgian and ecclesiastical policies that aimed at eradicating the national consciousness of the Georgian people. Theological schools were the first to be attacked by the exarchate. In 1881, the curator of the Caucasus Educational District, K. Yanovski, prohibited the teaching of Georgian in the lower classes of the theological schools. His decree of 1885 went on to declare that studies in all forms of theological education should be conducted in Russian alone. Teachers and students were even prohibited from using their mother tongue to explain Russian words.

Georgian periodicals published a stream of articles exposing Yanovski's schemes — there seemed to be no limit to his appalling actions. Increasingly relentless after receiving support from the highest ecclesiastical and secular officials of Russia, he decided to employ the Mingrelian language for the teaching of Russian at schools in Samegrelo with the motive of dividing the unity of the people. Accordingly, he instructed a Russophile Georgian teacher from Samurzakano, Tada Ashordia, to create a Mingrelian alphabet based on Cyrillic. He also translated the Lord's Prayer and other prayers into Mingrelian, but the words were "so alien and despised by the people that the listeners burst into laughter" (*Essays*, vol. V, p415).

Bishop Gabriel (Kikodze) of Imereti severely criticised Yanovski. In his appeal to the exarch, he argued that it was impossible to implement any kind of russification using these tactics. "Those who merely *speak* Russian are not Russians," he wrote. "Russians are those who think and feel in Russian, talk and grieve together with Russia." To disseminate the Russian language by force, he added, would simply set the oppressed people against the state. He advised the exarch and the Russian authorities to resist Yanovski's methods (*Jvari Vazisa*, 1906, p8). The priests and the faithful of Samegrelo, in agreement with Gabriel, were opposed to conducting church services in Mingrelian. They also demanded the restoration of Georgian at their schools. Since public indignation had grown to such a degree, the exarch was forced to retreat temporarily. Nevertheless, at a later date, further attempts were made to introduce the same practice in the church services of Samegrelo.

The Exarchate of Georgia applied a great deal of pressure on the students of the Tbilisi Theological Seminary. Punishment without cause became common practice and student discontent at the strict regime arose in the seminary. As a result of the official, imprudent policy of the ecclesiastical authorities, a number of seminarians turned to atheism and became actively involved in the Russian populist and marxist revolutionary organisations that arose in Georgia during the 1880s-1890s.

Tension in the theological seminary peaked in 1886 when an expelled student, I. Laghiashvili, mortally wounded the rector Chudetski. Admittedly this was a shocking and tragic incident, but the funeral speech of Exarch Pavel (1882-1887), where he cursed the Georgian people, was entirely unwarranted.

Prince Dimitri Kipiani, marshal of Kutaisi, was quick to respond to these anti-Georgian sentiments. In a letter to the exarch, he declared: "You were entrusted the Georgian people as your own flock; if it is true that you have condemned the Georgian nation, you must leave this country." The Russian administration of the Caucasus in turn was incensed at Kipiani's reaction and by a decision of the imperial court, the prince was arrested and exiled to Russia where, in 1887, he was murdered by imperial agents. Exarch Pavel, meanwhile, was given the highest possible commendation and was made metropolitan of Kazan.

The new exarch, Palladi Rayev (1887-1892), attempted a more liberal tack in order to abate the tension. However, it turned out to be impossible to maintain order among the discontented seminarians. In the 1890s, a secret student society was formed at the Tbilisi Theological Seminary in order to raise the political and nationalist consciousness of students.

At its first meeting, held on November 30, 1893, a decision was taken to oppose the Department of Religion of Georgia. In December of the same year, the students organised a strike, demanding that the exarch cease illegal student oppression, expel anti-Georgian teachers, and re-introduce the teaching of Georgian language and literature. The exarch became so alarmed at the riotous behaviour of the students that he cancelled lessons at the seminary for an entire year. Prominent students were expelled and subsequently spied upon by the Department of the Caucasian Gendarmerie and the exarchate. Notwithstanding these events, the harsh conditions endured by the students did not improve, even after studies recommenced. The administration of the seminary thereafter could only manage its affairs with the assistance of the police force.

The struggle to preserve ecclesiastical heritage

In the second half of the 19th century, progressive laymen and clerics fought actively to protect and preserve the old Georgian church traditions and cultural values. Their very survival was threatened by the powerful exarchs. Special attention was paid to Georgian church hymns, which, after the renunciation of autocephaly, were in danger of falling into disuse.

Because the Russian ecclesiastical authorities did nothing to conserve

St Gabriel (1825-1896)

Bishop Gabriel (Gerasime) Kikodze was born into the family of a priest in Western Georgia. He entered Tbilisi's Theological School (then Theological Seminary) and continued his studies in Pskov and in St Petersburg.

In 1849 he graduated from the Theological Academy of St Petersburg with a master's degree. On his return home, he was appointed inspector of the Theological Seminary in Tbilisi and a professor of maths and science. Later, at his own request, he was transferred to the Institute of Noble Young Ladies in Mstkheta.

Apart from his teaching activities, Gabriel published a monograph in Russian, *The Principles of Empirical Psychology*, which was used as a textbook at the theological schools.

In 1854-56 his wife and five children died one after another. Gabriel subsequently took monastic vows and in 1858 was appointed the bishop in charge of the Gori diocese.

From 1860 he was responsible for the Imereti diocese, while also managing church affairs in Abkhazia and Svaneti. His sermons became extremely popular — he spoke with immense love and helped listeners to believe in the value of Christian virtues. These homilies were published in Georgian, Russian and English.

Gabriel is buried in Gelati monastery near Kutaisi.

old Georgian church hymns, a Committee for the Restoration of Georgian Church Hymns was founded in 1860 at the initiative of the Georgian public whose intention was to record the melodies in notation, and to publish and to popularise them. This seemed to be the only way to save the hymns which were otherwise faced with extinction. The committee became especially active after 1879 when Bishop Alexander Okropiridze became its chairman. Through his financial support, the director of Tbilisi's Music School, I. Ippolitov-Ivanov, and the incomparable performer of old Georgian hymns V. Karbelashvili, recorded Kartlian and Kakhetian hymns. With the committee's approval of the music, Alexander financed publication of the scores in 1899 by Ippolitov-Ivanov. In 1897-1898, Karbelashvili had already published the Kartlian and Kakhetian melodies of the hymns for *mtsukhri* ("vespers") and *tsiskari* ("matins") at his own expense.

Bishop Gabriel Kikodze of Imereti contributed greatly to the restoration of hymns in Western Georgia. With his financial assistance, the musician P. Koridze recorded in notation Georgian hymns from Imereti and Guria. These were published in three volumes at the end of the 19th century (Bubulashvili, 2001, p193).

Throughout this period, the Georgian faithful also focused attention on the protection of Church artefacts and old Georgian manuscripts that had been left in abandoned churches and monasteries. In order to save them, there had been a proposal as early as 1870s to establish a Church Museum for the purpose of preserving precious church objects. The historian, Dimitri Bakradze, the initiator of the project, appealed for support in 1873 from the Academy of Sciences of the Imperial Court. Although the academy encouraged his proposal at that time, the museum at Tbilisi's Sioni cathedral was founded much later — in 1889 — because earlier exarchs had opposed its construction. The Church Museum, which functioned from 1889 to 1921, played a major role in saving old Georgian manuscripts and Church artefacts. Indeed, it became a kind of academic centre; the museum published more than twenty academic monographs.

In the last quarter of the 19th century, attention turned to Georgian church history, especially after the significant work of the priest Mikhail (Gobron) Sabinin. In 1877, he published, in Russian, *The History of the Georgian Church from Ancient Times until the 6th Century*, which was followed by *The Lives of Georgian Saints* in Russian and in Georgian. Mose Janashvili's *The Ecclesiastical History of Georgia*, which appeared in Georgian in 1886, was used as a manual for parish church schools.

St Alexander (Okropiridze; 1824-1907)

Born in 1824 into the family of a priest in the Gori district (Eastern Georgia). After graduating from Theological Seminary in Gori, he continued his theological education in Tbilisi.

In 1845 he took monastic vows and joined the monastery of the Transfiguration in Tbilisi. Soon after this he was sent to the Theological Academy of Kazan. After graduation from the academy he taught Latin, Holy Scripture, moral theology and archeology in Tbilisi.

His activity was most remarkable in Abkhazia, where he taught for three years at the seminary until 1854, when the school was closed as a result of the annexation of Abkhazia by the Ottoman empire. Later, in 1862, he became bishop of the diocese of Abkhazia. At various times he was made responsible for the dioceses of Guria-Samegrelo, David Gareja, Shiomgvime and Gori. In 1903, he was forced to resign, allegedly for reasons of old age.

He was a member of the Committee for the Rehabilitation of Orthodoxy in Georgia and chaired the committee for the critical edition of Biblical texts in Georgian.

St Alexander protected his people and severely criticised the "russifying" policies of Archpriest I. Vostorgov (see pp 126 & 173 ff).

Significant studies on specific themes on the history of the Georgian church were also written during this same period in Russian and in Georgian periodicals. These publications helped preserve the history of the Georgian church — increasingly ignored in the period of the exarchate — in the consciences of the Georgian people.

In 1883-1910, Archpriest David Gambashidze from the district of Zestaponi produced *Mtskemsi* (*"Pastor"*), a theological journal in Georgian, at his own expense. This publication had as its aim to heighten nationalist and patriotic feelings among the Georgian clergy and to strengthen the Christian faith of the people. Despite official decisions by the government that resulted in severe censorship, *Mtskemsi* not only concerned itself with matters relating to the history of the Georgian church and people, but also paid considerable attention to unbiased interpretations of politics during the late 19th and early 20th centuries. In order to stimulate the curiosity of non-Georgian readers, Gambashidze, from 1886 to 1903, also published the periodical *Pastyr* (*"Pastor"*) in Russian. Both magazines contributed greatly to the intellectual development of the new generation of clergy, many of whom published their first works in one or the other.

This "new generation of clergy" — nurtured on the ideas of the national-liberation movement — appeared in the public arena at the turn of the 1890s. Among them were Kirion Sadzaglishvili (catholicos-patriarch, 1917-1918), Leonide Okropiridze (catholicos-patriarch, 1918-1921), Ambrosi Khelaia (catholicos-patriarch, 1921-1927, later canonised), Kalistrate Tsintsadze (catholicos-patriarch, 1927-1952). They fought valiantly to promote the rights of the headless Georgian church. The aforementioned clergy, together with Bishops Gabriel and Alexander, served to buttress the unifying spirit in the Georgian church.

A new debate on autocephaly

In the years following the end of the 19th century, a section of the Russian church, both clergy and lay, demanded a series of ecclesiastical reforms, among them the abolition of the Holy Synod and the restoration of the patriarchate. In time, the call for a council to debate the situation resounded widely. For its part, the Georgians hoped that its exarchate would also undergo significant changes in the light of whatever decisions a local council of the Russian Orthodox Church would take.

Russian church circles were divided over the question of Georgian autocephaly. Defying the Russian Holy Synod's official stance, many Russians were openly critical of its policies. In 1896, for example, a collection of articles published in St Petersburg under the title *Tserkovnye Voprosy v Rossii* (*"Church Issues in Russia"*) contained an essay entitled "The Situation of the Orthodox Church of Georgia in the Tsarist Russia", written by "Brail" (probably a pseudonym; the author remains unidentified). The article exposes the anti-Georgian policies of the exarchs and highlights the pitiful situation of an unwillingly dependant Church. A similar criticism was voiced in "What Are the Needs of the Georgian Church?" in the periodical *Sankt-Peterburgskie Vedomosti* (*"Issues of St Petersburg"*, no. 207, 1898) by the canonical lawyer Nikolai Durnovo, professor at the universities of Moscow, St Petersburg and Kharkov.

When, in 1894, the future catholicos-patriarch of Georgia Kalistrate Tsintsadze, began issuing instalments in *Pastyr* of his post-graduate dissertation on the autocephaly of the Georgian church (this had been defended at the Theological Academy of Kiev), the exarch, Archbishop Vladimir Bogoyavlenski (1892-1898), threatened Gambashidze, then editor, by demanding the closure of the publication and a statement to the effect that the Orthodox Church of Georgia had never been autocephalous. The dissertation, however, attracted the attention of such contemporary canon legal experts as the professors I. Malyshevski and A. Olesnitski.

Treatment of Georgian monasteries outside Georgia

The condition of the Georgian Orthodox ecclesiastical foundations abroad were lamentable. As an independent state, Georgia gave considerable assistance to its monasteries in Syria and Palestine, on Mount Athos, and in other places. Often these monasteries had *metochia* (dependent) churches and monasteries with estates in Georgia. Throughout the period of imperial domination, Georgian monasteries ceased to exist.

With the abolition of statehood and church autocephaly in Georgia, the government of Russia was obliged to take care of Georgian historical possessions, but it neglected this important duty. In the first half of the 19th century, Greek monks on Mount Athos, encouraged by the passivity of imperial Russia, ousted the Georgian monks from Iviron monastery and took possession of it. In the 1860s, the number of Georgian monks on Mount Athos diminished considerably following oppression by Greek monastics. In 1861, by decision of the Monastic Council, Georgians were no longer admitted to the brotherhood of the Iviron (Natroev, 1909, p218).

The demoralized Georgian monks took up residence in different monasteries on the Holy Mountain and looked to Georgia for help. Both secular and church authorities in Georgia decided to set up a new Georgian monastic house on the Mountain. They then were faced with the struggle to restore their historical rights on the holy peninsula. In 1869, with the blessing of the bishops of Imereti, Samegrelo and Guria, the monk Benedikte Barkalaia, together with a twelve-strong brotherhood, left for Mount Athos. Using money donated for the purpose, they purchased from the Greeks the ruined 10th century Georgian church of St John the Theologian near the monastery of Iviron. Despite resistance by Greek monks, the Georgian brotherhood successfully restored the church.

With the founding of a new monastic settlement, the Georgian fraternity reunited and those Georgians who were scattered over Mount Athos gathered and attempted to restore their legal rights. For this purpose they applied for support to the ambassador for Russia in Constantinople and to the viceroy of the South Caucasus, but to no avail (Kalinovski, 1885, pp 45-46). All that the Russian government did in 1882 over the Georgian-Greek controversy was to suspend the rights of the Greek fraternity over the lands in Georgia donated to the monastery of Iviron (Central State Archives, Act 911, p6).

In their turn, the Georgian monks on Athos informed the Georgian and Russian public in 1884 of their hardships through a Russian-language monograph entitled *A Brief History of the Monastery of Iviron on Athos According to Georgian Sources*. In addition, they published a number of articles about Greek coercion and called for assistance and support. Some prominent members of the Russian public took the problems of the Athonite Georgians seriously, such as A. Kalinovski who wrote a monograph (in Russian), *Where is the Truth? A History of the Monastery of Iviron on Mount Athos* (St Petersburg, 1885). Indeed, Tsar Alexander III donated 15,000 roubles to the Georgian fraternity on the Holy Mountain (Central State Archives, Act 216, p15).

In spite of many determined efforts, the Georgian monks were unable to restore their ancient ownership of the monastery of Iviron. This was primarily because imperial Russia did not concern itself sufficiently with the fate of age-old Georgian property on Mount Athos.

Imperial church policies in the regions of Georgia
Abkhazia

The Society for the Restoration of Orthodox Christianity in the Caucasus intensified its activities in many regions of Georgia, and the

Russian authorities took advantage of its presence by enforcing its colonial religious policy in Abkhazia. Christianity had ancient roots in this part of the country. One need only refer to the bishop of Pitiunt (today's Bichvinta or Pitsunda), present at the Council of Nicaea in 325 to demonstrate this. By the mid-19th century, however, under Ottoman rule, a section of the population had converted to Islam and some even reverted to paganism. Consequently, the Christian presence was considerably weakened. The Russian authorities had intended to commence missionary activities in Abkhazia even before the establishment of the society — immediately, in fact, after the abolition of the Georgian church's autocephaly. Opposing Russian influence in Abkhazia at that time was Ottoman Turkey, which secretly spread anti-Russian propaganda not only among Muslims but also among Christians.

In 1851, Viceroy Vorontsov approved St Petersburg's decision to initiate missionary activities in Abkhazia. He asked the Over-Procurator of the Holy Synod of Russia to authorise the exarch to send into the mission fields Georgian hierarchs, those who knew the customs and traditions of the local population well. It was his opinion that such a decision would be concomitant with the political interests of the Russian state. Thereupon, the eparchy of Abkhazia was restored and its see was principically occupied (until 1885) by co-operative Georgian ecclesiastics. The following Georgian leaders of the Abkhazia eparchy — Germane Gogolashvili (1851-1857), Geronti Papitashvili (1857-1862), Alexander Okropiridze (1862-1869) and Bishop Gabriel Kikodze (head of the Abkhazia eparchy subordinated to the Imereti eparchy) — were effective in carrying out missionary work in Abkhazia. Other experienced Georgian clergymen, such as Besarion Zhordania, David Machavariani, Nikoloz Kirtadze, Konstantine Topuridze, were also chosen for the mission. Unlike the colonial policy of Russia, the Georgian missionaries were purely concerned with the revival of Christianity in Abkhazia and the conversion of many Abkhaz Muslims back to the faith.

The head of the Imereti eparchy, Bishop Gabriel, made a special contribution to the revival of Christianity in Abkhazia. During his episcopacy in Abkhazia (1869-1885) the region was placed under the jurisdiction of Imereti. His sermons made a great impact on the people, as did the fact that he conducted church services in the Abkhaz language. He proposed to the Society for the Restoration of Orthodox Christianity in the Caucasus that, following in his own footsteps, Abkhaz-speaking candidates for the priesthood should be provided with a theological education. The society rejected his proposal because, since

The Georgian exarchate

its agenda was the gradual introduction of Church Slavonic, the Abkhaz language would have been an obstacle in the path of russification of the local population.

The activities of the Georgian missionaries resulted in the opening of churches and schools. The authorities now permitted teaching in the Georgian language in parish schools and Georgian clergy were invited to teach because of the shortage of qualified individuals. The Russian government also planned to substitute Georgian with Abkhaz which, in turn, would be substituted by Russian. A special commission headed by the well-known linguists Bartolomey and Uslar was convened in order to create an Abkhaz alphabet. This was accomplished in 1864 on the basis of the Cyrillic alphabet and was subsequently introduced into the schools. In a few years, however, the commission came to the conclusion that it was impossible to translate theological literature into Abkhaz. It took until 1899 for the society to return to the problem, when it had the liturgy of St John Chrysostom and the Book of Prayers translated into Abkhazian. But once again the translations were not up to standard and they soon fell out of use.

From the 1880s the Russian government changed its policy in Abkhazia since missionary activities there did not comply with general colonial aspirations in the Caucasus. For example, in 1885 the Abkhaz eparchy was separated from Imereti and became an independent Sokhumi eparchy with the objective of reinforcing russification in Abkhazia. Ten years earlier, in 1875, the very large Russian monastery of Simeon the Canaanite was built in Akhali Atoni (New Athos) and inhabited by Russian monks. Within the enclosure of the monastery a theological school was founded where Abkhaz youth received the appropriate education (*Abkhazia and Novy Afon...*, 1885, p51).

On September 30, 1898, the Holy Synod of Russia decided to enforce by law the conduct of church services in Church Slavonic as opposed to Georgian throughout Abkhazia. Through another decree, issued a few months earlier, the teaching of Georgian in any kind of school in Abkhazia and Samurzakano was prohibited.

In the 1890s, the reality that Russian monks occupied most of the monasteries in Abkhazia led to protests all over Georgia. In 1900, in his secret report to the Chief Ruler (as the viceroy was now known) of the Caucasus, the governor of Kutaisi noted that in order to avert protests and disorder, it was necessary "to seize schools and churches from the hands of the Georgian clergy and hold divine services in churches and schools in Church Slavonic. This measure will help us to protect the local population from Georgian influence . . . In long run, these measures will completely change the difficult situation in the Sokhumi district and things will develop in favour of the interests of the state" (Central State Archives, Act 69, pp 1-3; cf. Khaburdzania, 1991).

At the end of the 19th century Russian officials set about reorganising the Exarchate of Georgia with the intention of separating Abkhazia from the rest of the country. According to this scheme, Abkhazia was to be united with the Kuban district, and the Sokhumi eparchy with the eparchy of Kuban. In 1901, both the exarch of Georgia and the Chief Ruler of the Caucasus lent their support to the project as a way of isolating Abkhazia from Georgia. The venture, ready for implemention, was nevertheless delayed by the political situation in Russia at the beginning of the 20th century.

Samtskhe-Javakheti

With the the Society for the Restoration of Orthodox Christianity in the Caucasus as support, the Exarchate of Georgia attempted to effect a similar policy to that of Abkhazia in other regions of the country. But, thanks to the resistance of the local population and of the Georgian public in general the schemes failed.

Active missionary work was initiated by the society in South Georgia (Samtskhe-Javakheti) but was faced with the obstacles of religious and ethnic diversity. When this ancient region was reunited with Georgia in 1828, the majority of its inhabitants were not Orthodox Christians but either Muslim or Catholic. Russian colonial policy pursued after 1828 effectively nurtured both religious and ethnic diversification. When Catholic Armenians emigrated from Ottoman Turkey and sects from inland Russia began to settle in the region, the demographic situation changed significantly and the Georgians there soon found themselves greatly outnumbered. Georgian missionary-priests who came to Samtskhe-Javakheti attempted to exploit the activities of the society in favour of the Georgians but under the circumstances this was not always possible.

Saingilo

A similar situation developed in Saingilo where non-Georgians, especially Muslim Daghestanis, lived alongside the Georgian Muslims who comprised the majority of the local population. Russia treated missionary work in Saingilo with prudence. As a result of the work done there, a number of these Muslim Georgians decided to return to the Christianity of their forefathers and to join the Orthodox Church.

In 1850, a small group of around a dozen Ingilos (ethnic Georgian converts to Islam) travelled to Tbilisi to meet personally with the viceroy Vorontsov who later visited Saingilo himself. He had the situation in the area assessed and he took practical steps to help newly christianised Ingilos. At their request, the Exarchate of Georgia sent a priest to the village of Kakhi in 1851.

Orthodox Christian churches were built in Kakhi and Koraghani by Vorontsov's direct order. Aware of the viceroy's benevolence, Christian Ingilos, under the leadership of the village elder of Kakhi, Ioane Bululashvili, sent a delegation to Tbilisi in 1853. They asked the Russian administration of the Caucasus to exempt the Ingilos from taxes and unfair levies and requested permission for Christian Ingilos to settle in the vicinity of Christian churches. Though Vorontsov was favourably disposed to these appeals and had attempted to resolve matters promptly, satisfaction was only received by a decree of December 6, 1859. The Ingilos were declared to be state peasants and relieved from their dependence on the Muslim Daghestanis. This political course of action initiated by the government turned out to be favourable for the dissemination of Christianity in Saingilo. When the Ingilos increased in number, the Russian government decided to use them for advancing its political interests in the region.

Understandably, the Muslim population of Saingilo found this intolerable and they staged a revolt against the Russians in 1863. Though suppressed, the Russian administration in the Caucasus realised that missionary work among Ingilos had to be undertaken discreetly (Tartarashvili, 1981, p34). Henceforth, Georgian missionaries were despatched to the region by the 1880s and, with the support of local Ingilos, churches were built in Alibeglo, Kakhi and Kurkhumi. In the 1880s and 1890s, as a result of the missionary activities of the Georgian clergy in Saingilo, distinguished personalities such as I. Bululashvili, Giorgi Janashvili, Fr Dimitri Janashvili, Fr Mikheil Quloshvili, Konstantine Tarkhnishvili, Mose Janashvili came to the fore.

Ajara

Following the decisions of the Berlin Congress in 1878 (which reconsidered the terms of the Treaty of San Stefano which Russia had forced on the Ottoman Empire earlier in 1878), Ajara was returned to Georgia. Because Georgian clergymen and other public figures were well aware of the difficulties vis-à-vis the Georgian Muslims in Saingilo, they avoided inciting trouble over the issue of religious identity. According to a contemporary account, the Muslim Georgians in Ajara "are true Muslims with all their dispositions, character, traditions, heart and soul; moreover, they are uncompromising in their faith. Knowing nothing about nationality, they call themselves Tatars. If you ask them about Georgia, they will all but curse it, as they can make no distinction between being *Georgian* and *Christian Orthodox*" (*Droeba*, 1878, no. 174).

Russian policy, however, ordained the conversion of the Georgian Muslims by force and Georgians in general considered this to be reprehensible, whether by coercion or by argument. As the newspaper *Droeba* expressed it:

> It would be a good thing if they themselves understood or became convinced of the merits of the Christian faith. Otherwise, they should be left as they are in peace. Differences in faith will be neither obstacle nor hindrance for our fraternity and unity (*Droeba*, 1878, no. 146).

In this context the appeal of Ilia Chavchavadze in support of the Muslim Georgians was timely:

> Now, Georgians! You must show your best side to your newly rejoined brothers. Now must you understand your forefathers' dictum: "A friend in need is a friend indeed!" Then would it be evident whether their teaching is a mere word or a serious affair for you (Chavchavadze, 1965, p15).

With the reintegration of Ajara into Georgia, a delegation of twelve Georgian Ajar Muslims travelled to Tbilisi in November 1878. It was their wish to clarify the position of their Georgian brothers on matters of religion. The Georgian public, including the Orthodox clergy, welcomed them with great love and respect and the Georgian bishops Alexander Okropiridze of Gori and Gabriel Kikodze of Imereti addressed them with these words: "We, Georgian Christians, will always be the protectors of your faith . . . Nobody will ever infringe upon your faith, family rules or traditions" (*Mitsa*, 1920, no. 10).

These sentiments of the Orthodox laity and clergy prevented Russian imperial rule from carrying out its christianization of the Georgian Muslims upon the readmission of Ajara to Georgia. But later, in 1885, missionary activity commenced, first with the construction of a Russian Orthodox church in Batumi — an action that became symbolic for what was envisioned as the eventual conversion of the Muslim population in Ajara.

But the government's belief that the Batumi church would play a positive role in the process of christianizing the Georgian Muslims turned out to be baseless. The Russian officials presumed that they could repeat the example of Abkhazia where Christianity proved to be a valid means of awakening nationalist sentiments. While in Abkhazia the conversion to Orthodox Christianity of the non-Christian population had not provoked a crisis, in Ajara things turned out to be different: ethnic Georgians wished to be recognized as part of the Georgian nation but did not wish to give up their Muslim faith.

Samegrelo (Mingrelia) and Guria

In 1885, following a decision of the exarchate, a missionary department based on the model of the Guria-Samegrelo eparchy was formed in order to carry out the evangelization of non-Christians in Ajara under the guidance of the Special Committee.

On February 21, 1890, however, the Missionary Department of Guria-Samegrelo opted to cease its activities in order to avoid further antagonism. Instead, it advanced cultural and educational work, and to this end, Father Ekvtime Talakvadze, a priest from Ozurgeti, and Iona Meunargia, a member of the Missionary Department, were given the task of restoring churches and monasteries and to find property on which to build schools. Such a programme was considered unthinkable by the Russian rulers, whereupon Exarch Palladi Rayev (1887-1892) deprived the bishop of Guria-Samegrelo of the right to appoint missionaries and placed himself at the head of the christianization project.

Between the two revolutions, 1901-1917

The activities of Archpriest Ioan Vostorgov

The Russian tsarist regime continued to follow its rigid masterplan for Georgia after the turn of the 20th century. The state administration of the Caucasus collaborated with the Exarchate of Georgia in acting against the wishes of the Georgian people and the Georgian church. In pursuing their goals, the administration pinned great hopes on the Russian clergymen already active in Georgia.

One of these, Ioan Vostorgov, a Russian archpriest who operated in Georgia between the late 19th and early 20th centuries, loyally imitated the work pattern of his predecessors. From 1894 to 1905, he was employed as a teacher of theology at the First Tbilisi Gymnasium for Girls, and from 1900 he was made an inspector of theological schools and a member of the Georgia-Imereti Synodal Office. At the same time he functioned as editor-in-chief of the *Ecclesiastical News of the Georgian Exarchate* — the official organ of the exarchate.

Vostorgov's activities and manner, upheld by the Russian government, were intended to perjure the spiritual experience of the Georgian nation: "I hate nobody more than Georgians, who have always been a repulsive lot," he declared. "Even if the country has fallen under the protection of the Blessed Virgin, she has not even dared to approach this abysmal race but sent others as apostles. Georgians are the eternal enemies of the Russians; all Georgians are our betrayers" (Rogava, 1996, pp 158, 212). To the exarchs of Georgia, he advocated the following: "First of all they must always remember that it is their responsibility to do their best, making every effort and sparing no pains to assimilate Georgians with Russians" (Rogava, 1998, p158).

This arrogant way of thinking — ingrained throughout the empire — was not limited solely towards the Georgians, for Vostorgov even brought the exarch Alex I (Opotsky) (1901-1905) under his influence — so much so that the archpriest himself became the actual administrator of the exarchates.

Vostorgov made unilateral decisions in matters of church administration: he rewarded or punished clergymen and was supported in this by Archimandrite Nikandr Fenomenov, rector of the Tbilisi Theological Seminary, Archpriest Sergei Gorodtsev, and others. Together they pursued a course of eradicating the Georgian language from parish schools. Indeed, in their efforts to russify the Georgian population, Russian officials concentrated especially on reorganizing the Georgian educational system according to the Russian model. This was the system under which officers loyal to the tsarist administration were trained. As such, Georgia's language and traditions were systematically discriminated against and, finally, altogether removed from Georgia's schools.

At the same time (early 20th century) the Georgian language was also forbidden to be used at state schools; it was maintained solely at parochial educational institutions. Naturally, the Georgian people had a preference for the latter and, as a result, the native language was targeted for elimination at the parish schools. Enforcing the obligatory use of Russian for all subjects became the chief preoccupation of the imperial officials. In 1904, on the basis of Vostorgov's recommendations, the Holy Synod decided to build up the teaching of Russian at Church schools throughout the country. Consequently, teachers of the Georgian language were victimized and strictly limited in number and their activities while only Russians were now appointed as teachers at parish schools (Paviliashvili, 1995, p76).

Vostorgov, in league with similar-minded individuals, ruthlessly opposed Georgia's language and church. They knew full well that spiritually weakened young Georgians with no knowledge of their native tongue would no longer be true Georgians.

Owing to tsarist policies and the decisions of the Holy Synod at the turn of the century, there was a significant number of russified Georgian clerics who were indifferent to all native traditions. Moreover, they were vociferous in demonstrating their devotion to the Russian government as a way of disguising their feelings of inferiority in the eyes of the Russian clergy. One particular example was the Georgian bishop Dimitri Abashidze, who became notorious for his ruthless struggle against his compatriots (Rogava, 1998, p93).

Receiving instructions from the Russian authorities, Vostorgov and his accomplices attempted not only to eradicate Georgian from church schools, but also set the provinces against one another, thereby facilitating the disintegration of the nation and the gradual assimilation of every region. They also prohibited the fostering of close relations between Georgian Muslims, Georgian Catholics and Georgian Orthodox Christians. Till today Georgia is plagued with the problem of ethnic divisions in its historic regions — especially in Abkhazia and Samachablo (South Ossetia) — owing to the interference of a Russian government that had acted on the principle of "divide and rule". As Vostorgov noted:

> All teaching in Abkhazia had hitherto been conducted in Georgian; the Church liturgy was also in Georgian. But today Russian is taught at schools and the church services are being held in Church Slavonic. Lately the Georgian language has been eliminated from the schools and churches of Ossetia (Tsintsadze, 2001, p7).

There was no one to prevent Vostorgov from also fleecing Georgian churches and monasteries of their treasures or from appropriating their wealth. For example, he blatantly sold ancient and irreplaceable manuscripts from Svaneti to the British Bible Society (Rogava, 1998, p97) since he knew all too well that no one would question him. Nevertheless, Germogen, bishop of Saratov, openly declared that "Vostorgov is in truth a cruel enemy of the Georgian people whom we must support because of our political goals." Germogen was in no doubt of the difficulty of separating the conflicting loyalties posed by his fellow Russian.

Dawn of the 20th century and war with Japan

During the Russian-Japanese War (1904), the Russian Orthodox Church, its Holy Synod and the Exarchate of Georgia lent their full support to the tsarist leadership. Upon receiving instructions from the Holy Synod, representatives of the exarchate attempted to rally support for the war among the Georgians.

Slogans with patriotic sentiments, for example, were published in Georgian magazines and newspapers. But the war proved to be a hard and heavy burden for the population everywhere in the empire, contributing to growing social protest and precipitating civil revolt. Besides, it became quite evident that Russia was ill-prepared for any kind of large-scale military action. Its armed forces were shamefully defeated and as a result, the people grew restless — and the stirrings of revolution now grew ever stronger.

Chavchavadze's campaign for autocephaly, 1905-1906

Restoration of autocephaly of the Orthodox Church of Georgia was integral to the movement for the restoration of national independence. Ilia Chavchavadze (1837-1907), writer, public figure and "Father of the Nation", stood at the forefront of the campaign, while other prominent Georgians who participated included Iakob Gogebashvili (1840-1912), Niko Nikoladze (1843-1928), Niko Marr (1864-1934) Ivane Javakhishvili (1876-1940), Alexander Tsagareli (1844-1929), Alexander Khakhanashvili (1864-1912), Tedo Zhordania (1854-1916), Bishops Kirion Sadzaglishvili (1855-1917) and Leonide Okropiridze (1862-1921), Archimandrite Ambrosi Khelaia (1861-1927), and Archpriest Kalistrate Tsintsadze (1866-1952).

In the struggle for autocephaly, besides practical action, the Georgian church also had to use theological and historical arguments to prove that the 19th-century abolition of the church's independence had been an illegal act. Those who supported autocephaly accordingly directed their efforts in the areas of theology and history and, by 1905, a number of monographs, booklets, and articles had already been published in both the Georgian and Russian presses. These were instrumental in creating a significant pro-autocephaly wave of support in public opinion. Basing themselves on historical sources and documents the writers used the following lines of reasoning:

—Before the 19th century the Georgian church's autocephaly existed not only *de facto*, but also *de iure*; that is, in accordance with the canons of the Orthodox Church.
—In 1811 the Russian government, by an administrative order, illegally put an end to the autocephaly of the church, thus abrogating the 30th and 34th of the Apostolic Canons and the 22nd Canon of the Synod of Antioch.[1]
—In order to revive the faith of the population it was necessary to revive the autocephalous administration of the Orthodox Church of Georgia (Papuashvili, 1996, p5).

Alongside their research into the historical and canonical sources, Georgian academics and public figures also exposed the tsarist, anti-Georgian policy of the russification of the Orthodox Church of Georgia and its leaders. The nationalist Iakob Gogebashvili declared:

1.   The Apostolic Canons are 85 canons attributed directly to the Apostles, and appear in a concluding chapter of the Apostolic Constitutions (late 4th century). The 25 Canons of Antioch are believed to have been worked out at the Council of Antioch in 341.

For more than a century the Church of Georgia has been subjected to so great a servitude as never experienced by any of the pagan religions within a Christian state. For a hundred years degeneration, deterioration, and denationalization have been what the foreign governors of our Church have aspired to. Now is the time to elude this illness; now is the time to liberate ourselves from the claws of church bureaucracy; to cure our ulcers; and to attain freedom of conscience. The single, pre-eminent remedy is the autocephaly of the Orthodox Church of Georgia (*Iveria*, no. 199, 1905, p3).

Publications of 1905 included *Short Historical Notes on the Autocephaly of the Orthodox Church of Georgia* by the historian Tedo Zhordania, and Archpriest Kalistrate Tsintsadze's *The Autocephaly of the Orthodox Church of Georgia*, both of which were translated into Russian. Writings such as these alarmed Russian public figures, such as Vostorgov, who wrote an article for the magazine *Narodnoe Obrazovanie* ("Public Education") in which he criticized the Georgians for their "ingratitude" and separatist agenda.

As mentioned above, prominent Georgian figures also initiated a number of public incidents in 1905 in order to reinstate autocephaly. Laymen and clergy held meetings in different towns of Georgia where they discussed the means and opportunities for restoring the church's autocephaly. At one of these gatherings, held at the parish school of the church of St Nikoloz, Chavchavadze reminded the public that they should be prepared for all kinds of provocation from the side of the Russian government (Bukurauli, 1920, p6).

In due course a petition was drawn up by the clergy which was designed to be sent to the Russian civil and church authorities. It presented, on the one hand, historical and canonical arguments for autocephaly, and, on the other, practical arguments for renewing local church life in the parishes with the participation of all the people of God. The petition ran as follows:

The deprivation of the autocephalous and property rights of the Orthodox Church of Georgia and the establishment of a church administration spiritually alien to the flock has resulted in the total disorganization of the ecclesiastical and religious life of the Georgian people. With the loss of the Catholicos-Patriarch, the spiritual father of the country, Georgians are without their patron and protector. Cathedrals, centuries-old, have been razed, temples and churches of outstanding architectural significance destroyed, monasteries deserted, monastic schools closed. They have been replaced by Russian theological educational institutions that offer candidatures for a clergy quite unsuitable for Georgian parish life. This clergy is trained with aspirations for a bureaucracy far from the native land; it is a clergy that has disseminated political ideals among the population and is lacking in the charisma of earlier Georgian pastors. Among the Georgians, Orthodox Christians from time immemorial, whose lives are spent in prayer and who struggled against Islam, one can now meet the protagonists of humiliation, murderers of clerics, evictors of pastors, blasphemers of old sanctuaries, robbers and burners of sanctuaries, and so on.

Aside from these, other Georgian clerics pointed out that the Orthodox Church of Georgia was still canonically autocephalous, since no legal resolution eliminating its autocephaly had ever been passed. Furthermore, only those churches which are intrinsically free are able to serve the Word freely and can manage all their activities and duties responsibly. Only a liberated self-ruling Church is able to defend its glorious Sacred Creed and have the required voice to implement its divine task which inflames human hearts.

Sensitive to the need for physical security for the independent functioning of their church, the clergy demanded that:

1. The Orthodox Church of Georgia should restore its autocephalous rights; that the rank of Catholicos-Patriarch should be reinstated; and that the Catholicosate of Mtskheta (Iberia) be restored within its former borders, i.e. within the provinces of Tbilisi, Kutaisi, Batumi, and in parts of the Black Sea provinces (Abkhazia, Samurzakano and the district of Zakatala).

2. The tradition of appointing clergymen to vacant positions by local election should be restored:
   a) the faithful should elect competent candidates for the parish council and for the parish clergy; that the Catholicos and the bishops be elected by clergymen and public lay representatives; that elected bishops be ordained at the council of all the bishops of Georgia, presided over by the Catholicos-Patriarch and the Holy Synod; and as for the Catholicos, he should be elected by the supreme temporary government;
   b) following discussions on the question of appointing candidates for the clergy at the eparchial committee under the bishop, the local bishop is to ordain them.

3. The Holy Synod should be established under the Catholicos as its chairman; standing committees of all eparchies under their bishops,

laymen and clergy should be elected for a determined period of time.

4. All governance of charity and ecclesiastical educational institutions, the Church, monastic and ecclesiastical affairs should be placed in the hands of the Holy Synod under the Catholicos.

5. All Church estates transferred to the state should be returned to the Orthodox Church of Georgia (Tsintsadze, 2001, pp 79-82).

As noted previously, this petition was debated and refined at meetings held throughout the towns of Georgia. Its final version for presentation to Russia was elaborated and announced at the Georgian Clergy Assembly on May 31, 1905.

Russian reactions to pleas for autocephaly

Russians who lived and worked in the Caucasus were now becoming anxious about the nascent struggles for Georgian statehood and church independence. Seeing this part of their imperial federation on the point of collapse filled them with dismay.

To mark the birthday of Tsar Nicholas II, Archpriest Sergei Gorodtsev delivered a defiant speech in one of Tbilisi's churches:

Russia has become weakened not because of the defeat by Japan, but because of its internal enemies. All Russia is agitated, the peripheries are worried. Our unassailable motherland is being interred before our very eyes; the ancient origin of autocracy, so dear to our Russian hearts, is being buried (Lominadze, 1959, p39).

Yet Gorodtsev, Vostorgov, Exarch Alex, Archimandrite Nikandr and so many others had no intention of wasting their time by standing back and doing nothing. In May 1905 they set up the Party of the Adherents of Order in Tbilisi with around 800 men joining up. Its members carried out attacks on revolutionaries and clergy; they murdered innocent people in the name of law and order, and stirred up national hatred between Russians and Georgians.

The Russian church officials too were swift to react. In 1905 they closed down the Kutaisi Theological Seminary, it being one of the main centres of dissent (it should be noted the theological seminaries in Russia, where far more serious civic unrest and chaos reigned during this period, were not closed).

On May 31, 1905 police invaded the Assembly of Georgian Clergy being held in the Tbilisi Theological Seminary and authorized by the exarch himself. The Georgian clergy there had been discussing restoring the Church's autocephaly. Niko Marr, the well-known Georgian academic and professor of St Petersburg University, happened to be in Tbilisi at the time and was an eye-witness to this barbaric act. He stood up on behalf of the Georgian clergy, appealing to the policemen with the words: "How dare you insult Christian clergy of the ancient Church!" (Takaishvili, 1991, p118).

News of the police raid spread round the world and created considerable injury to the international prestige of the Holy Synod of Russia. Twenty-seven Georgian clergymen refused to carry out their duties until the aggressors were identified and punished. The *mepisnatsvali* (the tsar's viceroy) was forced to appoint a special committee to investigate the incident after which, in the summer of 1905, Exarch Alex I and Archimandrite Nikandr, rector of the Tbilisi Theological Seminary, were summoned back to St Petersburg.

Vostorgov had already left earlier for Russia, but — as we shall see later — his struggle against the Orthodox Church of Georgia and the Georgian people was not over when he eventually became a leader of the church organization, the Moscow Union of the Russian People (Vardosanidze, 1987, p151).

While Vostorgov, Alex and others openly opposed the Georgian nation, the viceroy, Count Ilarion Vorontsov-Dashkov (1905-1915), chose different tactics to achieve the same goal, namely the russification and assimilation of Georgia. In his opinion, all things Russian had to be offered to the Georgians without the application of any force, without the traditional compulsion so dear to and characteristic of the Russians. By not degrading the local population, they in turn would express their gratitude and respect for the Russians; then, they could be easily russified and assimilated (Khutsishvili, 1972, p126).

There existed yet another line of Russian response to Georgia's struggle for state and church independence. The Georgian leaders of the self-rule movement acquired a number of unexpected supporters within Russia itself. In 1905, for example, during the debate on church reform, demands to restore the old Russian Patriarchate were widely propagated. In 1721, Tsar Peter I had abolished the patriarchate and in its place had established the Holy Synod in order to strengthen the dependence of the Russian Orthodox Church on the state. Members of the Russian Slavophile Movement, particularly Nikolai Durnovo (1856-1920), the scholar and authority on canon law, demanded restoration not only the patriarchate of Russia but also Georgia (Khutsishvili, 1972, p20).

The liberal yet traditionalist Slavophiles condemned the Holy Synod's policy of russification of non-Slavs as well as the existence of a Russian exarchate in Georgia (Vardosanidze, 1993, p13).

Even a number of Russian clerics working in Georgia came forward to protest against their anti-Georgian Russian compatriots. In one instance, Iona Brykhnevich, the priest of one of the Russian churches in Tbilisi, published an "Appeal to the Russian People" in the newspaper *Arise the Sleeper*:

> We should neither dominate nor suppress anyone. No one should be obliged to obey us. We should not be the masters of anyone. We should not take for our own other people's lands, houses, property or labour; that is, we should not rob anyone. Following this path, we will have no need to fight for anything or become enemies of anyone. We should not throw sand in the wheels of any nation or even of an individual person. In this way, we shall be able to achieve a situation whereby no one will wish to dominate us. The great historical mission of the Russian people consists not in conquering the lands of others, not in robbing and oppressing other peoples, but in using its power sent from God for the deeds prescribed by Him; that is, for the protection of the weak.
>
> Were we to behave so, were we only to act in order to protect the weak, why should the Georgians, Poles, Armenians, Jews, Tatars and other peoples fear us? Why should they shun the force that protects them? The great future of our people lies not in conquests, or doing evil, but in protecting freedom. We are protectors of freedom. Hence, all peoples of the world will bless us for this. And if the peoples bless us, this will be a sign that we are following the path of Our Lord to protect freedom. But if peoples curse us, this will be a sign that we are doing evil, that we are enslaving others (Rogava, 1996, 212).

Georgian-Russian talks on autocephaly

After recalling Alex I, the Russian Synod appointed as the next exarch of Georgia, Nikolai Nalimov (1905-1906), who was comparatively compassionate towards those striving for autocephaly and for the restoration of independence. On October 11, 1905, a special deputation led by Chavchavadze visited the *mepisnatsvali*, asking him to intercede with the Holy Synod and the tsar in their negotiations concerning the problem of autocephaly.

Viceroy Vorontsov-Dashkov gave his consent yet could not help asking: "How can two different Catholicoses exist within one Orthodox

State?" Clearly he was ignorant of the fact that in the mediaeval Byzantine Empire there had co-existed four distinct autocephalous patriarchates: Constantinople, Jerusalem, Antioch and Alexandria (Sharadze, vol. II, 1990, pp 307-309).

On November 16, a number of bishops, including Kirion, Leonide and Peter, petitioned Tsar Nicholas II over the restoration of Georgian autocephaly. The tsar instructed the Holy Synod to discuss the issue and a special committee was established to this end. In January 1906 two meetings were held to this end with the participation of Bishops Kirion and Leonide. The outcome was undecided owing to radical differences of opinion (*Jvari Vazisa*, no. 3, 1990, pp 56-63); unsuccessful, too, were meetings in April by Chavchavadze, an elected member of the Russian State Duma (Parliament), with the Synod's over-procurator A. Obolensky and its chairman Anthony, metropolitan of St Petersburg. They assured Chavchavadze, however, that they were inclined to make certain changes in the management of the Georgian exarchate on the matter of autocephaly, but this was complicated by the fact that Russian officials would acknowledge only the authority of an All-Russian Church Council, which had not met since the church reforms of Peter the Great.

Chavchavadze mentioned a further problem to Metropolitan Anthony in their discussions: the appointment of a new exarch in Georgia. He informed the Synod's chairman that the Georgian clergy were now intending to boycott Nikon (1906-1908), the latest exarch to be appointed. The churchmen had even sent a petition to St Petersburg demanding that Nikon should not be sent to Georgia since he would not be acknowledged by them (Sharadze, vol. II, 1990, pp 307-309).

When, despite such resistance, Nikon did turn up in Tbilisi in August 1906, it was only state officials, members of the Russian clergy and police detachments who turned out to greet him. The Georgians had decided that none of their clergy should have either official or private contact with the newly arrived exarch. The Russian state authorities were greatly alarmed at this show of resistance, as evidenced by the letter sent shortly after by *Mepisnatsvali* Vorontsov-Dashkov to Over-Procurator Obolensky. In order to pacify the Georgians' anger he asked the Holy Synod to restore the teaching of the Georgian language in the theological schools and to nominate more cautious candidates for bishops. "Using this method", he added, "we can avoid the kindling of the people's national self-esteem under the Georgian exarchate" (Rogava, 1998, p39).

Run-up to the 1906 All Russian Church Council

In the summer of 1906 deliberations on the issue of the autocephaly of the Georgian church entered a new phase. On August 11, on the basis of the Georgians' petitions and the report of the Synodal over-procurator, Tsar Nicholas II issued a decree asking the Local Council of the Russian Orthodox Church to deal with the matter. A preparatory meeting for the forthcoming All-Russian Church Council, established by the Holy Synod, was divided into several departments, the second of which was responsible for regulating church affairs in the Caucasus.

On two occasions in the autumn of 1906 this department considered the question of Georgian autocephaly (Vardosanidze, 2001, p118). Bishops Kirion and Leonide, as well as the Georgian historians and the-ologians Niko Marr, Alexander Tsagareli and Alexander Khakhanashvili participated in the preparatory committee on behalf of the Orthodox Church of Georgia.

Bishop Kirion submitted four reports: historical and canonical foun-dations of the Georgian church problem; the motivation behind Georgia's struggle to restore the autocephaly of its own Church; the sit-uation of Georgia when it was granted autocephaly in the 11th century; and the national principle within the Church. The key point linking all of these was that:

> Every nation should enjoy the freedom of its own Church. There must be no domination in the Church, as Church domination is the hardest, most dangerous and ruinous of all types of servitude. The Christian Orthodox Church grants no privileges to any one nationality. No nation may set itself up over and above the others for the purposes of superiority (Nikoladze, 1918, pp 212-216).

In his report, Bishop Leonide noted:

> At present, Christianity in Georgia is at an extremely critical stage. People do not go to church . . . Both clergy and believers consider that the only way to preserve Christianity in Georgia and to enjoy confidence at the parish level is to solve the problem of the restoration of autocephaly for the Orthodox Church of Georgia. It must be solved by a system of elections .
> . . the head of the Church must be the Catholicos-Patriarch, who will know the language of his own flock, their traditions, manners, psychology
> . . . This is the final decision of the people and the clergy; it is fixed,

and no opinions should make them change their beliefs (Vardosanidze, 1987, p9).

Marr raised objections to Vostorgov's anti-Georgian policies, published in 1905, and in his report *A Historical Review of the Georgian Church from Ancient Times*, the Georgian academic noted:

> Vostorgov has no idea either of the authentic Georgia or of the authentic Georgian church. The Christian spirit is foreign to him. He is an obvious enemy of the Georgians and Armenians. The sting of his absolute loathing is directed against the Orthodox Church of Georgia (Nikoladze, 1918, p227).

Tsagareli's paper essentially comprised the argument that from 1811 until 1906 the Georgian faithful were completely demoralized, which was the precise intention, deliberately and gradually achieved, by Russian church officials. Tsagareli formulated his thoughts on the situation in the following clauses:

1. There is no questioning the autocephaly of the Georgian church before 1811.
2. *De iure* the Georgian church did not lose its autocephaly after the establishment in 1801 of the Russian exarchate in Georgia; it was simply unable to exercise its canonical rights *de facto*.
3. The Georgian church did not join the Russian church to form a united entity; it was managed by exarchs sent by the Holy Synod of Russia.
4. The policy of managing a central, regional Church by exarchs of another country contradicts both ecclesiastical law, the praxis of the Orthodox Church in general, and in particular the tradition of the Orthodox Church of Georgia.
5. There is no doubt that the faith of the Georgians deteriorated following the introduction of rule by the exarchs.
6. No canonical grounds for the ecclesiastical overturning of 1801 were mentioned in the report by the Holy Synod sent to Tsar Alexander I; it simply demanded the substitution of the Georgian catholicosate by the Russian exarchate. In fact, justifiable grounds plainly did not exist.
7. The official acts of that period make it clear that the bolstering of the Church's economy served as a pretext for the Holy Synod to send exarchs to Georgia. Church lands were transferred to the state, a part of them was sold, Church peasants were freed, the number of

eparchies was reduced in order to save money, and so on. Consequently, there are no legal grounds for the existence of the Exarchate of Georgia.

8. In legal terms, neither the Holy Synod nor an All-Russian Church Council can grant autocephaly to the Georgian church nor deprive the Church of it. Only the decisions of the Emperor may be followed and these must be made in accordance with the canons and laws of the Ecumenical Church and based on the will of the clergy and faithful of Georgia who, in fact, firmly desire to retain the autocephalous rights of their Church.

9. The Church of either nation should be managed by the assembly of its own bishops.

10. Neither Church laws nor civil legislation provides for the dependence of Church or secular management of a given ecclesiastic area on one and the same central ecclesiastic authority.

11. The aspiration for an autocephalous Orthodox Church of Georgia does not imply state or ecclesiastical separatism.

12. No complications will follow the restoration of the autocephalous management of the Georgian church (Varazashvili, 2000, p93).

In addition to these reports for the preparatory council, other publications devoted to the problems of Georgian autocephaly and to the oppression of the Georgian people by Russian imperialism were published throughout 1906. Notable titles are Archpriest Kalistrate's monograph *A Historical Document on the Autocephaly of the Georgian Church*, and that of the great Georgian historian Ivane Javakhishvili (assistant professor at St Petersburg University and later founder of the Tbilisi State University), *Political and Social Movement in Georgia in the 19th Century*. In his study, Javakhishvili criticised the Russian empire for its religious tyranny:

> Once Georgia had joined with Russia, the Georgian people were deprived of the right to hear sermons in the cathedral of Sioni in the capital of Georgia in their native language, the language in which they had been tirelessly praying to the Blessed Virgin for 1,400 years. None of the Persians, fire-worshippers [Zoroastrians], Muslims, Arabs, idolatrous Mongols nor Turks did as much harm to the Apostolic Orthodox Church of Georgia as the Russian government and its exarchs (Rogava, 1996, p175).

From the depth of the reports and published works produced at the time by Georgian historians, theologians and church figures the conclusion is a clear one: that the Russian administration was neither canonically authorized to deprive the Georgian church of its autocephaly nor empowered to transfer rights of management to the Russian Holy Synod. These decisions violated all of the acknowledged and received norms of Orthodox Church management. Traditions and customs were violated, the only solution was to give back to the Orthodox Church of Georgia its autocephalous rights.

This is precisely what the Russian government had feared. It had every reason to believe that following the restoration of autocephaly Georgians would then move for political independence. Hence the preparatory meetings of the All-Russian Church Council would not meet the legitimate demands of the Orthodox clergy and people of Georgia.

When it became obvious that no legal basis existed for the current state of non-autocephaly of the Georgian church, Vostorgov, Archpriest T. Butkevich amongst others therefore attempted to force the issue into another domain: they now accused the Georgians outright of political separatism. Vostorgov submitted two propositions for the future administration of the Georgian church: to establish a Caucasian metropolis instead of a Georgian exarchate, and a call for the total abolition of the Georgian exarchate and the establishment of eparchies only of the Georgian church. These proposals provoked stiff opposition, even from some Russian academics, and Vostorgov, Butkevich and their supporters abandoned their plans — but only temporarily.

Finally, and as expected, the members of the preparatory meeting resolved to table the question of autocephaly for the forthcoming All-Russian Church Council. Already in 1906 following these meetings, the Georgian clergy became aware of the true intentions of the Russian Holy Synod. As a result they began to express opinions and did their utmost to prevent the matter of autocephaly from being raised at the All-Russian Church Council. Their reasoning was as follows:

1. The All-Russian Church Council was not authorized to resolve this particular question; it was only within the competence of the Eastern Patriarchs.
2. It was clear that the Holy Synod, having considered the issue, would respond negatively to the Orthodox Church of Georgia.
3. Were Georgians to consent to having the matter of their autocephaly placed on the agenda of the All-Russian Church Council, they would

by this very act be recognizing the council's authority to resolve this issue.

And so the Georgian church made every effort to block submission of the autocephaly question to the council. Instead, the Georgians preferred to exercise patience and to wait for the appropriate time for their rightful restoration: for them, the decision had to be made freely and independently, without the Holy Synod's permission or consent.

In 1906, Ambrosi Khelaia, an active campaigner for autocephaly, wrote to Bishop Leonide in St Petersburg:

> I believe that the coming church council will not yield any results and we must not agree to submit our affairs to it. It is not the council that has deprived us of the autocephaly of our Church; hence it cannot restore that which we possessed *de iure* and which in reality was taken away from us violently (Saitidze, 2000, p93).

The age of repression, 1907-1910

Such were the feelings of the leading voices of the Georgian church, when a sudden sea change in politics caused the All-Russian Church Council to be indefinitely postponed — and with it any discussion of Georgian autocephaly. On June 3, 1907, Nicholas II dismissed the Second State Duma which had proved even more hostile to his autocratic beliefs that the First Duma of 1906. Electoral changes allowed the Third Duma, under the conservative leadership of Pyotr Stolypin, to become the tool of the imperial government until 1912. Church and state policies now became increasingly harsh across the board: their main target was the periphery of the empire, especially Georgia where the Russians started to repress the leaders of the national-liberation movement. The actions, backed by Stolypin's government, were faithfully supported by the Georgian exarchate and its leader Exarch Nikon.

This policy put the Georgian clergy in a difficult situation. The leaders of the 1905-1906 movement for autocephaly, including Bishops Kirion and Leonide and Archimandrite Ambrosi, were subject to extreme persecution. And though there were some patriotic members of the Georgian clergy who refused to back down or compromise with the government, and who continued to campaign for restoration, there were others who feared the reprisals and so courted reconciliation with the Russian authorities, acknowledging Nikon as exarch of Georgia and promising him their loyalty and submission.

In 1907 Vorontsov-Dashkov informed Tsar Nicholas that "at present the Georgian clergy attaches less importance to the question of autocephaly than before, and they are ready to ignore most of their former demands" (Lominadze, 1959, p69). Aware he now had the advantage, Nikon acted. He prohibited the conduct of services in Georgian in the country's main churches — such as Sioni in Tbilisi, Bodbe, Batumi, and so on — and took action against any clergy who defended notions of autocephaly.

Writing on January 20, 1908 to Metropolitan Anthony of St Petersburg, Nikon declared:

> If the clergy are permitted to use Georgian, they should respect the principles of the state. As I wrote to the Holy Synod, a seminary where lessons are taught in Georgian shall be supported no longer by the Exchequer, and the students must be deprived of the rights they had enjoyed when it was entirely Russian. Once aware of their errors, the Georgians, remorseful and weeping, shall beg our pardon. Renouncing their national rights, they shall plead for the recovery of what they had before (*Kavkasioni*, 24/10, 1996, p9).

Although Nikon did his best to carry out Russia's interests in Georgia, the government remained dissatisfied: it wanted all hopes for national and ecclesiastical independence to be dashed forever. In the government's opinion, if national leaders in Georgia were to be harshly punished, the Georgian rank and file, shocked and demoralized, would never again dare to follow anti-Russian activists.

An obvious pretext, however, was necessary in order to put such extreme measures into action — for only then, it was believed, would anti-Georgian measures taken by the Russian authorities be regarded as lawful and righteous in the world's eyes. A sacrifice was needed therefore to further the state's interests (indeed, Russian officials tended to take decisions with the assumption that the end always justifies the means). The Russian government therefore chose to offer up Nikon, its most devoted servant and second fiddle to the *mepisnatsvali* in the Caucasus.

*

Oppression after Nikon's killing

On May 28, 1908, as he proceeded up the stairs to the Georgia-Imereti synodical office, Exarch Nikon was assassinated by an unknown assailant. Denounced as an act of terrorism, it was the talk of the day in every corner of the empire. The Russian clergy denounced the killing as an action directed against all Russians, scores of articles were published on the event and sermons eulogizing Nikon's policy of russifying Georgia were delivered. Investigations were held according to ecclesiastical and criminal legislation. The Synod over-procurator A. Izvolsky forced Vostorgov, synodal officials and others to study the situation of the Georgian church. Vostorgov appealed to Russians living in Georgia to defend their interests in the Caucasus, even if they had to fight to the bitter end (Khutsishvili, 1972, p126).

As for the criminal investigation, members of the Social Federalist Party first came under suspicion. Although this was the party that used nationalism to fight for the restoration of the autonomous rights of Georgia in Russia, its representatives denied the charge categorically (Laskhishvili, 1992, pp 226-228). When the investigation proved inconclusive, the Russian authorities turned their attentions to the Georgian clergy. Armed with neither evidence nor proof, they accused the pro-autocephaly element of the murder: Bishop Kirion was singled out as the "intellectual organizer" of the assassination. The authorities justified the accusation with the statement: "Exarch Nikon was against the autocephaly of Georgia, hence the Georgian autocephalists decided to get rid of him. Vostorgov even boasted: 'I will kill Bishop Kirion and flush all Georgia with his blood!' " (Saitidze, 1990, p10). Later, on December 10, the deputy V. Purishkevich delivered a speech to the Third State Duma of Russia, where he openly blamed Georgian autocephalists for the killing.

In the 1990s, Georgian historians working through the archives brought to light a number of secret documents. Only then did was it revealed that Nikon's murder was organized by the government and the secret police (Guruli, 1993, pp 89-96). However, Nikon's murder occurred at the beginning of the 20th century, when patriotic Georgian church dignitaries were placed under very difficult conditions, and so Bishop Leonide had his residence searched and he was then kept under permanent police surveillance. Archimandrite Ambrosi was exiled without trial to the monastery of the Holy Trinity in Ryazan, southeast of Moscow. Bishop Kirion, exiled to the desert of Sanakhar in the Russian province of Tambov, survived under the appalling conditions. Both Ambrosi and Kirion were deprived of their religious rights, i.e. they were forbidden to conduct church services. Since the arrest of an Orthodox clergyman was not permitted in Russia, these were the kinds of punishment that were used instead.

Such persecution of their clergy appalled those Georgian and

Russian dignitaries who were critical of the Russian administration. Pavle Tumanishvili, one of the leaders of the Georgian nobility, appealed to the *mepisnatsvali* to alleviate the oppression of the clergy, but to no avail — he was incapable of putting an end to the repressions against Kirion, Ambrosi and Leonide. Shortly before his death, one bishop asked:

> Can you not see how Bishop Kirion, an innocent, hardworking, energetic man, and beloved by all, is being persecuted on the grounds of auto-cephaly, which is merely a canonical problem? He is as pure as a candle burnt for the Lord. Where now are law, justice and conscience? These are under persecution as well and have been dismissed for foul motives at the hands of morally corrupt men. But God is merciful. Before its union with Russia, our country had always been surrounded by aggressive enemies, but none could ever achieve their aims. Not one could eliminate the Church, the faith or the people. Russia too will never succeed in this! (Durnovo, 1909, p12)

It was, indeed, impossible for the Russians to crush the spirit of the Georgians, who managed to publicise their cause in the rest of the world. Oliver Wardrop, Britain's High Commissioner for the Transcaucasus, was one of the foreigners who offered his help. He founded, on his own initiative, the "Society in Defence of Kirion", which collected signatures in the United Kingdom and Europe in a petition to set the bishop free. On March 10, 1909, George Loran, chairman of the League of Defence of Human Rights in Brussels, appealed to the chairman of the Russian State Council, or Upper House, in defence of Kirion's rights.

Actions such as these produced some results: Kirion and Ambrosi regained their canonical rights. Kirion was appointed bishop of Polotsk and Vitebsk while Ambrosi became igumen (abbot) of the Starya Russa monastery in the Russian province of Novgorod. They were, however, denied their most important right and objective, that of returning to Georgia. Their subsequent requests in this respect were repeatedly turned down on the grounds of it being too dangerous for Russia. Only after the 1917 February Revolution were they able to return (Gurgenidze, 1981, p37).

The Georgian public never forgot Kirion and Ambrosi during their exile. They sent letters and offered them spiritual encouragement. Below is a typical example, sent by Georgian students at Kharkov university to Bishop Kirion and providing evidence of the great esteem that they held for their compatriot:

Your Grace, you are inspired with enormous love for your motherland. Your boundless care for your people is ever seen in your deeds. The prosperity of your dearest motherland is the object of your constant thoughts. You do not even spare your strength for it, and you are ready to sacrifice even your life. You take the pain of your country as your own, its welfare as your own welfare. In all your deeds, your desires and your life as a hermit one could always see your endeavours to console the oppressed and overthrow the oppressors. When after the revolution the oppressed people began to express their ideas freely, your voice became louder and you eagerly joined the movement for freedom. In it you saw an opportunity for rehabilitating the oppressed people, but especially for setting your country free from the hard lot of slavery. When the flames of revolution died away, you, the greatest patron of the Georgians, were made victim of violent reaction . . . We promise you, that the youth of your native land, your younger brothers, will struggle together with you against the common enemy. Defeating it, we shall make our humiliated motherland, our oppressed nation, flourish. Let us hope for the speedy defeat of the enemy so that our oppressed nation can be set free, our Church receive its autocephaly, and you become its first Catholicos-Patriarch (Jvania, 1994, p16).

Despite being in exile and existing under the most difficult conditions, Kirion did not lose spirit but hoped for a better future. This is evident from one of his letters sent to Georgia: "Do not forget the autocephaly. Such questions are not solved quickly. We must rise to the opportunity of an advantageous situation" (Jvaridze, 1988, p16).

In 1909 Innokenti Belyaev (1909-1913) was appointed as the new exarch of Georgia. At his first meeting with the Georgian clergy, they acknowledged his appointment and expressed the hope that he would assist in finding a positive solution to the problem confronting the Georgian church. His reply was that he recognised only the integrated Russian church and did not accept the existence of any so-called "Georgian church". Moreover, Innokenti was of the firm conviction that if he restricted the rights of the Georgian clergy (those who had not been exiled) they would abandon their demand for autocephaly. He felt especial animosity towards Bishop Leonide (Vardosanidze, 1987, p7). The new exarch now ordered the Georgian clergy to baptize Georgian children with the names of saints familiar to the Russian church in order to eradicate Georgian national names.

Despite these repressive measures (which, however, lessened after 1911, when Pyotr Stolypin was assassinated in Kiev), a number of

Georgian and Russian intellectuals refused to give up the fight but continued to defend the Georgian language and Church interests, using every possible means. They issued reports to the State Council, published monographs, articles, disseminated magazines, made declarations and so on.

Between 1907 and 1910, Nikolai Durnovo produced a string of influential pamphlets defending the church: *The Fate of the Georgian Church, The Speech of Archpriest I. Vostorgov, The Alleged Decision over the Problem of the Georgian Church, A Historical Essay on the Autocephaly of the Churches of Iveria and Imereti.* In these, Durnovo warned the Russian authorities categorically that Georgia was a country that had fallen under the protection of the Blessed Virgin, that on many occasions the oppressed church had been defended by world Christianity, and that none of their "perfidious actions" could destroy it.

In *The Georgian Church from its Beginnings to the Present Time* (written in French and published in Rome in 1910) the Georgian Roman Catholic historian Mikheil Tamarashvili made a key attempt to draw the attention of the European public to the problems endured by Georgia. In addition, *Klde* ("*The Rock*"), a strongly nationalist periodical, was also launched. Its editors paid particular attention to issues such as the history of Georgia, the restoration of autocephaly and returning unfairly punished clergymen to Georgia.

On March 6, 1910, Karlo Chkheidze, a leader of the Social Democratic faction and a Georgian deputy, delivered a speech to the third Russian State Council. To those gathered at the assembly, he boldly stressed the importance of teaching Georgian in Georgian schools:

> The Georgian language is neither dangerous to the integrity of Orthodoxy and the state system nor to Russia. You must know, gentlemen, that Georgian is a language in which the New Testament was translated as far back as in the 4th century — at a time when the forefathers of the present "monsieur nationalists" were roaming the forests! (Saitidze, 1999, p26)

Imbued with the same sentiments was the speech of Evgeni Gegechkori, another Georgian deputy, made at the State Council on March 6, 1912. He pointed out that the ancient Orthodox Church of Georgia had for a century received nothing but insults, oppression and violence from the Russian Orthodox Church, and that the Russian government had led the Georgian church to the brink of annihilation (Saitidze, 1999, pp 164-167).

Exarch Innokenti died on September 9, 1913 and was replaced by Alex II Molchanov (1913-1914), an individual who has remained in the memory of the Georgians for his response to their aspirations towards autocephaly, which, to use his own words, was "a fabulous hallucination of Georgian intellectuals" (Saitidze, 1990, p9). Alex died on May 22, 1914.

The First World War and the exarchate

It was political expediency that now began to change tsarist attitudes towards the Georgian church. On August 1, 1914, the First World War broke out and, with it, the involvement of Russia. Because Russia needed the support of its own conquered peoples, it appointed as the new exarch Pitirim Oknov (1914-1915), a man who was highly knowledgeable about the history of Georgia and of its church.

The church leader was comparatively lenient with the Georgians and they for their part trusted him. Pitirim spoke a little Georgian, he had travelled over different regions of the country, observed local circumstances, and even tried to improve the financial lot of the clergy. His soft approach resulted in his being sent back to Russia by Viceroy Vorontsov who shortly afterwards was himself replaced by a representative of the ruling Romanov dynasty, Grand Duke Nikolai Nikolaevich (1915-1917).

But Pitirim did not forget imperial state interests either. After the outbreak of the First World War, the exarchate assured the population that Russia had not favoured the conflict but was forced into it by foreign countries, particularly its allies the Ottoman Empire (denounced as "the greatest enemy of Christianity") and Germany together with Austria-Hungary. He also instigated a sacred liturgical service for the victories achieved by the tsar and his army in the field of battle (Pavliashvili, 1995, pp 154-156).

The position of exarch in Georgia turned out to be a good starting point for Pitirim's future career — he benefited from being under the patronage of the priest Grigol Rasputin, the scandalous favourite of the Imperial family. At the end of 1915, Pitirim was suddenly promoted to the post of metropolitan of Petrograd and Ladoga. Platon Rozhdestvenski (1915-1917), who replaced him as exarch, upon learning the true situation of the Georgian church, called it "a total tragedy" and "on the brink of destruction".

But now Russia had made the decision to abolish the Exarchate of Georgia and to join it with the Metropolitan Province of the Caucasus —

this was officially announced by the Synod over-procurator A. Voljin on February 25, 1916 at the Fourth State Council. Henceforth, the words "Church of Georgia" were never to be mentioned again.

The move resulted in violent protest by the Georgians, and a flood of articles and books were printed in protest. Of these, an article by Archpriest Korneli Kekelidze deserves special mention: *The Metropolis of the Caucasus and the Exarchate of Georgia (a Historico-Canonical Observation)*. Platon marched with the Georgian clergy as an expression of his sympathy and support. However, it should be noted that his personal interests also came into conflict under the circumstances, since his position as exarch would have become redundant under the proposed "Metropolitan Province of the Caucasus". At all events, through the joint efforts of Platon and Georgian society the difficulties of the situation were taken into account and the plan was not implemented (Pavliashvili, 2000, p65).

Meanwhile, Russia was gaining nothing from its involvement in the First World War. The low levels of the national economy were nowhere near sufficient to meet the requirements of the war effort — in fact, the rapid disintegration of the Russian economy had already started prior to 1914 and the nation's entry into the conflict precipitated the crisis to even deeper levels.

The government now feared the growing prospect of revolt and, sure enough, in February, 1917 a people's revolution erupted throughout Russia. Tsar Nicholas II abdicated, the reins of government passed into the hands of a temporary government that was ordered to hold general elections for the Constituent Assembly of Russia demanded by the people. On March 3, freedom of conscience and of religious belief was declared, together with a decree on the self-determination of nations.

Against the background of these political upheavals and changes, realistic conditions had finally been created for the restoration of the autocephaly of the Orthodox Church of Georgia.

Restoration of autocephaly and times of trial, 1917-1952

A note on sources

Any study of the most recent history of the Orthodox Church of Georgia is fraught with difficulties owing to the extreme paucity of archival materials for the period 1917 to 1950. During the anti-religious campaigns of the first years of Bolshevik rule, Communist Party and Komsomol activists systematically destroyed religious books and documents both in Tbilisi and in the provinces. Scholars working in this field have therefore had to retrieve documents from widely-scattered holdings.

In the early 1970s an unexplained fire broke out in the patriarchate and destroyed most of its archives. The archives of the eparchies are lost, while the whereabouts of the minutes of the Catholicosate Council are unknown. Although the patriarchal archives are closed, however, the personal archives of the Catholicos-Patriarchs Kirion, Leonide, Ambrosi, Kristepore, Kalistrate and Ephrem, kept in the Institute of Manuscripts in Tbilisi, can be consulted.

One of Kristepore's manuscripts, dated 1926, that has survived carries the title *Bitter Memories of the Most Recent History of Georgia*, and runs to 456 pages. Other personal notes left by Kalistrate were recently published in Tbilisi, in 2001, under the title *From My Memories*. Other perceptions can be gained from the personal files of former Bishop Gaioz Keratashvili, who was defrocked and arrested by the authorities. The records of the Communist Party are now kept in the Central State Archive. In addition to official documentation, family collections as well as personal documentation were used in researching the following chapters.

Restoration of autocephaly

The revolutionary political changes taking place in Russia offered new hope to those who supported the restoration of autocephaly.

Restoration of autocephaly

On March 8, 1917, a secret meeting was held at the monastery of St Darya (today of the Transfiguration) in Tbilisi to prepare the ground. This was attended not only by church representatives but also by political figures who had a vested interest in an independent Georgian church. Besides Bishop Anton Giorgadze and Archpriest Nikita Talakvadze, Noe Zhordania, Alexander Lomtatidze and Ipolite Vartagava were also present.

Zhordania urged the church to take advantage of the current precarious situation of the Russian empire and to declare the autocephaly of the Georgian church without delay. The participants agreed to draft a statement to be read at a ceremony at Svetitskhoveli cathedral in Mtskheta; they sent telegrams to all the provinces inviting priests to attend a "special service" at the cathedral on March 12 for the "preservation of peace in the country". Many, realising that something extraordinary was about to happen, travelled to the ancient Iberian capital.

An enormous crowd gathered on March 12/25, 1917 in the cathedral. At noon, Leonide, then bishop of Guria-Odishi, surrounded by other concelebrating hierarchs, ascended the pulpit and read out the following declaration:

> As from March 12/25, 1917 the autocephaly of the Church of Georgia is restored; Leonide, Bishop of Guria-Odishi is appointed temporary administrator of the Church until such time as the election of a Patriarch-Catholicos takes place; a Provisional Executive Committee comprising both ecclesiastical and secular figures will supervise the Georgian church.

The people reacted to this news with great rejoicing. Bishop Kirion, who at the time was exiled in Vitebsk, welcomed the action warmly with these words:

> Congratulations on the autocephaly. Shackles have been removed from the Church of Iberia. Our national sanctuary had been enslaved and Georgians were treated as uncouth people. Slavery caused many tears and much suffering but now we shed tears of joy. Long live our free Church in our liberated country!

The day following the celebration, Leonide, on behalf of the Provisional Executive Committee, went to the former viceroy's palace. There he met B. Khatisov, representative of the chairman of the Extraordinary Transcaucasian Committee, and handed him a copy of the Act of

Autocephaly. The reaction of the latter's committee, and also of the interim government in Russia, was clearly negative.

On March 14, the members of the Executive Committee went to the former exarch of Georgia, Platon Rozhdestvenski, with the intention of informing him that, by virtue of the act, he had to relinquish his post. The exarch listened to them carefully before informing the Georgian hierarchs that he would wire the Holy Synod in St Petersburg about developments in Georgia and act in accordance with any instructions he might receive. At the same time, he warned the delegation that it would not serve the interests of the Georgian church to expel him forcefully and reminded them that he could count on the support of the Russian government and army. Unsurprisingly, both the ecclesiastical and secular authorities in Russia sought to boycott the restoration of autocephaly.

The question of autocephaly for the Orthodox Church of Georgia was on the agenda of the Local Council of the Russian Orthodox Church from the very beginning. However, various factors delayed the convening of the local council, including the diligent preparation of the lengthy list of matters to be debated. As it turned out, the council only commenced on the Feast of Dormition of the Mother of God, August 15, 1917, by which time the Orthodox Church of Georgia had already re-proclaimed its autocephaly and elected a new catholicos-patriarch as its primate.

From this point on, the focus had changed for the Local Council. Now the question was: how would the Russian Orthodox Church react to a newly emerged autocephaly? This was taken seriously by some of the participants; towards the end of the council, on September 7/20, 1918, Metropolitan Arseni (Stadnitski) reported:

Although the Supreme Church Council has received a report about the ecclesiastical regions, the matter has not been studied well enough and the council is unable to make a decision concerning the Caucasian metropolis/metropolitan regions. In my opinion, the issue of the autocephaly of Georgia as well as the address of His Holiness the Patriarch Tikhon, which differs from the aforementioned report, is important and has a great significance for the Russian Orthodox Church. Therefore, no decisions or resolutions should be made by the council without careful preparation (The Holy Council, 2000, 1/III, p371).

The interim government in Russia sent an official telegram congratulating the Georgian church on the restoration of its autocephaly but indicated that Russia understood this autocephaly not to be "territorial" but rather "ethnic". In other words, the patriarchate of Georgia would not oversee all of Georgia but only those parishes of Georgian Christians within its territory. The catholicos-patriarch would be in charge of these Georgians but the Russian exarch would retain jurisdiction over all non-Georgian Orthodox Christians within Georgia as well as the rest of the Caucasus. Accordingly, Rozhdestvenski was declared metropolitan of Tbilisi and exarch of the Caucasus. To affirm his authority, he made attempts to create division among the Georgian clergy, refused to leave his palace, and authorised the convening of several meetings against the authority of the Georgians.

At its meeting of March 29, 1917, the Provisional Executive Committee of the Autocephalous Church of Georgia issued an official protest against the position of the Russian ecclesiastical and secular authorities, making it clear that the Georgian nation would never agree to the notion of an ethnic autocephaly. There was no basis for such "national autocephaly" in its tradition and, historically speaking, the autocephaly of the Georgian church had always been territorial. To impose this kind of autocephaly would inevitably lead to religious and ethnic conflict.

To settle the dispute, the interim government of Russia sent Vladimir Beneshevich, an academic from St Petersburg university, to Georgia. There he met with representatives of the clergy, Fr Korneli Kedkelidze and Archpriest Nikita Talakvadze, and two specialists in Georgian history, Ivane Javakhishvili and Zurab Avalishvili. The Georgians attempted — but failed — to convince Beneshevich, on the basis of historical documents and the canons of the Orthodox Church, that there was no other choice except to recognize the territorial autocephaly of the Church of Georgia.

Delegated by the Provisional Executive Committee, Bishop Anton Giorgadze, Archimandrite Ambrosi Khelaia and Archpriest Kalistrate went to St Petersburg to hold talks with both the interim government and the Holy Synod. They were supported by secular leaders including Professor Zurab Avalishvili and the Social-Democrats Karlo Chkheidze and Erekle Tsereteli. Chkheidze held authority in the interim government and, although an atheist, he actively defended the position of the Church of Georgia. He firmly rejected the idea of national autocephaly and demanded that the Patriarch of Georgia should have his seat in Tbilisi where the Russian exarch was now residing:

> The Patriarchate of Georgia should have its see in Tbilisi. And what has a foreign language to do in the cathedral of Sioni? Is it not a matter of

concern to the Church of Georgia whether the highest dignitary of Tbilisi is called "Tbileli" [i.e. "of/from Tbilisi"] or by some other name?

Discussions in St Petersburg took place between June 18 and August 2. The delegation met with Lvov, the over-procurator of the Russian Synod, Kartashev, the minister for religious affairs, and Kerenski, the head of the Provisional Government of Russia (formed after the abdication of Tsar Nicholas after the 1917 February Revolution). It soon became clear that the Russian authorities completely concurred with Beneshevich's position — they were not prepared to go beyond the recognition of a "national" or "ethnic" autocephaly.

The Kerenski government also issued the following guidelines on the administration of the Georgian church:

1. Provisional rules on the status of the Church of Georgia within the Russian empire should be developed.
2. A special commission should be formed by the government to implement this task; this commission would decide which responsibilities shall be transferred from the exarchate to the catholicosate.
3. The over-procurator of the Synod would have the same authority with regard to the Church of Georgia as that held over the exarchate (*Svetitskhoveli*, 1917, p3).

The Provisional Executive Committee of the Church protested once more about these guidelines and issued a statement that it would not obey them. On August 13, 1917, the decision was taken to restore the Eparchy of Tbilisi and both a date and an agenda for the first council were set. Exarch Platon left Tbilisi on August 23 and the Provisional Executive Committee, led by Leonide, the locum tenens of the patriarchal throne, moved into the palace.

The first church assembly, September 1917

More than 430 delegates participated in the First Council of the Church of Georgia, held in Mtskheta from September 8 to 17, 1917. On the final day, the assembly elected a catholicos-patriarch. Of the two candidates proposed, Bishop Leonide and Bishop Kirion, the assembly chose the latter, the respected churchman and historian Kirion Sadzaglishvili. The official title was conferred of "His Holiness and Beatutude Kirion II, Catholicos-Patriarch of All Georgia", and his enthronement as catholicos took place on October 1 in Svetitskhoveli cathedral.

Restoration of autocephaly

The assembly engaged in lengthy discussions on the future structure of the Georgian church. It decided to establish thirteen eparchies and to adopt highly democratic rules for ecclesial administration. The highest authority of the Church was the Church Assembly, while between assemblies the Council of the Catholicosate, comprising twelve members and chaired by the catholicos-patriarch, would maintain control.

Kirion II (1917-18)

In addition to the patriarch, the council included two bishops, three archpriests and six laypersons, among whom also were women members. While clergy members of the council changed every three months, new laypersons were elected every six months. Prominent figures such as Ekvtime Takaishvili, Ivane Javakhishvili, Mose Janashvili and Pavle Ingorokva spent time serving on the council.

For decisions to be valid, at least eight members needed to be in attendance. The catholicos-patriarch, who had two votes, was also the chairman of the Catholicos Court, which consisted of canon law specialists and dealt with the Church's legal issues. Eparchial councils and courts, chaired by the hierarchs of each eparchy, were set up to deal with issues affecting the local churches.

Immediately after the restoration of autocephaly, the Orthodox Church of Georgia assumed an active role in the political life of the country. The independence of the Church had preceded the independence of the state, which took place on May 28, 1917 with the signing of the Act of Independence. The Council of the Catholicosate met on the same day and declared its full support for the initiative:

Participants at the First Council of the Church of Georgia, September 8-17, 1917

Restoration of autocephaly

To mark the Declaration of Independence of the Republic of Georgia, the clergy, led by His Holiness the Catholicos-Patriarch and Metropolitan of Tbilisi, will conduct a litany proceeding from the Sioni and Kashueti churches to Liberty Square, where a Service of Supplication will be celebrated (*Svetitskhoveli*, 1, 1917, p3).

From that day forward, Independence Day has been remembered every year by the Church of Georgia. Patriarch Kirion II also appealed to the members of the new National Assembly with the following words:

> You, the elects of Iberia, have the task to save the motherland from peril, to establish harmony in its midst and create fraternity, peace, decency and happiness among its members (Archives of the Girogi Leonidze State Museum, no. 207838).

Kirion II also participated in the opening ceremonies of the University of Tbilisi on January 28, 1918.

International recognition of autocephaly

One of the most pressing concerns now facing the Orthodox Church of Georgia was to ensure that its autocephaly was recognised by its sister Orthodox churches as well as by some non-Orthodox churches. Soon after his election, Kirion sent official messages to the Ecumenical Patriarch of Constantinople, the Pope in Rome and the Catholicos of All Armenians expressing the hope that the centuries-old relationship that had connected the Orthodox Church of Georgia with the Christian world would be restored and deepened.

The only reply was the one from the Armenian Church. Silence on the part of the others was due, to a large extent, to prevailing attitudes over the destiny of the Russian Orthodox Church where far-reaching changes had taken place. Shortly before the October Revolution, for example, the Moscow patriarchate had been restored and a council had been convened to engage in debates about the renewal of the church. The revolution, however, had ushered in an entirely unprecedented situation where Tikhon, the newly-elected patriarch, had to face a government fundamentally hostile to religion. In his eyes, the declaration of Georgian autocephaly was a further sign of disintegration: for him empire and church formed an indivisible whole.

Thus it was, on December 29, 1917, that he dispatched a curt letter to Catholicos Kirion and the bishops of the Georgian church demanding an apology and their complete submission to the Church of Russia. Clearly, this was contrary to Tikhon's usual style.

For Kirion and the Georgian church the Russian's appeal was unacceptable. Accepting his terms would have meant sacrificing autocephaly and, for the hierarchs, the Georgians' absolute alignment to the authority of the Russian Orthodox Church. But Kirion was never able to react officially. On June 17, 1918, he was murdered under mysterious circumstances in Martkopi monastery near Tbilisi.

Almost a century later it is still unclear how and why this happened. At about the same time, three individuals close to Kirion also met with tragic deaths: the metropolitan of Kutaisi Bishop Anton Giorgadze, the priest Timote Bakuradze and the monk Miran. These events only added to the mystery of their superior's murder.

A formal answer to Tikhon was sent by Kirion's successor Leonide on August 5/18, 1919. It was firm in substance and conciliatory in tone: "Both the Russian and the Georgian churches should make every effort to avoid conflict in the future." But the Russian Orthodox Church refused to restore eucharistic communion with the Orthodox Church of Georgia and even called on Russians residing in Georgia not to respect the jurisdiction of the new catholicos-patriarch.

Catholicos-Patriarch Leonide, 1918-1921

Several months following the death of Kirion II on November 28, 1918, the Council of the Catholicosate elected Leonide, then metropolitan of Tbilisi, as catholicos-patriarch. The council did not convene an assembly but proceeded on its own authority. A solemn consecration took place in Mtskheta the following year on February 23.

Leonide had to face an increasingly complex state of affairs. The Menshevik-dominated government of the Democratic Republic of Georgia, which had in the meantime come into office, was atheist and committed to putting its convictions into practice. On November 26, 1918, the National Assembly passed a new law, declaring that "the teaching of religion and the position of 'teacher of religion' are hereby abolished in every kind and in each grade of the public and private schools" (Legal Acts of the Georgian Democratic Republic, 1918, p110). The political authorities placed the Orthodox Church of Georgia on an equal footing with all other religions and began expropriating parts of its land holdings.

Catholicos Leonide pleaded with the head of the government, Noe Zhordania, to agree to a compromise:

Restoration of autocephaly

The Georgian government is socialist and has in principle no common ground with the Church. I can accept this as a fact. Let the Church and the socialists remain without reconciliation. Let them for a time go their separate ways. But fairness is called for even in separation. What we demand is a fair separation from the state — nothing more (Archives of the Georgian Patriarchate, no. 6443).

No measures, however, were taken by the government to protect

Leonide

the interests of the Church. In view of the fact that Zhordania played, as we have seen, an active role in the restoration of autocephaly, this may seem surprising. But as head of government he could not intervene in favour of the Orthodox Church or defend its position in society. The National Assembly and the government were convinced that the church should be independent from the state and not enjoy any advantages over and above other religious bodies.

Laws issued during these years make this quite clear. Indeed, the Georgian Constitution, adopted on February 21, 1921, stated that:

. . . Church and State are separate and independent from one another; that none of the religions can claim any privileges; that the State Treasury is forbidden to incur any expenses for religious needs; and that no religious instruction is permitted in schools.

The Bolshevik occupation

When the Red Army attacked Georgia in February 1921, all the Georgian churches held services and prayed for the salvation of the motherland from its enemies. Patriarch Leonide is said to have prayed as follows in Sioni cathedral: "If a sacrifice is needed for the salvation of the country, I am prepared to give up my life." Donations for the war effort were collected. As the Bolshevik troops approached Tbilisi, the Council of the Catholicosate decided to evacuate its most precious pieces from the Church Treasury to Kutaisi under the supervision of Bishop David Kachakhidze and Archimandrite Pavle Japaridze.

On February 25, 1921, the Bolsheviks entered Tbilisi and the capital turned into a scene of intense panic. Without delay, the occupying forces declared the Bolsheviks' Revolutionary Committee to be the highest authority in the country. On April 15, 1921 the same committee decided, with regard to the Georgian church, that "ecclesiastical and confessional associations have no right to property. They are not to be considered as legal entities. All property, at present in the hands of ecclesiastical and confessional associations, is transferred to the state" (Chronological Collection, 1955). In line with this decree, the patriarchate of Georgia was deprived of its only car. Increasingly, the church began to experience oppression once more. And then, as a consequence of the war, an epidemic broke out in Tbilisi and many died as a result. Among their number was Patriarch Leonide — he was buried in Sioni cathedral where the remains of Kirion II had also been laid to rest.

The memory of these two first patriarchs will be always honoured for their role in restoring the identity of the Church of Georgia for the benefit of the nation. Despite the enmity of the Provisional Government of Russia and the indifference of the new Georgian government, they succeeded in reviving the historical role of the Church among the Georgian people.

Catholicos-Patriarch Ambrosi (1921-1927)

Viewed as a symbol of Georgian ethnic identity, an autocephalous church was utterly unacceptable to the new rulers. The Bolsheviks therefore decided to replace Leonide with someone willing to collaborate with the expectations of both ecclesiastical and political circles.

The Council of the Catholicosate opted for Bishop Ambrosi Khelaia, metropolitan of Tskhum-Apkhazeti, who in due course was elected as primate by the Third Church Assembly held in Gelati from September 1-5, 1921. At the same time the assembly appealed to the political regime to recognise the Orthodox Church of Georgia as a legal entity. Rejection of this request, the assembly argued, would infer that the church had been reduced to the status of an oppressed religion. The assembly moved to condemn the attitude of the administrative bodies of the Soviet authorities and criticised Christians by declaring that, under such circumstances of oppression, the interests of the church could only be protected by discipline, holiness and unity.

The Orthodox Church of Georgia constituted, then, a force to be reckoned with. There numbered at that time 1,450 active churches and 25 monasteries; at least 1,600 clerics were involved in celebrating the divine services. Moreover, some of the faithful were calling for church reform — not of its doctrines, but for the modernisation of its organisation and traditions to contemporary life. The current political climate hardly allowed for serious debate on the subject; clearly the Council of the Catholicosate and the new catholicos-patriarch had other preoccupations, and their voices were especially raised over the protection of the people's national interests.

Ambrosi

The Bolshevik authorities were openly anti-Georgian. Every group except for the ethnic Georgians were satisfied as the country was divided into small administrative entities and the Autonomous Republics of Abkhazia and Ajara were established. Sections of Georgia became part either of Armenia, Azerbaijan or Russia. The future and integrity of the country were at stake.

Ambrosi's appeal in Genoa, 1922

The international peace conference in Genoa in April 1922 (see page 88) provided Patriarch Ambrosi with an opportunity to make the voice of Georgia and the Georgian church heard. This conference, convened to deal with reparation claims arising from the First World War, was attended by representatives from 28 European states, Japan and the

British Dominions. For the Soviet Union the matter of its recognition by the international community was at stake.

The patriarch succeeded in directing an open letter to the conference. It was carried by Dean Iason Kapanadze who subsequently chose to stay abroad and did not return to his homeland. In his letter, the patriarch urged the nations represented in Genoa to support Georgia and not to leave his country at the mercy of the Soviet Union:

> The occupiers seek to convince everybody at home and abroad that they have brought freedom to the Georgians and have made them happy. But I, as the spiritual father of the nation and as a priest, am aware of the secret threads coming from the heart of this nation and, hearing its moaning and lamentations, I know better than others just how "happy" the Georgian nation is (Central Historical Archives, 1955, no. 516).

He added that the social and political measures introduced by the Bolsheviks under the banner of socialism were bound to lead to moral degradation and, finally, to the nation's extinction.

The appeal had considerable impact at the conference. Chicherin, the Soviet Union's commissar of foreign affairs, who had been authorised by the Georgian Revolutionary Committee to speak on its behalf, was put in an embarrassing situation.

Persecution and arrests

The response by the occupying authorities to the open letter was harsh: anti-religious measures were immediately intensified. On June 13, 1922 the patriarch was taken for questioning before Kote Tsintsadze, chairman of the Extraordinary Transcaucasian Committee. He was accused of "instigating counter-revolutionary activities and attempting to deceive the government". The press was full of attacks against the Orthodox Church in general and against particular individual leaders.

A secret order was then given on June 2, 1923 to confiscate the patriarchal palace. The patriarch was literally thrown out onto the street. By way of response, Ambrosi, in a letter addressed to Pilipe Makharadze, head of the near-criminal Bolshevik government in Georgia, declared:

> My eviction from my apartments, the attacks on the Church, and the removal of the Church Chancellery will inevitably cause discontent among the Georgian people. I, as the father and spiritual leader of the Georgian nation, and you, the chairman of the government in the Republic of

Georgia, should avoid such conflicts. The nation is far bigger than you or I (Archives of the Georgian Patriarchate, no. 539).

Nevertheless, the anti-religious campaign continued with greater fury. Throughout 1923 the gradual dissolution of ecclesiastical life accelerated to the degree that more than 600 church buildings and monasteries were closed down. The authorities were eager to seize the precious gold and silver icons, chalices and processional crosses in order to sell them off.

On November 23, 1923, a meeting of the people's commissars of the Georgian republic adopted a resolution concerning the sale of church property — an act that resulted in widespread protest. A representative group of Georgia's intelligentsia, including such names as I. Javakhishvili, S. Kakabadze, G. Bochoridze, G. Chubinashvili, K. Kekelidze and D. Shevardnadze, formed a Committee for the Protection of Georgian Antiquities. They succeeded in saving many treasures of historical significance and placed them in the country's museums and libraries. Unfortunately, they failed to save the catholicos-patriarch's precious mitres, pectoral crosses and chalices that had been hidden in the residence of Metropolitan Nazar of Kutaisi. When the Bolshevik leadership of Kutaisi discovered their whereabouts, they were confiscated and melted down.

On January 11, 1923, Ambrosi was again ordered to appear for questioning before the Extraordinary Transcaucasian Committee. Before obeying the summons, the patriarch convened an extraordinary meeting of the Council of the Catholicosate and proposed that, in the event of his arrest Bishop Kristepore Tsitskishvili of Urbnisi be entrusted with the administration of the church.

The decision proved to be farsighted. Just one day later, all of the following church leaders were arrested: Patriarch Ambrosi, Metropolitan Nazar of Kutaisi, Frs Kalistrate Tsintsadze and Dimitri Lazarishvili (two archpriests at the Kashueti Church in Tbilisi), Fr Ioseb Mirianashvili (priest at Didube church), Fr Pavle Japaridze (priest at Svetitskhoveli cathedral), Fr Anton Totibadze (priest at Vere church) and Fr Markoz Tkemaladze (priest at the Sioni church). In addition, two members of the Council of the Catholicosate — Nikoloz Arjevanidze and Nikoloz Tavdgiridze — were taken into custody. The Church of Georgia now found itself in a highly dangerous position.

Even harsher anti-religious measures were carried out in the provinces. For example, on February 9, 1923, the public court in the town of Oni declared religion to be an "enemy" of the people. In Kutaisi, a somewhat baffling initiative was taken by V. Bakhtadze, head of the Communist Party. The relics of Ss David and Konstantine (canonised in the 8th century) were removed from the church at Motsameta and, in order to legitimise this action, a public court hearing was organised to demote the saints. In the Senaki district of Western Georgia all the churches were closed.

The Soviet authorities made every possible attempt to denigrate the incarcerated hierarchs, such as recruiting clergy who were willing to denounce their superiors. The very existence of opposition to Bolshevik ideology deemed by the Bolsheviks to be evidence of the church's moral decay. While the patriarch and members of the Catholicosate Council were held in Tbilisi's Metekhi prison awaiting the verdict of the Bolshevik court, some of their "colleagues", seeking to please the authorities, openly condemned them — singling out the patriarch for his unyielding stance — demanding that they recant his offences. But Ambrosi and his council, defenders of Georgia's national and religious freedom, stood firm and refused to collaborate with the occupying powers.

From March 10-19, 1924, the Bolshevik government organised a show trial at the Nazdaladevi theatre in Tbilisi. Patriarch Ambrosi and his fellow council members were accused of treason. To accompany the event, the press published predictably slanted articles with titles such as "The Evil Deeds of the Holy Fathers" and "Evil Counter-Revolution". Allegedly "on behalf of the Georgian people", individuals with clearly Russian names such as Orzumelov, Okoyev and Varlamov swore that Ambrosi and the Council of the Church had no right to address the Genoa Conference in the name of the Georgian people.

The catholicos-patriarch responded to these accusations with an impassioned speech:

I do not understand why I should be accused of an act whose purpose was to protect the Church and the nation and to raise my voice in condemnation of an ideology of power . . . I have simply fulfilled my duty. Any punishment by this court will be sweet; it will crown the cross which I have taken and borne throughout 37 years of my life. The voice I raised in protection of our national interests and the verdict of your court will find a place in the hearts of all Georgians who have not yet lost their religion and love of the motherland. As a believer, I will consider myself happy even with your verdict and say: "Let it be according to God's will!" (*Mnatobi*, 1988, p10)

Restoration of autocephaly

Dean Kalistrate Tsintsadze, himself destined to be patriarch, declared:

> Though I esteem and respect the authorities, I declare that I cannot and will not fulfil the laws issued by them. I beg you to dispense me from obeying them. If the government accepts my request, all will be good, if not, I prepare myself for crucifixion (*Mnatobi*, 1988, p10).

The Georgian version of Patriarch Ambrosi's letter to the Genoa Conference was later to be found in the archives of the Extraordinary Transcaucasian Committee. It carried several interesting notes: "Top secret", "Acquaint leading comrades with the content of this letter", "Discuss this letter", "Compare the handwriting of the catholicos and the manuscript", "Act in accordance with Soviet legislation".

The Bolshevik court passed severe sentences on charges that included composing the Genoa letter and resisting the transfer of Church possessions to the state authorities. Patriarch Ambrosi was given seven years' imprisonment, Iason Kapanadze nine years, Archpriest Kalistrate Tsintsadze and Nikoloz Tavdgiridze three years each, while Ioseb Mirianashvili and Markoz Tkemeladze received nine months apiece.

Despite the government's campaign of insinuation and slander, these men became symbols of the Georgian nation's struggle for independence. In recognition of his merits, Patriarch Ambrosi was canonized by an expanded Church Assembly, convened by His Holiness Ilia II in Mtskheta, in September 1995. March 16/29 was set as his day of commemoration. And so Patriarch Ambrosi entered history as an outstanding hierarch. The witness that he and his companions rendered contributed decisively to the survival of the Orthodox Church in the heart of the Georgian people.

On the basis of the earlier decision by the Council of the Catholicosate, Kristepore Tsitskishvili, bishop of Urbnisi, provided temporary leadership for the Church.

Resistance against the Bolsheviks

The Georgian people, unable to reconcile themselves with the Bolshevik regime, engaged in active resistance. In the spring of 1922, a Committee of Independence, representing every anti-Bolshevik political authority, was secretly launched. A clandestine military centre of command was also set up to prepare for a revolt against the occupying power and a plan of action was worked out.

A rebellion was intended to have started simultaneously all over

People gathered in Mtskheta for the enthronement of Catholicos-Patriarch Ambrosi (1921)

Georgia, but the Extraordinary Transcaucasian Committee learned of their plans. Nevertheless, in August 1924 insurgents began to instigate action in Chiatura (Western Georgia) and from there the uprising spread all over the country. But the movement was extinguished with bloody reprisals against both secular and religious figures and thousands of Georgians fell victim to the Bolshevik terror. A particularly barbaric incident took place in Kutaisi when Metropolitan Nazar Lezhava, the priests Germane Jajanidze, Ieroteoz Nikoladze, Roman Mchedlize and the deacon Besarion Kukhianidze were arrested and, in a summary trial, were accused of encouraging the anti-Soviet revolt. They were executed by firing squad.

The provisional leadership of the Church of Georgia issued, under the signature of Bishop Kristepore as the Church's temporary head, an appeal to the authorities to stop the persecution. They urged the government to stop closing churches, to stop harassing the clergy for no reason, to put an end to expelling clergy from their apartments, and to reexamine the indictments of imprisoned hierarchs and release them if not found guilty.

The government changed tactics. On March 10, 1925, when the justice ministry issued orders for the release of the imprisoned catholicasate members, the authorities made every effort to extract from them a declaration of repentance. The prisoners refused. Though physically weakened after months in prison, Patriarch Ambrosi celebrated the liturgy in the Sioni cathedral immediately after his release. A huge crowd gathered around him, and he received numerous letters of support very much in the spirit of the following:

> Your Holiness, the Parish Church of St Nicholas is filled with great love towards you. We have been waiting for your release from prison. We wanted to have you with us every day. Live long, our great Master, for the benefit of our nation! (Archives of the Georgian Patriarchate, no. 6581)

Thereafter Patriarch Ambrosi resumed his responsibilities for two more years. But the repressive situation remained as it was.

Recognition of autocephaly

The recognition of the Church's autocephaly continued to preoccupy the ecclesiastical leaders in Georgia but Bolshevik tactics relentlessly confused the issue. In the eyes of the Georgians, the independence of their church was a positive step for them since it reduced the authority of the Russian Orthodox Church. The Russians, on the other hand, categorically refused again to restore eucharistic communion with the Georgian church and even actively made efforts to destabilise its unity.

The synod in Moscow, for example, urged non-Georgian Christians in the Tskhum-Apkhazeti eparchy to defy their local bishop, and even asked the region's Bolshevik leadership to reduce the extent of his jurisdiction. In 1926, the Russian patriarchate sent Metropolitan Pyotr of Baku to Tbilisi with a mandate to gather the Russian Parish in the capital around himself and to subject it to his authority. His mission, however, failed because the Georgian church leaders managed to reject Pyotr's claims over their Church through carefully prepared arguments at every level.

Meanwhile, letters written by Patriarchs Leonide and Ambrosi to the patriarchs of the Eastern Orthodox Church remained unanswered. Clearly, the ecumenical patriarchate of Constantinople was anxious not to hurt the feelings of the Russian Orthodox Church and therefore refused to open relations with the Georgians. A letter by Patriarch Ambrosi addressed to Ecumenical Patriarch Basil III on July 26, 1926 contains the telling remark: "We would not wish to consider that your silence and lack of attention are caused by the fact that the legitimate interests of a small nation should be sacrificed in order to retain friendship with and receive benevolence from a large nation" (Archives of the Georgian Patriarchate, no. 6581). Pertinently, when the ecumenical patriarch convened a pan-Orthodox council in Constantinople in 1926, no invitation was addressed to the Church of Georgia.

Support did come, however, from the United Kingdom. The archbishop of Canterbury and primate of England demonstrated his solidarity with the Georgian church. On April 17, 1926, he wrote to Ambrosi with these words of support: "I am willing to do all I can to help you and others who guide your Church's faith under the present difficult and even dangerous conditions." There was no doubt that the archbishop was fully aware of the desperate situation in occupied Georgia.

Patriarch Kristepore III (1927-1932)

The Soviet authorities now became actively involved in the election of the new patriarch because they wanted the church to elect a leader who would co-operate with the regime. Their choice was Metropolitan Kristepore Tsitskishvili, then metropolitan of Tskhum-Apkhazeti.

Together with Bishop David Katsachidze, Kristepore headed a group of priests and hierarchs who were committed to reforming and modernising the church. A similar movement also existed in Russia — the Obnovlentsy or "Renovationists". Kritsepore's movement was essentially a Georgian version of the Russian group, and both felt that the Orthodox Church needed to adapt itself to modern times. They were openly critical of monastic life and sought to introduce changes in worship, such as reducing the length of church services and modernising the liturgical language. Although certain aspects of the Renovationists' programme had merit and were, in principle, shared by many of the faithful, they fatally undermined their cause by calling for one and all to accept Bolshevik rule, even condemning those hierarchs who felt it their duty to resist the atheist regime. As early as 1922 Kristepore had come out in favour of the Soviet authorities and publicly condemned the memorandum which Ambrosi had sent to the Genoa conference. For his part, he declared himself ready to collaborate with the Soviet authorities.

Kristepore went as far as risking a schism. He and Bishop David convened a council in Kutaisi on December 26 and 27, 1926, where the delegates agreed that the cause of the country's crisis was the anti-communist political stand of the patriarch and his council. Kristepore's council issued a statement addressed to "the Believers of the Georgian church" which was eventually distributed widely as a pamphlet. The national crisis, it stated, had happened for both external and internal reasons. First and foremost stood the church's unreasonable position — for Christians, socialism was a desirable code for society because of its commitment to equality for all human beings.

Upon Ambrosi's release from prison, the leaders of the Renovationist movement attempted to remove him from his post. Backed by the police, they issued an announcement to the Patriarch on March 23, 1927 to the effect that they would take over authority of the Church. Some days later, on March 29, the patriarch had a stroke and died. He was buried in Sioni cathedral.

The Fourth Church Council, held from June 21-27, had on its agenda issues that held great implications for the church's future. The assembly was asked, therefore, to consider the administration of the church; a declaration of understanding to be addressed to the Soviet government that aimed at eliminating conflict; an agreement on ways and means to implement the 1923 resolution of the government concerning the separation of church and state; the election of a new patriarch.

For reasons of convenience, the Council of the Catholicosate, at this

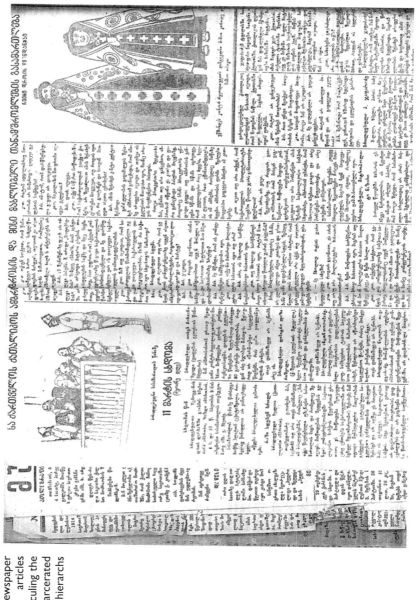

Newspaper
articles
ridiculing the
incarcerated
hierarchs

point the church's managing body, was replaced by the Synod of the Catholicosate under the direct authority of the patriarch. The Fourth Council then issued a statement criticising Ambrosi's attitude towards the Soviet authorities; instead pointing to the irreconcilable differences between the church's message and Soviet ideology, the council declared its full loyalty to the regime and offered to collaborate with it. Having taken these steps, the council then elected Metropolitan Kristepore as catholicos-patriarch.

Georgian Christians abroad

Georgians in the diaspora during this period were at their most numerous in Paris. In the first few years following the Bolshevik invasion, Georgian Christians abroad maintained eucharistic communion with the Mother Church. But after Kristepore was enthroned as catholicos-patriarch, they reacted negatively and saw the decisions of the Council as the beginning of the abolition of the Church "from within". They therefore severed communion.

To serve their spiritual needs, a Georgian parish was established in Paris in 1931. One of its founders, Grigol Peradze, was undoubtedly the most outstanding representative of the Church of Georgia in exile, and in honour of his memory the church canonised him in 1995.

Conflict over the calendar

It was only to be expected that, in contrast to his predecessor Ambrosi, Kristepore would ardently support the introduction of the Gregorian calendar proposed by Ecumenical Patriarch Basil III in 1923. This was an issue that had created a great deal of controversy in Georgia: should the church follow the state, which had adopted the new calendar in 1918?

On November 1, 1923 the Council of the Catholicosate voted in favour of abandoning the old Julian calendar. The ecumenical patriarchate's letter was seen as an official contact from abroad and the leadership of the Georgian church was eager to make use of every sign of recognition. The decision had been taken while Patriarch Ambrosi was still held in prison, but the reaction of the people to the innovation was strongly negative. Riots ensued and groups of believers barred access to certain churches in order to prevent the celebration of Christmas on December 25.

The council's decision was, therefore, not implemented at this point and it was not until 1927 that Patriarch Kristepore would move for the new calendar. Faced with stiff opposition, however, especially among the Russian-speaking laity in Georgia, he realised that the issue would cause a schism in the church and withdrew.

Oppression continues

Kristepore's hopes for progress remained unfulfilled. It turned out to be an unrealistic vision that the church would find its place in Soviet society through co-operation. Persecution continued and Kristepore was soon forced to admit that the situation was continuing to deteriorate. At a meeting of the Synod of the Church of Georgia held on May 22-23, 1928, less than a year after his election, he remarked that "the oppression of priests and believers has lately intensified, especially through administrative and physical measures" (Central Archives of Recent Georgian History, no. 284). One means of oppression was heavy taxation, another was the death threats frequently dealt out to priests.

The authorities, well aware of the fact that their anti-religious measures were unpopular and could possibly turn against them, eventually ruled that such acts of oppression were unlawful — their existence was, in fact, due to the actions of overzealous party activists, whereas, officially, the state respected the church. The reality was, of course, that persecution of the church continued to be encouraged by the government and taxation of the clergy grew to such exorbitant levels that, in a letter to the commissar for internal affairs, Kristepore himself had to ask for an exemption:

> I have declared my income for the year 1929-1930. But so many levies have been imposed on me that I am unable to pay the bill. Financial agents have drained my apartments and taken away my belongings in order to sell them . . . Since my income is low and my health very poor, I now request the commissariat of internal affairs for full exemption from taxes. If this cannot be granted, I ask that taxes will be levied in proportion to my real income as Catholicos-Patriarch of All Georgia and a member of the clergy (Central Archives of Recent Georgian History, no. 2100).

If the catholicos-patriarch himself had to face such difficulties, it is not difficult to imagine how desperate the situation was for ordinary members of the clergy.

In 1928 the Bolsheviks launched the Union of the Militant Godless, an association initiated by Stalin and Beria whose central aim was to eliminate religious belief. Speaking at a meeting with a delegation of workers from the United States, Stalin openly explained the Bolshevik position on religion: "The Party cannot remain neutral toward those who spread religious superstitions. Clergymen who poison the conscience of the workers' masses must be suppressed." As head of the Georgian OGPU (Obedinennoe Gosudarstvennoe Politicheskoe Upravlenie, "Combined State Political Directorate" or secret police), Beria held a leading role in the Soviet Union.

The aim of the new organisation was to emancipate each individual from his or her religious conscience, and to this end, the movement engaged in systematic anti-religious propaganda which included the forced attendance of citizens to sessions on atheist indoctrination. Frequently, the union went a step further by condoning anti-religious hysteria where the authorities would break into churches and monasteries and ravage them. The monasteries of Shiomgvime, Betania and Kakheti became scenes of such atrocities: unidentified raiders plundered such places of worship, in the process killing monks — the mere act of wearing a cassock or a cross could become a pretext for martyrdom. And while anti-religious activists were given unlimited freedom, priests had no right to even preach. Through official sanction, more than 600 churches were closed.

Protests and appeals from the Synod fell on deaf ears — its plea to put an end to the illegal moves was a cry in the wilderness. Any Georgian who identified with the church and defended its role in society fell victim to the terror of those dark years. Young people were nurtured in Bolshevik ideology and, as a consequence, Christianity ceased to hold a place in their lives. Moreover, anti-religious propaganda succeeded in creating an image of clergymen as counter-revolutionaries and dangerous relics of the past. And so the 1920s and 1930s came to be the most difficult decades in the entire history of the Orthodox Church of Georgia.

Catholicos-Patriarch Kalistrate (1932-1952)

After Patriarch Kristepore died on June 10, 1932, the hopes of the people turned to Kalistrate Tsintsadze, metropolitan of Manglisi. He was neither the natural choice of the Soviet authorities nor of the minority of clergy who pushed for collaboration with the state. Kalistrate did not toe Kristepore's line: he had been close to Ambrosi and had also been sentenced to three years' imprisonment for his views. Reformers within the Church had put forward as their new head the name of David Kachakhidze, bishop of Kutaisi, but the state authorities wanted someone with a certain degree of acceptance within the entire church. Kalistrate had an added advantage: he had been a fellow student of Stalin's at the Tbilisi seminary. The Sixth Church Assembly therefore elected Kalistrate as catholicos-patriarch on June 21, 1932 — and three days later he was consecrated at Svetitskhoveli cathedral.

Kalistrate faced a depressing situation. The majority of churches had been closed and out of the fifteen eparchies less than half continued to function. The clergy was divided. Although there was outright opposition in several circles to the patriarch, Kalistrate could count on the support of many others in other parts of Georgian society, where expectations were high. Characteristic in this respect was the welcome from Mariam Jambakur-Orbeliani, a prominent Georgian public figure and philanthropist, who declared: "Your Holiness, I join with pleasure and share the common joy of the sons of Georgia. I am happy that our Church has been given a leader of high merits and deserving of respect!"

Kalistrate began by concentrating his efforts on four main areas that often conflicted each other. He sought to stop the closure, destruction and theft of churches and monasteries, while attempting to maintain a loyal stance to the Soviet authorities. He also called for the alleviation of the stifling taxes imposed by the state, yet at the same time he continued to promote recognition of the autocephaly of the Orthodox Church of Georgia by the other Orthodox churches around the world.

It proved near impossible to achieve any these goals. The Soviets' campaign against religion continued unabated. In 1930 a University of the Union of Militant Godless and an Anti-Religious Museum were opened in Tbilisi. Members of the clergy were attacked in newspapers and magazines with titles such as *The Godless*, *The Militant Godless* and *The Militant Atheist*. According to its own reports the anti-religious State Security Committee held 25,624 lectures and seminars in the towns and villages of Georgia during the period 1932 to 1939. Members of the organisation secretly monitored religious services in the hope of discovering the churches' "real" income and so raise its taxes.

The arrests and killings of priests and monks continued. In October 1932, Kipriane and Ilarion, two monks from the monastery of Shiomgvime, were murdered while, in 1937, Metropolitan Varlaam (Makharadze) of Kutaisi and Gelati and Bishop Ephrem (Sidamonidze) of Urbnisi were arrested and exiled. From time to time the patriarch issued protests, such as his strongly worded letter, written in 1937 to the chairman of the Central Executive Committee of Georgia. In it, he referred to the desperate situation of the church at Anaga, a village in Sighnaghi district:

> In spite of the fact that the church has paid outright the full amount of tax imposed on it, the local authorities have placed all manner of obstacles in the path of the believers. At Easter, for example, the faithful were evicted from the church building. Please take measures to halt such actions (K. Kekelidze Institute).

Taxes imposed by the authorities constituted an intolerable burden. In 1939, Sioni cathedral faced the threat of closure and, in a bid to avoid the worst, Kalistrate sent a telegram directly to Beria, now head of the USSR's secret police, and Politburo member Mikhail Kalinin in Moscow. The documents that survive from this period, however, show that ordinary party members did not take the head of the Orthodox Church of Georgia seriously. On one particular occasion, the patriarch wanted to meet with the secretary of the Supreme Council of Georgia, Mirianashvili. The rendezvous proved to be a humiliating experience for Kalistrate: "I appeared at two o'clock but Mirianashvili did not meet me in person. He sent a secretary to inform me that the chairman had decided to refuse my request" (K. Kekelidze Institute).

At the turn of the year 1940/41, religious services in Sioni cathedral were discontinued. With pain in his heart, Kalistrate wrote to the secretary of the Central Committee of the Georgian Communist Party, Kandid Charkviani: "Hierarchs have been forced to stop celebrating the liturgy in Sioni, the only functioning cathedral, because it is poor and unable to meet the excessive demands of taxation."

There were some victories, small as they may have been. The Kashueti St George church in Tbilisi faced demolition: the initial intention was to build a bath house in its courtyard but the decision came later to demolish it entirely since, as it was built in the early 20th century, it had "no historical value". In the eyes of the faithful, however, the site meant a great deal. In the 6th century a monastery had been founded there by David, one of the Syriac Fathers. Kalistrate called on Beria, secretary of the Central Committee of the Communist Party, and urged him to intervene. Indeed, Beria did take measures to save the church. Another threat, this time to the Metekhi church in Tbilisi and to the famous churches in Gelati, Alaverdi and Nikortsminda, was averted by joint action between

Grigol Peradze (1899-1942)

Archimandrite Grigol, canonised by the Georgian church in 1995, was born into a priest's family in Bakutsikhe, Kakheti, and named after St Grigol Khandzteli. In 1922, the Holy Synod of the Orthodox Church of Georgia sent him to the University of Berlin to study theology and Oriental languages.

Realizing soon that he could no longer return to Georgia as a result of the worsening political situation throughout the USSR, he continued his studies in Belgium and Germany. In 1927 he was appointed as a lecturer at Bonn university to teach Old Georgian and Armenian studies. In the same year he attended the first World Conference on Faith and Order in Lausanne and drew attention to the situation of his church in a passionate speech.

In 1931 he took monastic vows and began pastoral activity in the Georgian church of St Nino in Paris, which he had founded. There he also launched the journal *Jvari Vazisa* ("The Vine Cross").

From 1932 he taught theology at Warsaw university. Poland became his second motherland and he remained there until his death in the Oswentzim camp in 1942. According to witnesses, he died in the gas chambers after saving the life of another.

He was an ardent protector of Georgian manuscripts and other church items scattered throughout Europe. He assisted Ekvtime Takaishvili in the task of rescuing some of Georgia's national treasures, comprising medieval church artefacts, which after the Red Army occupation of Georgia had been removed from the country by emigrants.

Among his writings are works on the history of Georgian monasticism, while humility was never far from his thoughts, as he declared in his diaries: "The greatest pain has been to be away from the motherland . . . but we should not make a god out of the motherland."

Kalistrate, the Georgian Committee of Antiquities, and the Georgian intelligentsia.

But additional tax increases after 1939 made the situation of the clergy more precarious than ever. In a message to Charkviani, Kalistrate wrote:

> The unlimited responsibility of the Inspector of the State Committee on Finance will soon lead to the extinction of the 1,600-year-old Church of Georgia. Priests will be forced to discontinue celebrating services . . . So long as Article 124 of the Soviet Constitution is not revoked ["Freedom of religious worship and freedom of anti-religious propaganda is recognized for all citizens"], no campaign should be conducted to suppress and destroy the Church by administrative means. This living remnant of the Georgian nation's ancient culture should not be wiped from the face of the earth (K. Kekelidze Institute).

In early June 1941, Svetitskhoveli cathedral was closed because it was unable to pay the taxes imposed by the state administration.

The Soviets' primary target was the Orthodox Church of Georgia since it was the main religious faith in the country, but other groups hardly fared better. German Evangelicals, Baptists, Pentecostals and Molokans went through hard times, and anti-religious measures were directed also against the Islamic communities, especially in Samtskhe-Javakheti and Ajara — whether of Georgian or Turkish origin, Muslims were considered to be untrustworthy especially during wartime. Many were consequently deported to Central Asia. By November 15, 1944, 15,574 Muslim families or 69,869 persons (59,780 Turks, 8,627 Kurds, and 1,462 Hemshins (Muslim Armenians) had been exiled. In the same period around 3,000 Lezgins and Muslims Abkhazians were also deported.

The Second World War

With the outbreak of the Second World War in 1939, a new set of circumstances arose to affect every religion. Under the threat of German invasion, the Soviet Union needed to unite its entire population in the fight against fascism. To help in this, Stalin recognised that he needed the various faiths, which, for their part, realised that they indeed had a role to play in society. Religious leaders assured the Soviet regime of the full support of their flocks in the defence of the motherland.

Reactions were similar both in Russia and in Georgia. Immediately after Germany attacked the Soviet Union on June 24, 1941, Patriarch

Kalistrate wrote to the Soviet government expressing the church's commitment to the patriotic cause. His letter was published in the Soviet press — both in Georgia and in the rest of the Soviet Union. The patriarch organised a collection in support of the Red Army which raised 2,000 roubles. In his reply of December 1941, Stalin asked Kalistrate to convey his greetings and thanks to the priests and believers for their contributions. The patriarch's letter was indeed of great importance for the future of the Church of Georgia. Kalistrate had correctly assessed the situation: there was a new role for the churches within the Soviet system. Expressing official support for the regime on behalf of the faithful, he at the same time made attempts to improve the legal standing of the Georgian church.

Although it is frequently reported that they first met at this crucial time in the Kremlin, this is not the case. Stalin and Kalistrate had known each other in the past — in their younger years they had spent time together at the Tbilisi Theological Seminary. There had been an exchange of letters but no meeting. In his letter of July 21, 1948 to the Soviet leader, Kalistrate wrote:

> The chosen one amongst all people, the greatest Georgian! It has always been my dream to see with my own eyes the greatest man in the world. Destiny, however, has deprived me of this joy. Perhaps I do not deserve it. Dear Ioseb, receive the sincere thanks of the Georgian church and its leader for the official recognition of our Church (Archives of the Georgian Patriarchate, no. 3998).

Relations with the Russian Orthodox Church

The new attitude of the Soviet Union towards the churches made it possible for the Georgians to resume negotiations with the Russian Orthodox Church. Earlier debates on the recognition of Georgian autocephaly had ended in an impasse. The Moscow patriarchate, refusing to recognise the Church of Georgia as an independent autocephalous church, eventually even terminated eucharistic communion with the Georgians.

But the issue continued to plague the spirit of the Georgian Christians. In a letter written in 1938 to the secular authorities in Georgia, Kalistrate explained in detail the causes of the discord between the two churches. A new point of departure was made possible with the change in church-state relations during the Second World War. The election and enthronement of Patriarch Sergei in Moscow (for years the

Russian Orthodox Church had been prevented from electing Sergei formally as patriarch) on September 14, 1943 gave Kalistrate the chance to re-open the debate. In his official message of congratulations to Sergei on his formal appointment, the Georgian primate expressed his hope that relations between the two churches could be normalised. By way of reply, the Russian patriarch agreed to settle the issue through negotiation.

On October 28, 1943, Archbishop Anton of Stavropol and Pyatigorsk arrived in Tbilisi and entered discussions with the catholicos-patriarch. Three days later, on October 31, 1943, the Russian Orthodox Church officially declared its recognition of the territorial autocephaly of the Orthodox Church of Georgia and restored eucharistic communion. This regularization of relations between the two churches was, without any doubt, due at least in part to Stalin. It seems that, discreetly, he had encouraged the Russian church to make such a move.

In 1946, the patriarch of Moscow, Alexi I, paid an official visit to the now formally autocephalous church and, two years later, when Kalistrate participated in the celebrations of the 500th anniversary of the autocephaly of the Russian Orthodox Church, he was named an honorary member of the Moscow Theological Academy.

A period of limited renewal

There were a great many changes during these years as pressure on the churches diminished in several areas. In Georgia, the authorities restricted the activities of the Union of Militant Godless by closing the anti-religious museum and the anti-religious publishing house. Clearly, the Church was enjoying new breathing space. But the antagonism between state and church persisted. Since religion was incompatible with Soviet ideology, the church had to conduct its activities covertly. Archival sources abound with reports of secret agents being active within the congregations in this period.

On October 8, 1943, the Soviet authorities restructured the relationship that had existed between the state and the religious communities. At both central government and republic level, Committees for Religious Affairs were set up whose purpose was to control the operations of churches and communities throughout the Soviet Union.

In the past religion was treated as if it did not exist, but now the new state organisations provided religious institutions with a "state address". The committees exercised tight control over the churches since one of their tasks was to register every house of worship — whether or nor it was functioning. In principle it became possible to re-open any of the churches that had been closed by the administration in the 1920s and 1930s. To do so required the comparatively simple acquisition of a permit — involving a list of 20 collected signatures to be registered at the local executive bodies — and the submission of a petition to the office of the attorney for religious affairs at the Council of Ministers of Georgia. This council, in turn, would pass these papers on to the Committee for Religious Affairs in Moscow which had the authority to grant permission for the opening of churches in the towns and villages of the republics.

But as soon as these new procedures were set in place, attention was focused on the Russian Orthodox Church to the detriment of the Orthodox Church of Georgia. Kalistrate dispatched a string of messages to Moscow requesting that the current committee delegate for the Russian Orthodox Church should be renamed delegate for the Russian and Georgian Orthodox churches or simply for the Orthodox churches. His intercession was ultimately heeded and, on August 22, 1947, a resolution was passed establishing the post of a representative for the Orthodox Church within the Council of Ministers of Georgia. The official's brief was to co-ordinate between the Georgian state authorities and the Church of Georgia.

On December 1, 1944, the Council of Commissars of the Soviet Union adopted a resolution, entitled "Orthodox Churches and Chapels", that prohibited the closure of registered Orthodox churches. In 1943, however, Georgia possessed only 15 working church buildings and the crucial question now was whether churches closed earlier could be *re-opened*. Kalistrate fought for the restoration of closed churches and monasteries in accordance with the new church laws. Congregations in the districts of Kutaisi, Batumi, Sokhumi, Lagodekhi, Gori, Tianeti and Sighnaghi demanded the re-opening of their ecclesiastical premises. Two years later, 29 churches in the country were once again functioning with a total of five hierarchs, 41 priests, two archdeacons and three chanters.

Having reinstated a dialogue between the secular powers and the Church, Kalistrate then turned his efforts to the protection of clergy rights. The Security Department of Georgia supplied him with a list of around 70 clerics who had been executed and twenty others who had perished in exile. Kalistrate managed to obtain official permissions for the return from exile of Bishop Ephrem, Archpriest Ivan Lozov and Archdeacon Ambrosi Akhobadze. Moreover, two new bishops, Gabriel Chachanidze and Anton Gigineishvili, were ordained. Kalistrate also sought to reclaim objects that had been removed from churches and monasteries — some were now held in state museums. In 1947, he also made an official request the return of the relics of St David and St Konstantine to Motsameta monastery in Kutaisi.

On August 18, 1949, the patriarch made a further attempt to secure a proper residence for himself — and, in time, the authorities agreed to make available a building near Sioni cathedral. Then, from 1941 onwards, the patriarchate was permitted to publish an annual calendar for the church, the church's rules of administration, a guide for Sioni cathedral, and a prayer book.

In return, Kalistrate went out of his way to praise the Soviet authorities. In 1950, for example, he sent a telegram of congratulations on the anniversary of the October Revolution to Stalin and also addressed his good wishes to the local authorities. With hindsight, such steps might be described as sycophancy but at that time there was no other option to obtain concessions for the church — the repression and terrible persecution of the 1920s and 1930s, after all, were still fresh in the minds of the faithful. Patriarch Kalistrate was obliged to play the diplomat in dealing with the state authorities; by voluntarily manifesting loyalty, he hoped to enlarge the manoeuvrable space of the church.

When Kalistrate died on February 3, 1952, it was an immense loss for the church. Spontaneous mourning erupted among his flock and, despite the communist regime's hostile attitudes, the most eminent of Georgia's intelligentsia openly expressed their sympathy by accompanying the patriarch's body at his funeral. The patriarch's death marked the end of one of the most troubled and contradictory periods of the Orthodox Church of Georgia in the 20th century.

Structural and organisational changes

In September 1917, not only was autocephaly restored but the church also underwent a radical re-organisation. To begin with, it was divided into eparchies, the eparchies into districts and the districts into parishes. Historically (i.e. from the 5th to 18th centuries), the number of eparchies had varied in number from 33 to 50 but, with the abolition of autocephaly in the 19th century, the Russian exarchs had worked to reduce this number. By 1811, the Georgian church still had 25 eparchies; after the abolition of autocephaly their number was reduced to three or five. The church order adopted by the Church Assembly in 1917 envisaged 13 eparchies.

In 1918 the titles of "bishop" and "metropolitan archbishop" were introduced and it was decreed that Church Councils would be convened once every three years. Representing the highest ecclesiastical authority, these were chaired by the catholicos-patriarch himself. The Church Council was also responsible for legislation; it acted as the supreme court of the Church and took final decisions on issues submitted by the Council of the Catholicosate. Typically, the issues raised related only to the affairs of the Council and the Court of the Catholicosate and to the determination of eparchial boundaries.

The governing system of the Council of the Catholicosate consisted of twelve members and headed by the catholicos or his deputy, was democratic. Serving hierarchs and clergy held two-monthly terms and meetings were conducted weekly. Decisions, binding for the catholicos-patriarch and for the eparchial hierarchs, were deemed to be valid so long as a minimum of eight council members attended. Laws and resolutions ensued from open debate among council members. The catholicos-patriarch was given two votes. The council also had the task of preparing church assemblies and establishing the agenda; it was also responsible for organizing relations with other Orthodox churches and, more generally, with other Christian churches. There was a chancellery, managing bodies accountable for the finances of the church and of monasteries, and a legal adviser.

The highest authority in the eparchies was the Diocesan Council. Each district sent four representatives to the Eparchial Assembly. The hierarch in charge of the eparchy normally chaired the assembly, though in his absence the plenary was entitled to name another person as chairman. The Eparchial Assembly elected the members of the Diocesan Council and the Eparchial Court. Its responsibility was to supervise Church life, divide eparchies into districts, and to establish educational institutions. The Eparchial Council, chaired by the hierarch of the eparchy, was the executive body of the assembly. Districts were constituted by ten to fifteen parishes and were led by an archpriest. Legal issues were dealt with by the Court of the Catholicosate chaired by the Catholicos-Patriarch. The Eparchial Courts were chaired by the Eparchial Hierarchs.

On July 20, 1920, the second Church Assembly decided to introduce certain amendments to the constitution:

—the eparchies of Mtskheta and Tbilisi were merged;
—following the demand of the eparchial hierarchs, the Diocesan Councils

and the Court of the Catholicosate were abolished;

—the Eparchial Courts continued to function but their authority was reduced;

—in order to strengthen central power, the functions of the Court of the Catholicosate were taken over by the Council of the Catholicosate.

Even more far-reaching changes were made in 1927. On January 21, the Council of the Catholicosate was abolished by the state authorities (it allegedly constituted "a shelter for counter-revolutionary elements") and was first replaced by a Provisional Managing Board. In due course, following the election of Kristepore as catholicos-patriarch, the Synodal Plenum and the Synod of the Catholicosate were established. In 1948, the Synod of the Catholicosate became the Synod of the Catholicos. The representative style of government which, for the church, had hitherto been typical, was now a part of history. These new regulations confirmed the personal rule of the Catholicos-Patriarch of All Georgia.

Until 1921 the eparchies established by the first Church Assembly functioned normally. Some problems occurred in the Tskhum-Apkhazeti eparchy where the Russian Orthodox Church had interfered in the form of an attempt to separate the eparchy from the Georgian church. Particularly after the Bolshevik takeover, local Russian residents gave the authorities to understand that the Orthodox Church of Georgia was anti-Soviet and had expressed the wish to sever its relations with the Russian church. Using his diplomatic skills, Patriarch Kalistrate succeeded in preventing the formation of a religious opposition within the eparchy and did what lay within his power to defend the interests of the diocesan clergy. Later, after the Russian Orthodox Church recognised the autocephaly of the Georgian church, the issue lost its relevance.

The eparchies of the Orthodox Church of Georgia went through especially difficult times in the 1930s. A number were abolished: that of Alaverdi in 1929, of Chkondidi in 1930, those of Ninotsminda and Manglisi in 1932, Batumi-Shemokmedi in 1934, and that of Atskuri in 1935.

As already mentioned, the Second World War marked a turning point in the history of the church. By a decree of April 15, 1921, the Revolutionary Committee had declared the church to be a non-legal entity, i.e. it was deprived of any juridical status and could therefore not own property. It was not until 1943 that its legal status was restored and the state recognized its existence. Although confiscated property was not returned, places of worship registered as "working churches" could no longer be closed down. In his letter to Stalin, Kalistrate explicitly expressed his gratitude for the restoration of the church's legal status. Despite this official recognition, however, the situation of the Church remained a precarious one.

From oppression to rebirth, 1952-2003

Patriarch Melkisedek III

The process of electing a new church leader following the death of Catholicos-Patriarch Kalistrate was also a choice of official church policies. Kalistrate's opinion had been that among the members of the Synod it was Melkisedek (Pkhaladze) who was the best candidate. The Ninth Assembly of the Orthodox Church of Georgia, held on April 5, 1952 in Sioni cathedral, Tbilisi, indeed elected Melkisedek, then metropolitan of Urbnisi, as Catholicos-Patriarch of All Georgia under the name of Melkisedek III. Under his rule, the church continued to follow the course defined by Kalistrate: co-operation with the authorities and maintenance of relations with believers within the framework of Soviet law.

With Stalin's death in March 1953, a process of limited liberalisation emerged in the Soviet Union under its new leader Nikita Khrushchev. Though the system was *de facto* maintained, this liberalisation had consequences for all aspects of life, including that of the churches. While religion continued to be considered an enemy of Soviet ideology, Soviet law nevertheless now recognised freedom of conscience. Emboldened by this, the Georgian church authorities made fresh attempts to regain those sacred items that had been looted from its churches and monasteries during the 1920s and 1930s. The return of the holy remains of Ss David and Konstantine Mkheidze (who had died fighting heroically during the Arab Umayyad invasion headed by Marwan ibn Muhammad in the eighth century) to Motsameta, was an important event in this respect. After the public trial by the Soviets to downgrade the saints' status, the relics had been kept in the local Museum of Natural Sciences. Melkisedek now obtained permission to bring them back to Kutaisi.

In principle, Soviet law permitted the exercise of religious life. It has already been noted, for example, that 20 individuals could ask for a church to be opened for worship. Very often, however, pressure was put on believers to not sign petitions of this kind or else to withdraw a signature already given. Despite such heavy-handed manipulation, religious services were restored at the churches of Motsameta, Bodbe, and Poti as a result of Melkisedek's efforts. Eventually, a new church was built in Khashuri.

The new patriarch promoted choral singing during church services and took measures to rescue the rich tradition of church hymnody from oblivion. In spite of dire financial stringencies faced by the Orthodox Church of Georgia, choristers were remunerated. But when Melkisedek asked the Georgian authorities for permission to publish an official church bulletin, his request was denied.

A pressing concern for the Georgian church was how to provide training for young priests; in 1957 only five of its fifteen eparchies had a senior hierarch, most of whom were of an advanced age. Indeed, over the years, effective anti-religious propaganda and, even more, administrative sanctions had led to a drastic reduction in the number of believers themselves. Signs of religious life were noticeable only on the major religious feast days — and even then authorities sent representatives to inspect churches to identify young people attending services. Schoolchildren were strictly reprimanded at schools if it was discovered that they had attended religious ceremonies while university students were excluded from studies.

Under such conditions it was difficult to remain faithful either to the church or to any religious belief. Melkisedek sent a letter to the Georgian government in which he underlined how testing the conditions of the Orthodox Church were, and he made a number of demands on the government:

> In order to train candidates for the clergy of the Georgian church, we need to arrange for short training courses. For that purpose, we request permission to place advertisements on church walls and to ask interested people to make known their willingness to participate to the person in charge of the courses (Archives of the Georgian Patriarchate, 2001/1).

In his wish to replace the older generation of clergy with a new one, Melkisedek made overtures to younger members of the intelligentsia. Indeed, he offered to ordain to the episcopate Ipolite Vartagava, the well-known literary critic, public figure and graduate of the Kazan Theological Seminary — but the latter refused. And unfortunately for all concerned, Georgian intellectuals, afraid of the authorities, withdrew from the Church during the 1950s and 1960s.

At the same time the church was in no position to sustain relations either with Orthodox or non-Orthodox churches beyond the borders of the Soviet Union, which itself continued to be so closed that it was almost impossible for clergy to visit foreign countries. Delegations from the Orthodox Church of Georgia, however, participated in meetings of religious organisations held within the Soviet Union. In December, 1952, at the Fourth International Peace Conference held in Moscow, the catholicos-patriarch was permitted to make an extended speech.

Catholicos-Patriarch Ephrem II (1960-1972)

Melkisedek III died on January 10, 1960 at the age of 88. It was expected that Metropolitan David (Devdariani) of Urbnisi, the choice of the deceased catholicos-patriarch, would become locum tenens of the patriarchal throne. But the majority of the Georgian clergy felt they had a more appropriate choice in Ephrem (Sidamonidze), metropolitan of Batumi-Shemokmedi and Chkondidi, who was the most senior clergyman. For his part, David reacted in a genuinely Christian manner. Opening the extraordinary meeting of the Holy Synod of the Orthodox Church of Georgia on January 11, he praised Ephrem as one of the most distinguished clerics in the Georgian church and himself proposed that Ephrem should be elected as locum tenens. The majority in the synod supported this.

At the 11th Assembly of the Orthodox Church of Georgia, held on February 19 and 20, 1960, Ephrem was accordingly elected Catholicos-Patriarch of All Georgia under the name of Ephrem II, and on the following day, a Sunday, he was enthroned at Svetitskhoveli cathedral.

Despite the more liberal attitude of the Soviet authorities during the 1960s, conditions continued to be grim for the Georgian church. Soviet political leadership regarded religion as a "harmful antiquated shibboleth" that hindered the "spacious edifice of communism". As a result, anti-religious propaganda was reinforced. In 1960, Khrushchev ordered the closure of more than 10,000 churches and monasteries in Russia and the Ukraine, while in Georgia, out of 1,550 religious buildings in 1921, only 48 churches and 80 clergy now remained.

However, a somewhat atypical event, that went unreported, occurred at this time. When the Glinski monastery, in the Sumy district of Ukraine, was closed down, the Orthodox Church of Georgia, supported by Vasil Mzhavanadze, First Secretary of the Georgian Communist

Party, gave shelter to twenty of its monks, offering them hospitality at Tbilisi's Alexander Nevsky monastery.

But during this period most of the Georgian church's eparchies existed in name only. Clergymen of the older generation were few, while there was no new generation to speak of. The speech made by the new catholicos-patriarch Ephrem II, at the funeral of the highly respected hierarch David Garsiashvili, soberly alluded to this:

> Here we are, all of us aged people about to leave this world, but there is no one to replace us . . . Why is the Georgian nation avoiding its Mother Church, treating it with reproaches? Has it not been of service to the motherland and to the nation? (Archives of the Georgian Patriarchate, no. 876)

By the 1960s the situation had improved with a total of seven hierarchs, one of them a metropolitan. The patriarchate had jurisdiction over eight parishes, one hundred active churches with 105 priests, and two monasteries. Among all the religious organisations of the Soviet Union, the Orthodox Church of Georgia was one of the most oppressed, being deprived of the rights that other similar bodies continued to enjoy. The Russian patriarchate, for example, was permitted to run two theological academies and several theological seminaries, and it published numerous journals and religious books. Closer to home, in Armenia, the Echmiadzin Theological Academy functioned together with its publishing house.

Ephrem persistently requested permission from the secular authorities to set up training programmes for priests. Eventually, he succeeded in convincing them of their indispensability, and courses for ordinands, named the Bishop Gabriel Courses (see page 153), commenced in 1963 in Mtskheta. Before long, these had evolved into a theological seminary led by the youngest hierarch of the Orthodox Church of Georgia, Bishop Ilia (Shiolashvili) of Batumi-Shemokmedi who, after graduating from the Moscow Theological Academy in 1960, had returned to Georgia. He was consecrated bishop on August 23, 1963, by Ephrem and, within a short period of time, he was able to raise the level of education at the Mtskheta Theological Seminary.

Ephrem's next step was to ask the Georgian authorities to return the patriarchal residence that had been confiscated in 1923, but in vain. Moreover, despite the desire of the Georgian faithful to have church services restored, the obstacles encountered were almost insurmountable. In 1960, Orthodox Christians in the town of Gori addressed Mzhavanadze, the Georgian Communist Party leader:

> We are ashamed. Why is it impossible to open a church in Gori when there are Orthodox churches elsewhere? Tbilisi alone has twenty functioning churches. Why is it that we in Gori are forced to reject our Georgian traditions when the citizens of Tbilisi are not? Nonetheless, we will never forget the venerable traditions of our ancestors for as long as we live. Do not torment us. Give us even a single church. We are even prepared to build a new one. The local authorities have intimidated us; they threaten to deprive the pensioners who have asked for a working church and to dismiss us from our employment. They claimed that it was absurd for us to want to open a church now that we have come so close to communism. But let such a church here be closed if we ever accept communism — let them be closed everywhere — we would not resist that! (Central Historical Archives, no. 1880)

Ephrem officially lent his support to the petition, but to no avail. The secular authorities feared that other districts in Georgia would also demand to open churches if the request of Gori's residents was satisfied. Hence they started to crack down on believers there. In a confidential letter sent to the chairman of Gori's town council, D. Shalutashvili, head of religious affairs at the Georgian Council of Ministers, complained about the petitioners:

> Citizen Prangishvili persistently makes applications to the most senior comrades that clearance be given for the former church building in Gori to re-open as a functioning church. He walks around among the people advocating the opening of the church. You must, therefore, have words with Prangishvili and his group to stop them campaigning for the church and to put an end to collecting signatures (Central Historical Archives, no. 1880).

In an attempt to coerce the faithful, agents of the Office for Religious Affairs infiltrated the gatherings of worshippers that assembled for the major Christian festivals. In March 1972, special efforts were made by the same office to prevent the mass gatherings of believers at holy sites on the territory of the Abkhazian Autonomous Republic. Measures taken against the monastery of Kamani were particularly appalling. This monastery was famous for its holy well and thousands of the faithful would visit it on feast days for cures from a range of ailments. By way of reaction, religious affairs bureaucrats demanded the local authorities to block the road leading to the monastery and to cut off the supply of the holy water. If these measures did not prove to have the desired effect, they threatened to build a pig farm on the site in order to keep people from bathing in the waters. Throughout the 1960s and 1970s similar acts of blasphemy were not uncommon in Georgia.

In the face of such pressure, Ephrem continued to act in the interests of the Orthodox Church of Georgia. During his ministry, he succeeded in ordaining three bishops in 1963, 1965 and 1972: respectively Archimandrites Ilia, Romanoz (Petriashvili) and Gaioz (Keratishvili). Some patriotically minded souls, however, wished even more determined action by the church. The writer Ipolite Vartagava wrote a letter of such spirit to the patriarch that the latter was moved to reply:

> We are today in a more difficult position than at the times of the Patriarchs Kalistrate and Melkisedek. For obvious reasons, I am unable from this position to commit all things to writing. Our Church is in a very difficult situation. Possibly it has a great many supporters, but I see no one prepared to take initiatives. In spite of these testing times, I have managed to establish the two-year Bishop Gabriel Courses for priests, to publish the Gospel and the Epistles of Mtatsmindelis, to produce a Book of Prayers, icons of Georgian saints, religious images, and a church calendar. I am convinced that the situation will calm down and the Church will once again occupy a respected position in society (*Jvari Vazisa*, 1978-1983, p197).

Participation in the ecumenical movement

In the late fifties and early sixties a new position had arisen with regard to contacts with churches — Orthodox and non-Orthodox — outside the Soviet Union. Khrushchev's regime was characterised by two general considerations. On the one hand, he pleaded for the peaceful coexistence of communist and capitalist ideologies and, for the sake of world peace, the two systems were to abstain from provocation and aggression. On the other hand, he promoted a renewed commitment to communist principles: communism in every aspect of society was to be achieved within a foreseeable timespan. To achieve this objective, its theories were to be applied with renewed vigour.

These two considerations found expression also in the attitude of the state toward churches and religion. On one level, the churches were, in the name of world peace, allowed to engage in international contacts and to participate especially in conferences and meetings for the promotion of peace. On another, anti-religious measures became more severe. Churches and religion in general were considered to be obstacles on the road to the full attainment of communism.

In the late fifties, informal talks had begun between the World Council of Churches (WCC) and the Russian Orthodox Church. While the Russian church in earlier times had severely criticised Western Christianity, it now showed an interest in participating in the ecumenical movement. It eventually applied for membership and became a full member at the Third Assembly of the WCC in New Delhi (1961).

Both the WCC and the Orthodox Church of Georgia moved quickly to use this window of opportunity. An exchange of letters was initiated between the WCC general secretary Willem Visser't Hooft and Ephrem. An invitation was made in 1960 to the Church of Georgia to send an observer to the New Delhi conference. However, although the patriarch accepted the invitation, he was not granted permission by the authorities to send a representative.

On May 4, 1962, the Orthodox Church of Georgia applied for WCC membership. In his letter to the general secretary, Ephrem wrote: "The Orthodox Church of Georgia has always attached great importance to issues of close relationship among all Christians on the basis of consolidating universal brotherhood, love and peace among the nations." Accompanied by a delegation, Ephrem travelled to Paris to attend a meeting of the WCC Central Committee where he delivered a speech on the history of the Georgian church. His presentation aroused the greatest of interest because, after so many years of isolation, most members of the Central Committee had only the vaguest ideas about the history and life of the Orthodox Church in Georgia. Soon after the admission of the Georgian church, an official WCC delegation visited Georgia.

It was Ephrem's fervent hope that membership in the WCC would entail international recognition of the Orthodox Church of Georgia and help restore relations with the other Orthodox churches. But for a number of years, participation in the ecumenical movement remained minimal. Representatives of the Georgian church took part in several WCC assemblies, such as those held in Uppsala (1968) and Nairobi (1975), while Bishop Ilia (Shiolashvili) was from time to time allowed to attend the meetings of one of the major WCC Commissions. Any additional active participation by the Georgian church in ecumenical activities was disapproved of by the state authorities in both Moscow and Tbilisi.

On many occasions, foreign church visitors were denied visas while Georgian delegates were blocked from leaving the country. On one occasion, Ephrem was invited to Bucharest for the celebrations in honour of the Romanian patriarch Justin for the 20th anniversary of his accession but Shalutashvili, at the Georgian Council of Ministers, informed the Committee for Religious Affairs of the Soviet Union that it was not expedient to grant Ephrem permission for this journey. On another occasion, a Georgian delegation wanting to participate at a pan-Orthodox conference met with insurmountable obstacles.

Repression continued its relentless pace. Church taxes were increased, as in 1958 when the government issued a decree stipulating that 87 per cent of church income was payable to the state. In protest, Ephrem referred to the decree as "a waxed noose on a heinous offender's neck". The dire conditions of the Georgian church were evident everywhere. When the Mtskheta Theological Seminary requested permission from the deputy chairman of the Council of Ministers of the Georgian Soviet Republic to use an official seal and stamp of their own, it was refused. And in 1979, when the Holy Synod of the Orthodox Church of Georgia decided to observe the 10th anniversary of Ephrem's accession, the communist authorities refused to issue a permit for any kind of celebration.

Catholicos-Patriarch Ephrem II died at the age of 76 on April 8, 1972.

Catholicos-Patriarch David (1972-1977)

The church's situation deteriorated even further in the period between 1972 and 1977, when David V (Devdariani) served as catholicos-patriarch. Only three of the fifteen theoretically active eparchies had their own hierarchs. David consecrated three new bishops — Giorgi (Gongadze) for Manglisi, Grigol (Tsertsvadze) for Alaverdi, and Ilarion (Samkharadze) for Bodbe. But this did not improve things overall since most of the Georgian hierarchs were aged and performed their duties in the churches of the capital Tbilisi.

Patriarch David was already elderly at his election. Voices had, in fact, been raised suggesting that Bishop Ilia (Shiolashvili) — who in due course became metropolitan of Tskhum-Apkhazeti — would have been the more appropriate candidate to succeed Ephrem. But the state authorities were pushing for a quick decision and the synod followed their instructions. Given the poor health and vulnerability of the new patriarch, younger hierarchs, such as Bishop Gaioz (Keratashvili), were able to play to his detriment. The disorder in the Church only served to promote the designs of the State and all attempts at re-establishing any kind of order were suppressed. Those believers who raised their voices in protest continued to be intimidated, and several found themselves arrested.

The situation was even worse in the eparchies. The local administrations, armed with directives from the central administration, severely persecuted the clergy and organised raids on religious festivals in order to identify believers present. Anti-religious literature was printed in the 1970s to spread the idea that Georgia was a country of mass atheism. Under such conditions, relations between the Orthodox Church of Georgia and Christianity at large became even more difficult. On several occasions, Moscow refused to permit representatives from the World Council of Churches to travel to Georgia to meet Patriarch David.

After several fruitless attempts, Lukas Vischer, director of WCC's Faith and Order Commission, succeeded in obtaining permission from the Soviet authorities to visit the church in Georgia. However, by the time of his arrival, Catholicos-Patriarch David had died. Vischer instead was received by Metropolitan Ilia, who had been named locum tenens — and who was shortly to succeed as head of the Georgian church.

Election of Catholicos-Patriarch Ilia II (1977–)

A new era had begun. At the time of his election, Ilia was metropolitan of Tskhum-Apkhazeti. His consecration, held at Svetitskhoveli cathedral on December 25, 1977, was attended by a large number of public figures, intellectuals and visitors from abroad. Among these were Patriarch Pimen of Russia, the Catholicos of All Armenians Vazgen I, Archimandrite Naum from the Bulgarian Church, and Archimandrite Grigorios from the Church of Alexandria.

Everyone sensed that a new point of departure had been reached. "I am aware of the painful and at the same time honourable duty God imposed on me today under the arches of this holy cathedral," pronounced Catholicos-Patriarch Ilia II at the ceremony (*Jvari Vazisa*, 1978-1983, p1).

In his speech at the reception organised on behalf of the Orthodox Church of Georgia, the Armenian catholicos Vazgen alluded discreetly to the pressurised position of the Georgian church. Speaking about his own early years and the difficulties faced in the 1950s by the Armenian

Church, he expressed the hope that the new Georgian catholicos-patriarch would be as successful in resolving his problems as the Armenians had been.

On April 14, 1978, a peaceful demonstration held in Tbilisi proved to be an important event for Soviet Georgia when thousands of Georgians raised their voices against Moscow's oppressive policies in ordering a revision of the constitutional status of the Georgian language as the republic's official state language. Bowing to pressure from the mass protests, Moscow approved the reinstatement the same year by the republic's leader Eduard Shevardnadze to retain the status of the Georgian language in the Constitution of Georgia. On the very same day the patriarchal residence caught fire. This was not a coincidence but a warning for the newly elected patriarch — a preparation for the major problems that he would soon be facing.

The church was facing increasing pressure from the public to support the national-liberation movement that was rapidly expanding in the republic. It was significant that Sioni cathedral was now attracting large congregations, including prominent nationalist figures who were among the patriarch's altar servers. Ilia set out to strengthen the fragile ties between church and people and to re-establish the church's traditional role in Georgia's life and destiny. To make this work, he knew it was necessary to train up a new generation of young, talented priests and to revive the closed churches and monasteries.

As a result of the patriarch's determination, seven young hierarchs joined the Holy Synod of the Orthodox Church of Georgia between 1978 and 1983: Nikoloz (Makharadze) for the Tskhum-Apkhazeti eparchy, Ioane (Ananiashvili) for Chkondidi, Shio (Avalishvili) for Kutaisi-Gaenati, Tadeoz (Ioramashvili) for Tsilkani, Atanase (Chakhvashvili) for Bodbe, Konstantine (Melikidze) for Urbnisi, Anania (Japaridze) for Samtskhe-Javakheti, and Ambrosi (Katamadze) for Nikortsminda. New choristers were selected for functioning churches and forgotten Georgian hymns were revived.

The Georgian church also reinforced its missionary and evangelical activities. Homilies were given greater emphasis in services while preachers gave sermons on a wide variety of themes that included every sphere of public life.

Raising an international profile

A new start was also made in international relations. The Orthodox Church of Georgia began to attach increasing importance to relations with Orthodox and non-Orthodox churches as well as with non-Christian religions.

In May 1978, an official conference dedicated to the 60th anniversary of the restoration of the patriarchate in Russia was held in Moscow. Ilia addressed the plenary and met Metropolitans Meliton and Bartholomeos from the Ecumenical Patriarchate of Constantinople, Patriarch Maxim of Bulgaria, Archbishop Chrysostomos of Cyprus, Metropolitan Vasili of Poland, Archbishop Dorotheos of Czechoslovakia, Metropolitan Theodosios of the United States and Canada, and Vazgen, Catholicos of All Armenians. Plans for future relations between the various churches were discussed at the meetings.

Between 1978 and 1988 delegations from the Georgian church led by Ilia were able to pay official visits to Bulgaria, Poland, Czechoslovakia, the United States, Constantinople, Echmiadzin, Alexandria, Jerusalem, and Yugoslavia. Equitable and fraternal relations were also restored with other Orthodox churches.

The profile of the Georgian church was raised not only because of such links but also as a result of its co-operation within the framework of the World Council of Churches. In 1975, the WCC Assembly in Nairobi had chosen Metropolitan Nikodim of Leningrad as one of the WCC's six presidents. After his sudden death, the WCC Central Committee, at its meeting in the Jamaican capital of Kingston in January 1979, asked Patriarch Ilia to take over the position since he represented the same "area" of Christianity. In September of the following year, Glen Williams, general secretary of the Conference of European Churches, visited Tbilisi and shortly afterwards the Georgian church also joined the Conference of European Churches.

The Georgian church continued to regularly participate in conferences held under the auspices of the WCC, with Ilia visiting its headquarters in Geneva several times as one of the presidents of the organisation. In the process, he strengthened his church's ties with the Armenian, Coptic, Anglican and other Protesant churches. He also paid formal visits to Protestant churches in Switzerland and Germany.

In 1980 it was the patriarch's opinion that the Georgian church needed to focus on greater co-operation between the Christian Churches: "In the ecumenical movement, many issues relevant to the Orthodox Churches are being addressed but at the same time the strong influence of Protestant elements can be felt. This is why we should attempt to strengthen Orthodox representation in this inter-Church movement (*Jvari Vazisa*, 1978-1983)."

In the 1980s the Church also initiated relations with the Roman Catholic Church, and in June 1980, Ilia visited the Vatican to meet Pope John-Paul II. "Our two Churches have always had good bilateral relations expressed in cultural, scientific, and spiritual co-operation," noted Ilia on this occasion. In November 1999, John-Paul visited Georgia — the first pope ever to do so — and there he met President Shevardnadze as well as Catholicos-Patriarch Ilia.

Efforts at renewal

The Georgian public approved of and supported the first cautious steps of their Church to provide a degree of breathing space after the stifling decades of Soviet ideology. But the authorities and their ideological forces remained wary: they reinforced anti-religious propaganda and strengthened the staff of the office for religious affairs at the Georgian Council of Ministers. Although this department was directed to constrict the activities of the Church, its efforts proved fruitless. Compared with the time of Patriarch Ephrem, a new mood had developed in the country and people from every level of society, including many young people, joined the ranks of parishioners.

Thanks to initiatives taken by Ilia, the fifteen previously nominal eparchies began once more to function as normal with the return of their hierarchs from Tbilisi. Grand religious celebrations were held in the cathedrals of Sioni and Svetitskhoveli; deacons, priests and bishops were ordained. Despite stiff resistance from the government leadership, churches shut down in the 1920s and 1930s underwent restoration. Moreover, new churches were built in Tbilisi and Batumi while monks and nuns returned to monasteries that had been abandoned for almost a century.

The Church also turned its attention to restoring severed relations with creative intellectuals and prominent academics. To begin with, the Patriarchate held regular meetings with Georgian scholars to discuss the country's political, religious, and cultural issues. Thanks to Ilia's efforts, the governor of Holy Mount Athos visited Georgia in 1978. At a meeting with researchers, the governor expressed his readiness to help Georgians in obtaining microfilms of Georgian manuscripts kept at the Georgian (Iviron) Monastery on Mount Athos. Microfilms of Georgian manuscripts held in the Vatican were also made available. All of these were presented by the patriarch to Tbilisi's K. Kekelidze Institute of Manuscripts.

The church also took bold initiatives in the processes underway in Georgia. The first such step was made in the autumn of 1978 when the remains of the celebrated Georgian historian Mikheil Tamarashvili were taken from Italy to Georgia for reburial. This event provided the opportunity for an initial, serious involvement with civil society. Leading the members of the Holy Synod in mourning ceremonies at the Didube Pantheon (the church in Tbilisi where eminent Georgians are buried), Ilia used the occasion to stress that the Georgian nation and the church had always been together and that this situation would not change in the future.

The Orthodox Church of Georgia now openly celebrated the feast days of Saint David Agmashenebeli, Saint Vakhtang Gorgasali and Saint Nino. It also participated in the 1,500th anniversary celebration of the first monument of Georgian literature *The Martyrdom of St Shushanik*, which was initiated by the secular authorities — an icon of St Shushanik was made with the patriarch's blessing. Then, in 1987, the church canonised Ilia Chavchavadze (see box on page 61).

The Georgian patriarchate also increased its efforts in the publication of theological works in Georgian. In the 1960s and 1970s, only a small number of church calendars had been permitted to be published, but now the church was able to produce the journal *Jvari Vazisa* ("The Vine Cross"), with its first issue appearing in 1978. Initially, the plan was for an issue to appear every two months but, due to governmental interference, it came out only twice a year. Moreover, state officials restricted the number of copies and resorted to various ploys to dissuade scholars from co-operating in such church-led initiatives. Regardless, the patriarchate managed to publish collections of theological studies covering ecclesiastic subjects, as well as histories of of the church and of Georgia.

Ilia also made further progress in restoring the eparchies, and on the major religious feasts he would visit them personally. Indeed, in 1978, he succeeded in participating — in the face of stiff resistance by the secular rulers — on the plain around Alaverdi cathedral in the great festival of Alaverdoba (the feast of the cathedral) where he appeared before a crowd numbering many thousands. As a result of such efforts, people started returning to the church.

Anti-religious measures

Leaders of the Georgian Communist Party held innumerable meetings and briefings on the subject of "improving anti-religious activities". An indication of the methods they employed in order to exercise pressure on the church is revealed in a report prepared for the government in 1980 by T. Maisuradze, who was at the time in charge of religious affairs at the Council of Ministers of Georgia. The report stated that the deputy secretary for religious affairs, I. Rurua, and the chief inspector, O. Jashi, made an appearance during the entrance examinations for Mtskheta's Theological Seminary. They noted with indignation that "unfortunately, the contingent that came to the seminary turned out to be far better prepared this time compared with previous years". The KGB paid particular attention to the incoming candidates, asking them why they had decided to enter a seminary. If the answers failed to convince, the authorities would spread rumours accusing the students of sexual misbehaviour.

A letter sent to Ilia on November 21, 1986 by the head of religious affairs is characteristic of the levels of arrogance and interference practised by the department:

> Based on reports available to us, we feel the need to call your attention to the frequency of violation of Soviet law on religious cults by the Orthodox Church of Georgia. Thus, in the immediate future, it will be necessary for us to carry out the following measures in order to suppress this abuse:
>
> 1. Prohibit priests and the staff of the patriarchate from appealing directly to different bodies of this republic and of the Soviet Union.
> 2. Restrict movement of priests to and from churches.
> 3. Strictly prohibit all regular priests or church hierarchs from interfering in financial and industrial activities as well as in organisational issues of religious communities.
> 4. Warn all hierarchs, priests, and other religious workers to discontinue the practice of participating in celebrations held in non-functioning and non-registered churches.

A conflict arose, for example, in 1979 over a celebration at the monastery of Shiomgvime, which at that time was still state property. Patriarch Ilia celebrated the liturgy in the abandoned building and then asked Archimandrite Ioakime to remain in the monastery. While it is not unknown in the history of the Georgian church for an individual monk to live in a deserted monastery, this was a provocative step in view of the soviet regime. Ioakime was subsequently thrown into prison at Shiomgvime by the state authorities. It required the strongest intervention on the part of the patriarch to free the incarcerated monk.

The Tbilisi Theological Academy

October 1, 1988 became a day of special note in the history of the Church since it was the day when the Theological Academy of Tbilisi was officially opened. Ilia noted:

> The academy must become a link between modern science and theology
> . . . The academy should become a training centre not only for educating
> future priest but also a research institute to be used by both ecclesiastic fig-
> ures and scholars (Chronological Collection, 1955, 1988, no. 4).

Departments were opened and chairs founded in theology and fine arts at
the academy and scholarly studies were initiated. Thanks to the efforts of
the patriarch, the Gelati Academy in Kutaisi, founded by King David IV
in the 12th century, also resumed activities. In addition, other theological
seminaries were opened in Akhaltsikhe, Batumi, Zestaponi and Bodbe.

Implications of independence
The processes of liberalisation and political reform in the Soviet Union
provided the Orthodox Church of Georgia with new opportunities.
From the 1980s the national-liberation movement found a home within
the church. Leaders of the organisation such as Zviad Gamsakhurdia,
Merab Kostava, Gia Chanturia, Erekle Tsereteli and Tamar Chkheidze
were frequently to be found at Sioni cathedral — with some of them
even assisting in the church services. The Sioni congregation was therefore a significant force for the movement. Prohibited literature was distributed within the cathedral and people debated national and religious
issues.

When on April 9, 1989 the Soviet Army used force to disperse the
peaceful demonstration outside the Government Building that demanded the restoration of Georgia's independence, the patriarch appeared in
the midst of the protesters in order to avoid bloodshed. He urged them
to go home and find a peaceful solution.

After the 1990 multiparty elections, the leaders of the national-liberation movement succeeded in forcing the authorities to return the patriarchal residence (confiscated in 1923) to the patriarchate, to dismantle
the Office of Religious Affairs in the Council of Ministers, and to abolish income tax on churches, monasteries and the clergy.

A greater role for independence
With independence in 1991, the role of the church in the life of
the Georgian nation became even more significant. An article in the
new state constitution even recognized the special position of the
Orthodox Church in Georgian history. But there were also unexpected

Ilia II

complications as tensions rose among the leaders of the national-liberation movement and efforts at mediation by the patriarch failed.

Moreover, newly elected president Zviad Gamsakhurdia had his own views on the place of the church in the nation. To evoke Georgian unity, he had romantic notions of convoking a church council in the spirit of the ancient Synod of Ruisi-Urbnisi, convened in 1103 by King David the Builder. For the patriarch, proposals such as this were unacceptable because they violated the present canonical tradition and limited the church's freedom.

The period of the civil war that erupted in the years that followed turned out to be one of the most challenging in Georgia's history. The Russians, yet again seeking to destabilise the Caucasian nations, helped to instigate ethnic conflicts in Abkhazia and South Ossetia (Samachablo). And so once more, the Georgian church found itself attempting to reconcile the conflicting parties in order to maintain political unity within the country.

With the removal from power of Gamsakhurdia, the former Soviet foreign minister Eduard Shevardnadze now came to the fore as the new head of state. Despite his past career as general secretary of the hostile Georgian Communist Party, Shevardnadze now sought to establish close relations with the church and began this by publicly accepting baptism. The following years saw the growth of mutual recognition by church and state. But as the president gradually lost control over the frage-menting nation, opposition grew. Many now felt that the church was too closely allied with the government and had failed to raise its voice to denounce the corruption that had become endemic to Shevardnadze's regime.

Growth of the church

The church nevertheless experienced growth and consolidation through-out the years immediately following independence. One indication of its renewed strength was the increase of eparchies, and today there exists the following eparchial division in the Georgian church, each of which is led by a hierarch: Mtskheta-Tbilisi, Alaverdi, Akhalkalaki, Akhaltsikhe, Batumi-Skhalta, Bodbe, Bolnisi, Borjomi, Chkondidi, Dmanisi, Gurjaani, Khoni, Kutaisi-Gaenati, Manglisi-Tsalka, Margveti, Mestia, Nekresi, Nikortsminda, Nikozi, Poti, Rustavi, Ruisi-Urbnisi, Sagarejo-Nikortsminda, Samtavisi, Senaki, Shemokmedi, Stepanetsminda, Tianeti, Tsageri-Svaneti, Tsilkani, Tskhum-Apkhazeti, Vani-Bagdati, Zugdidi-Tsaishi, and Western Europe.

In 1995 the Holy Synod of the Orthodox Church of Georgia decided to canonise the following victims of the Bolshevik regime: Catholicos-Patriarch of All Georgia Ambrosi (Khelaia), Metropolitan of Kutaisi Nazar (Lezhava), the priests Simon (Mchedlidze), Germane (Jajanidze), Ieroteoz (Nikoladze), and the deacon Besarion (Kukhianidze). Grigol Peradze, who was martyred at the hands of the Nazis and died at Auschwitz, was also made a saint.

In 1997, the Orthodox Church of Georgia and, indeed, all of Georgia celebrated the 20th anniversary of enthronement of His Holiness, Catholicos-Patriarch of All Georgia Ilia II. Shevardnadze, as the nation's president, presented His Holiness with the award of David the Builder — the highest such honour in Georgia.

The issue of autocephaly

Recognition of its autocephaly by the other Orthodox churches continued to be one of the pressing issues of the Georgian church. During his visit in May 1979 to the Patriarch of Constantinople Dimitrios, the foremost prelate of the Orthodox world, Ilia declared that:

> The hardships of past centuries weakened the close friendship of our two ancient Apostolic Churches and of the tradition of co-operation between them. However, the time has now come: thanks to God's providence and mercy we are together again (*Jvari Vazisa*, 1978-1983).

He then made a direct request for the patriarch to recognise the historical autocephaly of the Orthodox Church of Georgia:

> When the Ecumenical Patriarchate of Constantinople sends messages or congratulations, it does not accurately refer to the Catholicos-Patriarch of All Georgia. The Orthodox Church of Georgia should occupy its lawful place at ecclesiastic forums and conferences. We should like this problem to be resolved once and for all (*Jvari Vazisa*, 1978-1983).

The Patriarch of Constantinopole accordingly sent several delegations to Georgia to settle the issue, and in 1989 Dimitrios himself visited the country. The anxious discussions finally ended in 1990 when the Ecumenical Patriarchate recognised the historical autocephaly of the Orthodox Church of Georgia.

*

Internal tensions

In the 1990s a number of pro-Russian hierarchs declared the Russian Orthodox Church in Exile to be the only true Orthodox Church. They started a campaign against the catholicos-patriarch accusing Ilia of betraying "true Orthodoxy" by associating the Georgian church with the Ecumenical Movement. They demanded Georgia's immediate withdrawal from the World Council of Churches and all other ecumenical organisations which, they alleged, were populated by "heretics". In support of their views, they distributed brochures and books that condemned the ecumenical movement.

In violation of Orthodox canonical norms, hieromonks from the monasteries of Shiomgvime, David Gareji, Betania, Zarzma and Shemokmedi issued an ultimatum in May 1997, demanding that the Holy Synod and catholicos-patriarch withdraw the Georgian church from membership of the World Council of Churches on the grounds that it was forbidden for Orthodox Christians to pray with Protestants and Catholics. Faced with the threat of schism, the Holy Synod made the following decision at its extraordinary meeting on May 20, 1997: "The Orthodox Church of Georgia renounces its participation in the ecumenical movement; it withdraws from the World Council of Churches and from the Conference of European Churches" (*Dilis Gazeti*, May 21, 1997).

This decision may have headed off a terrible split in the church, but it also had the effect of reinforcing the position of fundamentalist circles within it whose views are alien to the Georgian people and Church alike. Public opinion continues to be divided and conflicting views are vigorously expressed. The attitude of the conservative minority has recently been articulated in a book entitled *Ecumenism: The Religion of the Antichrist* (Tbilisi, 2002), which labels the WCC as "an organisation of heretics, freemasons and satanists" and ecumenism as "an ecclesiological heresy". An opposing view is expressed in Tamar Meshki's *So That All May Remain Together* (Tbilisi, 2002). Meskhi's book is highly critical of those opposing the ecumenical movement and views the Georgian church's withdrawal from the council as a fundamental misjudgement.

It is a debate that also reflects the country's conflicting political views. While there are isolationist forces in Georgia, most people want international recognition and realise the importance of outside contacts. A renewed participation in the ecumenical movement is now on the increase, promoted by a number of bishops, and in a recent open letter, theological students appealed for a more inclusive attitude towards other churches. Clearly Ilia's primary aim is not to jeopardise the unity of the church, but despite the tensions, the patriarchate has continued to pursue informal ecumenical contacts.

Conclusion

Our concluding remarks, therefore, may be left to His Holiness, Catholicos-Patriarch of All Georgia Ilia II (Ilia, 1997, p414):

"The centuries-long history of the Georgian nation is filled with many tragic developments. Evil forces have always hindered the nation's peaceful growth. From the very beginning, our country found itself in hostile surroundings. It is a wonder how this very small but spiritually strong nation has managed to cope with such numerous enemies. Every one Georgian has had to combat ten opponents. The country bled profusely in its struggle against inequality.

"Our ancestors, however, continued the fight to preserve for us our God-given land, the Christian faith, and our mother tongue, Georgian. Scarcely managing to repel one enemy, our people faced another at the ready to overwhelm our lands. Alarm bells tolled from the Orthodox Church of Georgia's belfry calling one and all, again and again, to protect the Motherland. Young and old, laymen and priests, fought the enemy together.

"Every battle became a kind of testing ground for the nation on which the united Georgian soul was hardened and formed. The Orthodox Church of Georgia was at the helm for the Georgian nation."

*   *
*

Ilia II welcomes a new generation

Appendix I

Heads of the Georgian church since 1814

Patriarchs

Kirion Sadzaglishvili	1917-1918
Leonide Okropiridze	1918-1921
Ambrosi Khelaia	1921-1927
Kristephore Tsitskishvili	1927-1932
Kalistrate Tsintsadze	1932-1952
Melkisedek Pkhaladze	1952-1960
Ephrem Sidamonidze	1960-1972
David V Devdariani	1972-1977
Ilia II Shiolashvili	1977-

Exarchs

Varlaam Eristavi	1814-1817
Theophilact Rusomov	1817-1821
Iona Vasilevski	1821-1832
Moses Bogdanov-Platonov	1832-1834
Evgeni Bashenov	1834-1844
Isidor Nikolski	1844-1858
Yevsevi Ilyinski	1858-1877
Ioannike Rudnev	1877-1882
Pavel Lebedev	1882-1887
Palladi Rayev	1887-1892
Vladimir Bogoyavlenski	1982-1898
Flavian Gorodetski	1898-1901
Alexi I Opotsk	1901-1905
Nicholas Nalimov	1905-1906
Nikon Sofiiski	1906-1908 *(murdered)*
Innokenti Beliayev	1909-1913
Alexi II Molchanov	1913-1914
Pitirim Oknov	1914-1915
Platon Rozhdestvenski	1915-1917

Appendix 2

Selected church terminology

archdeacon — მთავარდიაკვანი *mtavardiakvani*
archpriest — დეკანოზი *dekanozi*
autocephaly — ავტოკეფალია *avtokepalia or* თვითმწყობა *tvitmtsqoba*
bishop — ეპისკოპოსი *episkoposi*
cathedral — (კათედრალური) ტაძარი *(katedraluri) tadzari*
catholicos-patriarch — კათოლიკოს-პატრიარქი *katolikos-patriarki*
church — ეკლესია *eklesia*
convent — დედათა მონასტერი *dedata monasteri*
deacon — დიაკვანი *diakvani*
hermit — დაყუდებული ბერი *daqudebuli beri*
hierarch — მღვდელთმთავარი *mghvdeltmtavari*
lavra — ლავრა *lavra*
metropolitan — მიტროპოლიტი *mitropoliti*
martyr — მოწამე *motsame*
monastery — მონასტერი *monasteri*
monk — ბერი *beri*
nun — მონაზონი *monazoni*
Orthodox — მართლმადიდებელი *martlmadidebeli*
Orthodox Church — მართლმადიდებელი ეკლესია *martlmadidebeli eklesia*
patriarch — პატრიარქი *patriarki*
priest — მღვდელი *mghvdeli*
saint — წმინდანი *tsmindani*
superior/abbot — წინამძღვარი *tsinamdzghvari*
synod — სინოდის კრება *sinodis kreba*

Bibliography

Abkhazia and the Novy Afon Simon Canaanite Monastery There, Moscow, 1885 (*Абхазия в ней Ново-Афонский Симоно-Кананистский монастырь*, Москва, 1885).

Acts Collected by the Caucasian Archeographic Commission, vol. i, Tiflis, 1866 (*Акты собранные Кавказкой Археографической Комиссией*, Т. I., Тифлис, 1866).

Acts Collected by the Caucasian Archeographic Commission, vol. ii, Tiflis, 1866 (*Акты собранные Кавказкой Археографической Комиссией*, Т. II., Тифлис, 1866).

Acts Collected by the Caucasian Archeographic Commission, vol. iii, Tiflis, 1869 (*Акты собранные Кавказкой Археографической Комиссией*, Т. III., Тифлис, 1869).

Acts Collected by the Caucasian Archeographic Commission, vol. iv, Tiflis, 1870 (*Акты собранные Кавказкой Археографической Комиссией*, Т. IV., Тифлис, 1870).

Amiranashvili, Sh., *Khakhuli Triptych*, Tbilisi, 1972 (ამირანაშვილი შ, ხახულის კარედი, თბილისი, 1972).

Antelava I., 'The Colonial Policies of Tsarism in Georgia in the 1830-1850s: Administration System', in *Essays on the History of Georgia*, vol. v, Tbilisi 1970 (ანთელავა ი., 'ცარიზმის კოლონიური პოლიტიკა საქართველოში მეცხრამეტე საუკუნის 30-50-იან წლებში: მმართველობის სისტემა', საქართველოს ისტორიის ნარკვევები, Т. V., თბილისი, 1970).

Asatiani, N., *The History of Georgia*, Tbilisi, 2001 (ასათიანი ნ. საქართველოს ისტორია, თბილისი, 2001).

Bakuradze I., *Tbilisi Theological Seminary. History of Education in Georgia. Collected Materials*, Tbilisi, 1937 (ბაკურაძე ი., თბილისის სასულიერო სემინარია, სწავლა-აღზრდის ისტორია საქართველოში. მასალების კრებული, თბილისი, 1937).

Berdnikov I., *The State Religion in the Roman-Byzantine Empire*, vol. i, Kazan, 1881 (Бердников, И. *Государственное положение религии в Римско-Византийской империи*, Т. I., Казань, 1881).

Berdzenishvili, N., V. Dondua, M. Dumbadze, G. Melikishvili, S. Meskhia, & P. Ratiani, *A History of Georgia*, vol. i, Tbilisi, 1958 (ბერძენიშვილი ნ., დონდუა ვ., დუმბაძე მ., მელიქიშვილი გ., მესხია შ., რატიანი პ., *საქართველოს ისტორია*, თბილისი, 1958).

Brail V., 'The Situation of the Georgian Orthodox Church in Tsarist Russia', in: *Ecclesiastical Affairs in Russia*, St-Petersburg, 1896 (Браил, Б., 'О положении Грузинской православной черкви в чарской России', из книги *Церковние вопросы в России*, СПБ, 1896).

Bubulashvili, E., *Catholicos-Patriarch of Georgia Anthony II*, Tbilisi, 2002 (ბუბულაშვილი ე. *საქართველოს კათალიკოს-პატრიარქი ანტონ მეორე*, თბილისი, 2002).

Bubulashvili, E., 'Georgian Church Hymns in the Period of Exarchate', in: *Collected Articles on Georgian Church Hymns, the Nation and Traditions*, Tbilisi, 2001 (ბუბულაშვილი ე., 'ქართული საეკლესიო საგალობლები ეგზარქოსობის პერიოდში', *ქართული საეკლესიო გალობა, ერი და ტრადიციია*, თბილისი, 2001).

Bukurauli, I., 'Memory', *Theater and Life*, 18/VI, no. 26, 1920 (ბუკუ-რაული ი., 'ხსოვნა', *თეატრი და ცხოვრება*, 18/26, 1920).

Butkov, P. G., *Materials on the New History of the Caucasus from 1722 to 1803*, vol. ii, St Petersburg, 1869 (Бутков, П. Г., *Материалы для новой истории Кавказа с 1722 но 1803*, Т. II., Санкт-Петербург, 1869).

Chardin, Jean (trans/ed. M. Mgaloblishvili), *Trip to Persia and Other Oriental Countries: Reports about Georgia*, Tbilisi, 1975 (ჟან შარდენის მოგზაურობა სპარსთა და აღმოსავლეთის სხვა ქვეყნებში, ცნობები საქართველოს შესახებ, ფრანგულიდან თარგმნა და კომენტარი დაურთო მ. მგალობლიშვილმა, თბილისი, 1975).

Chavchavadze, Ilia, *Works*, vol. v, Tbilisi, 1965 (ჭავჭავაძე ი., *თხზულებანი*, Т. V., თბილისი, 1965).

Chichinadze, Z., *The Georgian Jews in Georgia*, Tbilisi 1904 (ჩიჩინაძე ზ. *ქართველი ებრაელები საქართველოში*, თბილისი, 1904).

Chichinadze, Z. (ed.), *Speeches and Letters about the Most Reverend Alexander*, Tbilisi, 1907 (*სიტყვები და წერილები ყოვლად სამღვდელო ალექსანდრეზე, შეკრებილი და გამოცემული ზ. ჩიჩინაძისაგან, თბილისი, 1907).

Chronological Collection of the Laws of the Georgian SSR 1921-1940, Tbilisi, 1955 (*საქართველოს სსრ საკანონდებლო აქტების კრებული 1921-1940, თბილისი, 1955).

Bibliography

The Conversion of Kartli, Shatberdi Collection of the Tenth Century, Tbilisi, 1979 (მოქცევაი ქართლისაი, შატბერდის კრებული მეათე საუკუნისა, თბილისი, 1979).

Duguet, R., *Moscow and the Martyred Georgia*, Tbilisi, 1994 (დიუგე რ., მოსკოვი და წამებული საქართველო, თბილისი, 1994).

Dumbadze, M., *West Georgia in the First Half of the 19th Century*, Tbilisi, 1957 (დუმბაძე მ., დასავლეთ საქართველო მეცხრამეტე საუკუნის პირველ ნახევარში, თბილისი, 1957).

Durnovo, Nikoloz, *Destinies of the Georgian Church*, Moscow, 1907 (Дурново, Н., *Судьбы Грузинской Черкви*, Москва, 1907).

Durnovo, Nikoloz, *Towards a Possible Decision on the Question of the Georgian Church*, Moscow 1909 (ნიკოლოზ დურნოვო, ქართული საეკლესიო საკითხის სავარაუდო გადაწყვეტისათვის, მოსკოვი, 1909).

Essays in Georgian History, vol. v, Tbilisi, 1978 (საქართველოს ისტორიის ნარკვევები, T. V., თბილისი, 1978).

Faris John, *Eastern Catholic Churches: Constitution and Governance*, New York, 1992.

From the History of Georgia. Destruction of the Georgian Church, vol. i, Tbilisi, 1907 (საქართველოს ისტორიიდან. საქართველოს ეკლესიის აკლება, T. I., თბილისი, 1907).

Gamkrelidze, A., & S. Kaukhchishvili (eds.), *Georgica, Scriptorum Byzantinorum Excerpta ad Georgiam Pertinentia*, vol. i, Tbilisi, 1961 (გეორგიკა, ბიზანტიელი მწერლების ცნობები საქართველოს შესახებ, T. I., თბილისი, 1961).

The Georgian Soviet Encyclopaedia, vol. v, Tbilisi, 1978 (ქართული საბჭოთა ენციკლოპედია, T. V., თბილისი, 1978).

Gogebashvili, I., *The Basis of Nationality*, Tbilisi, 1903 (გოგებაშვილი ი., ბურხი ეროვნებისა, თბილისი, 1903).

Gogebashvili, I., *Works*, vol. ii, Tbilisi, 1962 (ი. გოგებაშვილი, თხზულებანი, T. II., თბილისი, 1962).

Gogoladze, D., 'The Struggle against Tsarist Domination during the First Two Decades of the 19th Century', *Essays in the History of Georgia*, IV, Tbilisi, 1973 (გოგოლაძე დ., 'ბრძოლა ცარიზმის ბატონობის წინააღმდეგ მეცხრამეტე საუკუნის პირველ ოცეულში', საქართველოს ისტორიის ნარკვევები, T. IV., თბილისი, 1973).

Gorgadze, S., 'Autocephaly of the Georgian Church', *Spiritual Messenger of the Georgian Exarchate*, no. 21-22, 1905 (С. Горгадзе, 'Автокефальность Грузинской Церкви, *Духовный Вестник Грузинского Эксархата*, no. 21-22, 1905).

Gurgenidze, Vakhtang, 'Kirion II', *The Theological Book*, 5, 1981 (ვახ-ტანგ გურგენიძე, 'კირიონ II', *საღვთისმეტყველო კრებული*, 5, 1981).

Guruli V., Vachnadze M., Shvelidze D, Kirtadze N., Tsotskolauri A., Piranishvili P., *History of Georgia in the 20th Century*, Tbilisi, 2003 (გურული ვ., ვაჩნაძე მ., შველიძე დ., კირთაძე ნ., წოწკოლაური ა., ფირანიშვილი პ., *საქართველოს ისტორია მეოცე საუკუნეში*, თბილისი, 2003).

Guruli, Vakhtang, 'The Murderers of Exarch Nikon', *Religion*, 1, 1993 (ვახტანგ გურული, ეგზარქოს ნიკონის მკვლელები, *რელიგია*, 1, 1993).

The Hierarchy of the All-Russian Church from the Beginning of Christianity in Russia until Present Times, Moscow, 1901 (*Иерархия всерасийской черкви от начала христианства в Росии и до настоящего времени*, Москва, 1901).

The Holy Council of the Orthodox Church of Russia in 1917-1918, 3 vols, Moscow, 2000 (*Священный Собор Православной Российской Церкви, 1917-1918*, три тома, Москва, 2000).

Ilia II (Catholicos-Patriarch of All Georgia and Archbishop of Mtskheta-Tbilisi), *Epistles, Addresses, Sermons*, vol. ii, Tbilisi, 1997 (სრულიად საქართველოს კათოლიკოს-პატრიარქი და მცხეთა-თბილისის მთავარეპისკოპოსი ილია II, *ეპისტოლენი, სიტყვანი, ქადაგებანი*, წიგნი 2, თბილისი, 1997).

Japaridze, A., *The Armenisation of the Georgians*, Tbilisi, 1998 (ა. ჯაფარიძე, *ქართველთა გასომხება*, თბილისი, 1998).

Jvaridze, T., (Kirion II, Catholicos-Patriarch of All Georgia), *Jvari Vazisa*, 1, 1988 (თ. ჯვარიძე, 'კირიონ II კათალიკოს-პატრიარქი სრულიად საქართველოისა', *ჯვარი ვაზის*, 1, 1998).

Kacharava, Y., A. Kikvidze, P. Ratiani, & A. Surguladze, *A History of Georgia*, vol. ii, Tbilisi, 1973 (Ю. Качарава, А. КиКвидзе, П. Ратиани, А. Сургуладзе, *История Грузии*, Т. II, Тбилиси, 1973).

Kalinovski A., *Where is the Truth? A History of the Iveria Monastery on*

Bibliography

Mount Athos, Saint Petersburg, 1885 (Калиновский, А., *Где правда? История Афонского иверского монастыря*, СПБ, 1885).

Kelenjeridze M., *The Truth about the Autocephaly of the Georgian Church*, Kutaisi, 1905 (Келенджеридзе, М., *Правда об автокефалии Грузинской Черкви*, Кутаиси, 1905).

Khaburdzania V., 'Kutaisi Governor Reports to the Viceroy', *Gantiadi*, 1991, no. 3, pp 188-189 (საქართველოს ცენტრალური სახელმწიფო საისტორიო არქივი, ფონდი 13, აღწერა 1, საქმე № 69; შდრ. ვ. ხაბურძანია, 'ქუთაისის გუბერნატორი მეფის ნაცვალს მოახსენებს', ჟურნალი განთიადი, 1991, № 3, გვ. 188-189).

Khundadze T., 'Newspaper Droeba and the Tbilisi Theological Seminary', *Review of I. Javakhishvili Institute of History of the Academy of Sciences of the Georgian SSR*, vol. ii, Tbilisi, 1951 (ხუნდაძე ტ., 'გაზეთი „დროება" და თბილისის სასულიერო სემინარია', საქართველოს სსრ მეცნიერებათა აკადემიის ივ. ჯავახიშვილის სახელობის ისტორიის ინსტიტუტის მიმომხილველი, Т. II., თბილისი, 1951).

Khutsishvili, Mirian, *The Social and Political Position of the Georgian Church in the 19th and 20th Centuries*, Tbilisi, 1972/1987 (ხუციშვილი მ, საქართველოს ეკლესიის სოციალურ-პოლიტიკური პოზიცია მეცხრამეტე-მეოცე საუკუნეებში, თბილისი, 1987).

Kikvidze, A, *A History of Georgia from 1801 to 1890*, Tbilisi, 1977 (კიკვიძე ა., საქართველოს ისტორია 1801-1890, თბილისი, 1977).

Kirion, Bishop, *A Short Outline of the History of the Georgian Church and the Exarchate in the 19th Century*, Tiflis, 1901 (Епископ Кирион. *Краткий очерк истории Грузинской Церкви и Экзархата за XIX столетие*, Тифлис, 1901).

K. Kekelidze Institute of Manuscripts, personal archive of Kalistrate Tsintsadze (კალისტრატე ცინცაძის პირადი არქივი, კ. კეკელიძის სახელობის ხელნაწერთა ინსტიტუტი).

Kochlavashvili A., 'Policy of Socialist Industrialisation and First Measures to Implement it', in *Essays in the History of Georgia*, vol. vii, Tbilisi, 1976 (კოჭლავაშვილი ა. 'კურსი სოციალისტური ინდუსტრიალიზაციისაკენ და მისი განხორციელების პირველი ღონისძიებანი', საქართველოს ისტორიის ნარკვევები, Т. VII., თბილისი, 1976).

Korelov, I., 'Greek Speakers of Other Languages (Urums) on Georgian Territory', *Matsne*, Tbilisi, 1989 (კორელოვი ი., 'სხვა ენაზე მოლაპარაკე ბერძნები, ურუმები) საქართველოს ტერიტორიაზე', მაცნე, თბილისი, 1989).

Kutalia, G., *Martin Luther's Social and Political Views*, Tbilisi 1993 (კუტალია გ. მარტინ ლუთერის სოციალური და პოლიტიკური შეხედულებანი, თბილისი, 1993).

Lang, David M., *The Georgians*, London, 1966.

Laskhishvili, George, *Memoirs*, Tbilisi 1992 (გიორგი ლასხიშვილი, მემუარები, თბილისი, 1992).

Legal Acts of the Georgian Democratic Republic, Tbilisi, 1990 (საქართველოს დემოკრატიული რესპუბლიკის დოკუმენტების კრებული, თბილისი, 1990).

Leonide, Catholico-Patriarch, 'Epistle of his Holiness Leonide, Catholicos-Patriarch of all Georgia, towards Tikhon, Patriarch of Moscow and all Russia', *Caucasus*, 24/10, 1996 ('ეპისტოლე სრულიად საქართველოს კათოლიკოს პატრიარქის უწმინდესი ლეონიდესი, მოსკოვისა და სრულიად რუსეთის პატრიარქის ტიხონის მიმართ', კავკასიონი, 24/10, 1996)

Leonti Mroveli, 'The Life of the Georgian Kings', in S. Kaukhchshvili (ed.), *The Life of Kartli*, vol. i, Tbilisi, 1955 (ლეონტი მროველი, ცხოვრება ქართველთა მეფეთა, ქართლის ცხოვრება, ტ. I., ს. ყაუხჩიშვილის რედაქციით, თბილისი, 1955).

Lominadze, Babilina, 'Autocephaly of the Georgian Church', in *Essays in Theology*, vol. xii, Tbilisi, 1981 (ლომინაძე ბ. 'საქართველოს საპატრიარქო და მისი ავტოკეფალია', საღვთისმეტყველო კრებული, ტ. XII., თბილისი, 1981).

Lominadze, Babilina, *The Reactionary Role of the Church in the 1905-1907 Revolution*, Tbilisi, 1959 (ბაბილინა ლომინაძე, ეკლესიის რეაქციული როლი 1905-1907 წლების რევოლუციაში, თბილისი, 1959).

Lortkipanidze, M., *Essays in Georgian History*, Tbilisi, 1994 (ლორთქიფანიძე მ., ნარკვევები საქართველოს ისტორიიდან, თბილისი, 1994).

Maisuradze, G., *Relations between the Georgians and the Armenian Georgians*, Tbilisi 1928 (მაისურაძე გ. ქართველ და სომეხ-ქართველთა ურთიერთობა, თბილისი, 1928).

Manjgaladze, G., *German Colonists in the Transcaucasus*, Tbilisi, 1974 (მანჯგალაძე გ. გერმანელი კოლონისტები ამიერკავკასიაში, თბილისი, 1974).

Melikishvili, L. (ed.), *The Pankisi Crisis*, Tbilisi, 2002 (პანკისის კრიზისი, ლ. მელიქიშვილის რედაქციით, თბილისი, 2002).

Melikset-Begi, I., 'The Armenian Epigraphy and the Polyglot Georgian-

Bibliography

Armenian-Persian-Yulur Inscription on Mount Gareji', *Moambe*, Tbilisi, 1940 (მელიქსეთ-ბეგი ი. 'გარეჯის მრავალმთის სომხური ეპიგრაფიკა და პოლიგლოტური წარწერა, ქართულ-სომხურ-სპარსულ-იელურული)', მოამბე, თბილისი, 1940),

Metreveli, R., *Georgia*, Nashville, Tennessee, 1995.

Mgeladze, V., *The Return of Russia to Georgia. From the Archives of Georgian Emigration*, Tbilisi, 1991 (მგელაძე ვ., რუსეთის მობრუნება საქართველოში, ქართული ემიგრაციის არქივიდან, თბილისი, 1991).

Natroev, A., *The Iveria Monastery on Mount Athos*, Tbilisi, 1909 (Натроев, А., *Иверский монастырь на Афоне*, Тифлис, 1909).

Nikandr, Archimandrite, 'On the Autocephaly of the Georgian Church and Church Life in Georgia under Catholicoses', *Spiritual Messenger of the Georgian Exarchate*, no 13-14, 1905 (Никандр, архимандрит. 'Об автокефальности Грузинской Церкви и церковной жизни в Грузии при католикосах', *Духовный Вестник Грузинского Экзархата*, No 13-14, 1905).

Nikoladze, Evsevi, *History of the Georgian Orthodox Church*, Kutaisi 1918 (ევსევი ნიკოლაძე, საქართველოს მართლმადიდებელი ეკლესიის ისტორია, ქუთაისი, 1918).

Nozadze, G., 'The Georgian Enamels', in *Kavkasioni*, Paris, 1967, no XII. p. 161 (გ. ნოზაძე, 'ქართული მინანქრები', ჟურნალი კავკასიონი, პარიზი, 1967, № 12, გვ. 161).

Paichadze, G. (ed.), *Georgievsk Treaty*, Tbilisi, 1983 (გეორგიევსკის ტრაქტატი, გ. პაიჭადის გამოცემა, თბილისი, 1983).

Papuashvili, Nugzar, *The Church of Georgia between the Two World Wars*, Tbilisi 1996 (ნუგზარ პაპუაშვილი, საქართველოს ეკლესია ორ მსოფლიო ომს შორის, თბილისი, 1996).

Pashayeva, L., *The Family and Family Life of the Greeks in Tsalka District*, Tbilisi, 1992 (Пашаева, л., *Семья и семейный быт греков Цальского района*, Тбилиси, 1992).

Pavliashvili Ketevan, *The Georgian Orthodox Church in 1917-1921*, Tbilisi, 2000 (პავლიაშვილი ქ., საქართველოს ეკლესია 1917-1921 წლებში, თბილისი, 2000).

Pavliashvili, Ketevan, The *Exarchate of Georgia 1900-1917*, Tbilisi 1995 (ქეთევან პავლიაშვილი, საქართველოს საეგზარხოსო 1900-1917, თბილისი, 1995).

Percival, Henry R. (ed.), *A Selected Library of Nicene and Post-Nicene*

Fathers of the Christian Church — Vol. xiv: The Seven Ecumenical Councils of the Undivided Church, Oxford, 1899.

Petrushevsky, L. (ed.), *The Colonial Policy of Tsarism in Azerbaijan in the Twenties to Sixties of the 19th century*, vol. i, Moscow-Leningrad, 1936 (Петрушевский, Л., ред., *Колониальная Политика Царизма в Азербайджане в 20-60 гг. XIX в.*, Т. I., Москва-Ленинград, 1936).

Regulations of the Orthodox Church with Interpretations by Bishop Nikodime, vol. i, Moscow, 1996 (*Правила Православной Церкви с толкованиями Никодима Епископа Далматинского и Истринского*, Т. I., Москва, 1996).

Review of the Activities of the Society for Restoration of Orthodox Christianity in the Caucasus in 1860-1910, Tiflis, 1910 (Обзор деятельности об щества восстановления православного христианства на Кавказе за *1860-1910* гг., Тифлис, 1910).

Rogava, G., 'The Struggle of the Russian Clergy against Georgian National Culture', *Mnatobi* 5, 1998 (გოგი როგავა, 'რუსი სამღვდელოების ბრძოლა ქართული ეროვნული კულტურის წინააღმდეგ', *მნათობი* 5, 1998).

Rogava, G., *History of the Church of Georgia*, Tbilisi, 1996 (როგავა გ. საქართველოს ეკლესიის ისტორია, თბილისი, 1996).

Saitidze, Gela, 'Evgeni Gegechkori, 'Deputy of the II Russian State Council', *Klio*, 5, 1999 (გელა საითიძე, 'ევგენი გეგეჭკორი, რუსეთის II სახელმწიფო სათათბიროს დეპუტატი', *კლიო*, 5, 1999).

Saitidze, Gela, *Ten Years as the Leader of a Section of the Russian State Council*, Tbilisi, 2001 (გელა საითიძე, *10 წელი რუსეთის სახ-ელმწიფო სათათბიროს ფრაქციის სათავეში*, თბილისი, 2001).

Saitidze, Gocha, 'Life of a Martyr Kirion II', *Public Education*, 30/08, 1990 (გოჩა საითიძე, 'ცხოვრება მოწამისა, კირიონ II', *სახალხო განათლება*, 30/8, 1990).

Saitidze, Gocha, 'The Martyr of the Native Country and the Church, The Catholicos-Patriarch of all Georgia Ambrosi Khelaia', *Collection of Articles dedicated to the 60th anniversary of the academician Roin Metreveli*, Tbilisi 2000 (გოჩა საითიძე, 'წამებული მშობელი ქვეყნისა და ეკლესიისათვის სრულიად საქართველოს კათალიკოს-პატრიარქი ამბროსი ხელაია', *ისტორიანი სამეც-ნიერო კრებული, მიძღვნილი აკადემიკოს როინ მეტრეველის დაბადების 60 წლისთავისადმი*, თბილისი, 2000).

Sanikidze, L., *Glimpses of the History of Georgia*, Tbilisi, 1994 (სანიკიძე

Bibliography

ლ. საქართველოს ისტორია თვალის ერთი გადავლებით, თბილისი, 1994).

Sharadze, Guram, *Ilia Chavchavadze*, vol. ii, Tbilisi, 1990 (გურამ შარაძე, ილია ჭავჭავაძე, T. II., თბილისი, 1990).

Surguladze, A., & P. Surguladze, *A History of Georgia: 1783-1990*, Tbilisi, 1991 (სურგულაძე ა., სურგულაძე პ., საქართველოსო ისტორია 1783-1990, თბილისი, 1991).

Surguladze, A., 'Victory of the Soviet Power in Georgia', *Essays in the History of Georgia*, vol. vi, Tbilisi, 1972 (ა. სურგულაძე, 'საბჭოთა ხელისუფლების გამარჯვება საქართველოში', საქართველოს ისტორიის ნარკვევები, T. VI., თბილისი, 1972).

Tadumadze, M. *Social and Economic Conditions of Church Peasants in the First Half of the 19th Century*, Tbilisi, 1993 (თადუმაძე მ. საეკლესიო გლეხების სოციალურ-ეკონომიკური მდგომარეობა მეცხრამეტე საუკუნის პირველ ნახევარში, თბილისი, 1993).

Takaishvili, Ekvtime, *Academician Niko Marr*, Tbilisi 1991 (ექვთიმე თაყაიშვილი, აკადემიკოსი ნიკო მარი, თბილისი, 1991).

Takaishvili, Ekvtime, *Archeological Findings, Research and Remarks*, Tbilisi, 1913 (თაყაიშვილი ე. არქეოლოგიური ექსკურსები, ძიებანი და შენიშვნები, თბილისი, 1913).

Tamarashvili, M., *History of Catholicism among the Georgians*, Tbilisi 1902 (მ. თამარაშვილი, ისტორია კათოლიკობისა ქართველთა შორის, თბილისი, 1902).

Tamarashvili, M., *In Response to the Armenian Writers*, Tbilisi 1904 (მ. თამარაშვილი, პასუხად სომხის მწერლებს, თბილისი, 1904).

Tartarashvili, V., 'Ecclesiastical and Missionary Activities of Tsarism in Saingilo', *History, Society, Geography at School*, 1981, no. 2 (ვ. ტარტარაშვილი, 'ცარიზმის საეკლესიო მისიონერული საქმიანობა საინგილოში', ჟურნალი ისტორია, საზოგადოება, გეოგრაფია სკოლაში, 1981, № 2).

Toidze, L., *Intervention, Occupation, Forceful Sovietisation, Actual Annexation*, Tbilisi, 1991 (ლ. თოიძე, ინტერვენციაც, ოკუპაციაც, ძალდატანებით გასაბჭოებაც, ფაქტობრივი ანექსიაც, თბილისი, 1991).

Tsintsadze, I., *The Protecting Treaty of 1783: Material on the History of Russian-Georgian Relations*, Tbilisi, 1960 (ცინცაძე ი., 1783 წლის მფარველობითი ტრაქტატი: მასალები რუსეთ-საქართველოს ურთიერთობის ისტორიისათვის, თბილისი, 1960).

Tsintsadze, Kalistrate, *From My Memories*, Tbilisi 2001 (კალისტრატე ცინცაძე, რაც მახსოვს, თბილისი, 2001).

259

Vachnadze, M., & V. Guruli, *A History of Georgia in the 19th and 20th Centuries*, Tbilisi, 2001 (ვაჩნაძე მ., გურული გ., საქართველოს ისტორია მეცხრამეტე-მეოცე საუკუნეებში, თბილისი, 2001).

Varazashvili, Akaki, *Georgian Historians in the Struggle for the Autocephaly of the Georgian Church, from the early 20th Century to 1917*, Tbilisi, 2000 (აკაკი ვარაზაშვილი, ქართველი ისტორიკოსები საქართველოს მართლმადიდებელი ეკლესიის ავტოკეფალიისთვის ბრძოლაში, მეოცე საუკუნის დასაწყისიდან 1917 წლამდე, თბილისი, 2000).

Vardosanidze, Sergo, *The Patriarch of All Georgia, Leonide, 1918-1921)*, Tbilisi, 1987 (სერგო ვარდოსანიძე, სრულიად საქართველოს პატრიარქი ლეონიდე, 1918-1921), თბილისი, 1987).

Vardosanidze, Sergo, *Kirion II, Catholicos-Patriarch of all Georgia, 1917-1918*, Ozurgeti, 1993 (სერგო ვარდოსანიძე, კირიონი, სრულიად საქართველოს კათალიკოს-პატრიარქი, 1917-1918, ოზურგეთი, 1993).

Vardosanidze, Sergo, *The Orthodox Church of Georgia from 1927 to 1952*, Tbilisi 2001 (სერგო ვარდოსანიძე, საქართველოს მართლმადიდებელი ეკლესია 1927-1952, თბილისი, 2001).

Zhmakin, V., 'The Georgian Catholicos Anthony II in Russia', *Christian Reading*. Part I, Petersburg, 1905 (Жмакин, В. 'Грузинский Католикос Антоний II в России', *Христтианское Чтение*, Часть I, Петербург, 1905).

Zhvania, Zviad, *Georgian Catholicos-Patriarchs and Bishops since 1917*, Kutaisi, 1994 (ზვიად ჟვანია, საქართველოს კათოლიკოს პატრიარქნი და მღვდელმთავარნი 1917 წლიდან, ქუთაისი, 1994).

Zurabashvili, L., *Traditions of Interethnic Relations in Georgia*, Tbilisi 1989 (ზურაბაშვილი, ლ., ეროვნებათაშორისი ურთიერთობის ტრადიციები საქართველოში, თბილისი, 1989).

Periodicals

Dilis Gazeti, 21 May 1997 (დილის გაზეთი, 21 მაისი, 1997).

Droeba, 1878, no. 146 (დროება, 1878, № 146).

Droeba, 1878, no. 174 (გაზეთი დროება, 1878, № 174).

Droeba, 1880, no 164 (გაზეთი დროება, 1880, № 164).

Georgica, vol. viii, Tbilisi, 1970 (გეორგიკა).

Iveria, 199, 1905 (ივერია, 199, 1905).

Jvari Vazisa, 1988, no 1, p.17 (შდრ. ჟურნალი ჯვარი ვაზისა, 1988, № 1, გვ. 17).

Bibliography

Jvari Vazisa, 1906, no 9 (ჯვარი ვაზისა, 1906, № 9).

Jvari Vazisa, 1978-1983 (ჯვარი ვაზისა, 1978-1983).

Jvari Vazisa, 3, 1990 (ჯვარი ვაზისა, 3, 1990)

The Messenger of the Georgian Exarchate, 1912, no 16 (*Вестник Грузинского Экзархата*, 1912, 16).

Mitsa, 1920, no. 10 (გაზეთი მიწა, 1920, #10).

Mnatobi, 1988 (ჟურნალი მნათობი, 1988).

Mogzauri, 1901, no 4 (ჟურნალი მოგზაური, 1901, № 4).

Sveticxoveli, 1917, 1 (ჟურნალი სვეტიცხოველი, 1917, 1).

Archives

Archives of the Georgian Patriarchate (საქართველოს საპატრიარქოს არქივი).

Archives of the Giorgi Leonidze State Museum of Literature (გიორგი ლეონიძის სახელმწიფო მუზეუმის არქივი).

Central Historical Archives of Recent Georgian History (საქართველოს უახლესი ისტორიის ცენტრალური საისტორიო არქივი).

Central State Archives of Georgia, f. No 12, 4, Act no. 911 (საქართველოს ცენტრალური სახელმწიფო საისტორიო არქივი, ფონდი № 12, აღწერა 1, საქმე № 911).

Central State Archives of Georgia, f. No 1438, descr. 1, Act no. 216 (საქართველოს ცენტრალური სახელმწიფო საისტორიო არქივი, ფონდი № 1438, აღწერა 1, საქმე № 216).

Central State Archives of Georgia, f. No 493/ 1, Act no 3 (საქართველოს ცენტრალური სახელმწიფო საისტორიო არქივი, ფონდი № 493, აღწ. 1, საქმე № 3).

Central State Archives of Georgia, file no 488, Act no 62523. See: K. Pavliashvili, *Exarchate of Georgia in 1900-1917*, Tbilisi, 1995 (საქართველოს ცენტრალური სახელმწიფო საისტორიო არქივი, ფონდი 488, საქმე № 62523; შდრ. ქ. პავლიაშვილი, *საქართველოს საეგზარქოსო 1900-1917*, თბილისი, 1995).

Central State Archives of Georgia, file no. 13/ 1, Act no 69.

Index

Index

Index

Index

Index

Index

RELATED TITLES FROM BENNETT & BLOOM

GEORGIA
A Short History
Edited by Nicholas Awde

THE WELLSPRING OF GEORGIAN HISTORIOGRAPHY
The Early Medieval Historical Chronicle
'The Conversion of Kartli' and 'The Life of St. Nino'
Translated with introduction, commentary and
indices by Constantine B. Lerner

THE GEORGIANS
People, Culture and History
Edited by Nicholas Awde

THE MEDITERRANEAN LEGACY IN EARLY CELTIC CHRISTIANITY
A Journey from Armenia to Ireland
Jacob G. Ghazarian

THE HISTORY OF BISHOP SEBEOS
Redefining an Ancient Armenian History
Gabriel Soultanian

RACISM IN RUSSIA
Edited by Nicholas Awde & Fred James Hill

WOMEN IN ISLAM
An Anthology from the Qur'an and Hadiths
Translated & edited by Nicholas Awde

BENNETT & BLOOM
PO Box 2131, London W1A 5SU, UK
www.bennettandbloom.com
info@bennettandbloom.com